RENEWALS 458-4574

TALES OF
CROSSED DESTINIES

D0770817

WORLD LITERATURES REIMAGINED

MODERN LANGUAGE ASSOCIATION OF AMERICA

Brazilian Narrative Traditions in a Comparative Context
Earl E. Fitz. 2005

Tales of Crossed Destinies:
The Modern Turkish Novel in a Comparative Context
Azade Seyhan. 2008

TALES OF CROSSED DESTINIES

THE MODERN TURKISH NOVEL IN A COMPARATIVE CONTEXT

Azade Seyhan

THE MODERN LANGUAGE ASSOCIATION OF AMERICA

NEW YORK 2008

Library
University of Texas
at San Antonio

© 2008 by The Modern Language Association of America
All rights reserved
Printed in the United States of America

For information about obtaining permission to reprint material from MLA book
publications, send your request by mail (see address below), e-mail (permissions@mla.org),
or fax (646 458-0030).

Library of Congress Cataloging-in-Publication Data

Seyhan, Azade.
    Tales of crossed destinies :
the modern Turkish novel in a comparative context / Azade Seyhan.
        p. cm — (World literatures reimagined)
    Includes bibliographical references and index.
    ISBN 978-1-60329-030-2 (hardcover : alk. paper)
    ISBN 978-1-60329-031-9 (pbk. : alk. paper)
    1. Turkish fiction—20th century—History and criticism.   I. Title.
    PL223.S44 2008
    894'.3533—dc22   2008022976

World Literatures Reimagined 2
 . ISSN 1553-6181

Cover illustration for the paperback edition: *Istanbul Painting*, by Ali Demir.
Used with permission of the artist

Published by The Modern Language Association of America
26 Broadway, New York, New York 10004-1789
www.mla.org

CONTENTS

Wrld literature: for many years, this concept has been little under-stood and even less agreed on. Since Goethe's invention of the term *Weltliteratur*, in 1827, readers have tended to invest world literature with both an impossibly ideal character and an inconceivable mate-rial scope. For some, it is a highly selective canon of works that transcend their national literatures and languages. For others, it is everything—the sum of all the national literatures considered together. For still others among a spate of recent theorists who have embraced the topic, world literature is the outcome of a confrontation between received forms and local conditions, a mode of reading and exchange between works of different times and places, or a met-ropolitan construction that ensures the maintenance of categories such as "major" and "minor" literatures.

Meanwhile, world literature has become increasingly prevalent in de-partments of literature, as the rubric for a kind of course that—despite its name—usually reflects local institutional notions of what might be rele-vant. While the concept has been undergoing considerable intellectual revi-sion in recent years, little has changed for teachers or students who seek to expand their reach.

The series World Literatures Reimagined, sponsored by the MLA's Publications Committee, seeks to redress this gap by exploring new concep-tions of what world literature—or literatures—might mean. Written by specialists but addressed to a wide audience, books in the series consider particular literatures in an international context. They seek to develop new articulations of the connections among literatures and to give a sense of the ways in which literatures and their cultures might be like and unlike one an-other. Among other things, volumes in the series look afresh at works that might expand or complicate our notions of world literature; make compar-isons between less well known works and their better-known counterparts; and deal forthrightly with translation, showing teachers and students what is (and what should be) available in English. A shelf of these volumes should go far to encourage the reimagining of world literatures in our conscious-ness as well as our classrooms.

Roland Greene
Series Editor

ŞAİR VE BİLGE OĞLUM KERİM YASAR İÇİN

Jeder Schlag des Herzens schlägt uns eine Wunde, und das Leben wäre ein ewiges
Verbluten, wenn nicht die Dichtkunst wäre.

—Ludwig Börne

ACKNOWLEDGMENTS

I would like to extend my sincere thanks to Roland Greene, of Stanford University, editor of the MLA's series World Literatures Reimagined, for his support of this study, his vision, and his extensive knowledge and appreciation of world literatures. I would also like to commend the MLA for its timely efforts to reintroduce the many lesser-known literatures of the world to American and international readers, critics, and teachers.

Many friends and colleagues have supported my work on this book in ways they may not be aware of. I am grateful to Maria Alter, Nora Alter, Susan Bernofsky, Anne Boyden, Jean Carey, Jodi Eisenberg, Ülker Gökberk, Sabine Hake, David Kenosian, Peter Koelle, Sooyong Kim, Francisco LaRubia-Prado, Anna Kuhn, Serap Menda, İnci and Yüksel Pazarkaya, John Pizer, Roberta Ricci, Enrique Sacerio-Garí, Ken Seigneurie, Amy Spangler, Süheyla Toker, James Tupper, and Marc Weiner for their counsel, encouragement, and friendship. Special thanks also go to Ambassador Robert Finn, of Princeton University, and Venkat Mani and Susan Sanford Friedman, of the University of Wisconsin, Madison, who invited me to lecture on work in progress and provided valuable feedback.

As always, my family encouraged me at every step of the project and kept my spirits up. *Canım annem Hazime Seyhan, sevgili kardeşim Selim ve biricik oğlum Kerim, size ne kadar teşekkür etsem azdır.* I thank my cousin Ayşe Gürsan Salzmann and niece Han Salzmann for making sure that I took time from work to celebrate events big and small. I am grateful to my sister-in-law Tülây for her interest in the progress of the manuscript and for her help in finding rare and out-of-print books in Istanbul's antiquarian and used-book stores.

The completion of this book was made possible by a grant from the National Endowment for the Humanities given to the American Research Institute in Turkey. The Office of the Provost at Bryn Mawr College and the Mary Patterson McPherson Fellowship matched the grant to provide me with a full year's sabbatical. My sincere thanks go to our former provost Ralph Kuncl, former associate provost Suzy Spain, and the grants administrator Nona Smith for their help in arranging for the much-needed sabbatical, without which this book could not have been written. In the absence of research assistants, Oliva Cardona, our competent and resourceful program assistant, helped out with every detail during the writing process.

In the last stages, David G. Nicholls, director of MLA Book Publications, shepherded the manuscript through a long and rigorous review process; Michael Kandel did a meticulous and thoughtful job of copyediting; and Paul J. Banks, the production manager, facilitated the task of obtaining rights to the cover painting. The two anonymous specialist readers provided extremely informed and thoughtful criticism. I am most grateful for their feedback. I would also like to thank Ece Kıyat Gödek, owner of the Doku Sanat Galerisi in Istanbul, for her generous cooperation in obtaining permission to use the *Istanbul Painting* for the cover of the book and in providing high-quality images of the painting.

This acknowledgment would not be complete without my mentioning Walter G. Andrews's extraordinary scholarship in Ottoman and Turkish literature and his stewardship of Turkish studies in American academe. Andrews has trained and mentored a generation of scholars who teach Ottoman Turkish literature and culture at major research universities. In some small measure, I hope that this book will be a tribute to his work, to the valiant efforts of those translators who have introduced Turkish literature to English readers, and to all the scholars of Turkish language and literature in the English-speaking world.

CHAPTER 1

Introduction: Novel Moves

Poetry is the art of inner fortification. Language becomes
the inner fortress of a nation, not when it is used for
communication but when it becomes the material and texture
of that fortress. As such, language is the very essence of a
nation's people, its history, and its culture. . . . The art that
language creates is the art of inner fortification. From there, it
slowly marks its victories. The poet's Rome gradually lets its
eagles out of the fortress walls.

> —Ahmet Hamdi Tanpınar,
> *Edebiyat Üzerine Makaleler,* "Articles on Literature"

Literature is one of society's instruments of self-awareness—
certainly not the only one, but nonetheless an essential
instrument, because its origins are connected with the origins
of various types of knowledge, various codes, various forms of
critical thought.

> —Italo Calvino, *The Uses of Literature*

Nothing allows us a more insightful access into other times and cultures than narratives. The relentless passage of time brings in its wake inevitable surges of amnesia and awakens in human consciousness a sense of irredeemable loss. From the desire to reclaim what is lost or beyond reach spring narratives that connect us to our pasts and to others in webs of intimacy and memory as well as in webs of enmity and error. Such narratives respond to the universal human need for identification or affiliation with a clan, a community, a religious or ethnic group, or a state. Contingencies of history and politics, however, pose a constant threat to any stabilization of collective identity, for these entangle us in the histories of numerous others, leading to fragmentation and reconfiguration of allegiances. It is precisely because of the unstable and unpredictable nature of life and history that we draw on fiction to lend in retrospect sense, unity, and dignity to fragmented lives and times. Within multiple frames of narrative, characteristic of many literary texts, operates a dialectic of remembrance and anticipation. In a world where tides of globalization threaten the specificity of local cultures and ethnic and religious strife is an all too common occurrence, the question of identity writ large has acquired an unprecedented intensity. Literature, as an institution par excellence of memory and a universally employed mode of human expression, untiringly explores ways of articulating who we are and of understanding both the incommensurability and the interconnectedness of our histories.

Writing in the first half of the nineteenth century, at a time when Germany was a conglomerate of numerous small states, the German poet Heinrich Heine maintained that the only institution to lend Germany a sense of unity in the absence of any unifying political structure was modern German literature, born of the language Martin Luther created in his translation of the Bible by synthesizing myriad German dialects (*Zur Geschichte* 79). Cultures and customs change far more slowly and reluctantly than do political and ideological formations. Historical, political, and sociological studies record the events and trends of the times, whereas literary texts remember what is often forgotten in the sweep of history. The vast amount of journalistic reporting and political commentary on the ethnic strife that fractured the former state of Yugoslavia does not begin to tell the story of the troubled legacy that turned a once peaceful country into killing fields. It is a literary work, the Yugoslav Nobel laureate Ivo Andrić's epic novel *The Bridge on the Drina*, that captures the complex relation of life stories and local culture with political histories and offers some clarification of this bloody conflict at the end of the twentieth century in the heart of Europe. *The Bridge on the Drina* is an accomplished synthesis of fact and fabulation that shows the role of multiple factors—language, faith, communal memory—in identity formation.

The bridge on the Drina River in Višegrad, Bosnia, was built by the son of a Bosnian peasant who grew up to become the Grand Vizier Sokullu (born Sokolović) Mehmet Pasha (1506–79) of the Ottoman Empire in the mid–sixteenth century. Sokullu, recruited into the sultan's army as a youth, wanted to pay homage to his Bosnian origins by having a bridge built over the Drina. He also appointed his blood brother as the patriarch of the Serbian Church, another gesture of wishing to be remembered in his place of birth. As long as the Ottoman power remained secure in Bosnia, Muslims,

Orthodox Christians, and Roman Catholics lived side by side in relative harmony. But as that power declined, the religious divisions in Bosnian society became increasingly explosive. Andrić narrates how the Bosnians and the Serbs, Muslims and Christians, respectively, living side by side in a remote outpost of the Ottoman Empire, begin to attribute different symbolic meanings to the larger political changes that descend on their lives. When in the course of time they begin to remember their pasts differently, their conflicting memories turn coexistence into turmoil and violence.

Through his masterful portrayal of the Ottoman civilization as experienced in his native Bosnia, Andrić investigates the role of Ottoman-Islamic culture in the formation of Bosnian identity. Modern-day Turks, the direct descendants of this civilization, are engaged in an ongoing effort to articulate their relation to the Ottoman legacy in the historical continuum. In its broadest sense, this effort, exemplified in contemporary Turkish fiction, represents a desire to restore a past erased in the interest of creating and maintaining stability and unity during the early years of the Republic of Turkey. A newcomer to the league of nation-states, the Turkish state was (re)built on Asia Minor and parts of Thrace, on the reclaimed territories of the Ottoman Empire (1299–1923), which was defeated and occupied by the Allied powers in the First World War. Both the distinguished writer-intellectuals of the early republic, including Halide Edib (later Adıvar), Reşat Nuri Güntekin, and Yakup Kadri Karaosmanoğlu, and writers of the more recent Turkish literary scene, such as İhsan Oktay Anar, Abidin Dino, Ahmet Altan, and Orhan Pamuk, have tried in complementary and opposing ways to assess the enduring legacy of Ottoman culture in modern Turkish life.

The history of modern Turkish literature is a vast archive that remains understudied and largely unexplored. Lack of knowledge about the cultural life of Turks and of their language; the scarcity of translations; and the widely held perception of the Middle East, in Victoria Holbrook's words, "as an exclusively sociological area where humanities never happen" all hinder access to a rich literary tradition that not only synthesizes the oral storytelling practices of Middle Eastern cultures and Western forms but also complements our understanding of the travails of modernity. In the introduction to her theoretically sophisticated study of the eighteenth-century Ottoman Turkish poet Şeyh Galip's philosophical romance *Hüsn ü Aşk* (*Beauty and Love*), Holbrook states, "A marvelous maze of absences is point of departure for writing about Ottoman literature in the United States today" (1). The same may be said of modern Turkish literature.

Although Holbrook and Walter Andrews (Andrews; Andrews and Kalpaklı), the prolific American scholar of Ottoman and Turkish literature, have broken the silence of cultural history with regard to Ottoman poetry and resituated it in a framework of important historical and critical paradigms, the history of modern Turkish letters still awaits critical remembrance. To be sure, there are published dissertations on genres, periods, and individual figures and important articles in specialized journals, mostly in *Edebiyat: The Journal of Middle Eastern Literatures*. Talat Sait Halman, poet, professor, and former minister of culture, has single-handedly translated volumes of Turkish poetry and prose into English and edited several anthologies. In Germany, another poet-translator, Yüksel Pazarkaya, has produced a vast body of Turkish literature in German translation and paved the way to the spectacular emergence of award-winning literature by Turkish writers. Turkish critics—among them Hasan Âli Yücel, who was arguably Turkey's most accomplished and admired minister of education, Berna Moran, Hilmi Yavuz, Fethi Naci, as well as the renowned novelist Ahmet Hamdi Tanpınar—have produced informative and powerful analyses of modern Turkish literature. They have seen this literature as a response to the trials of a rapid and unexamined embrace of Western values, as an intervention in social spaces, and as a form of resistance against the institutionalization of cultural memory. In the contemporary Turkish cultural scene there is certainly no shortage of review journals and book-length studies on specific topics of modern literature and culture. A recent special issue of the *South Atlantic Quarterly* on contemporary Turkish culture offers a series of outstanding articles of an interdisciplinary nature by prominent literary and cultural critics (Güzeldere and Irzık). But there is as yet no significant study in English that offers a (re)view of modern Turkish literature in a critically nuanced literary history. This study is intended to offer a synthesis of this accumulated intellectual labor.

Any venture in this other "marvelous maze of absences," however, will inevitably generate other absences and fall short of reader expectations. Nevertheless, the point of departure is in sight and beckons the critic. Orhan Pamuk's international renown and his status as the first and only Turkish Nobel laureate in any field, increasing public interest in the Turkish novel as an expression of diverse historical and aesthetic concerns, and the small but promising increase in the availability of Turkish literary works in translation call for a closer investigation of the cultural spaces from which modern Turkish literature has drawn intellectual and aesthetic sustenance.

Academic interest in Turkish affairs has traditionally and obstinately remained focused on socioeconomic and political questions. But literary texts, inclusive of literary memoirs, biographies, and letters, remember stories that history has forgotten and complement our understanding of the past. The authors of the early Republican period (1923–50) have had a decisive influence on our views of that time, as they portrayed with deep insight the young nation's struggle to refashion a new westernized Turkish identity and its precarious adoption of secular modernity in the shadow of a suppressed but powerful religious tradition. They were committed to the task of building the new nation; to the success of its educational and social reforms; and to the Enlightenment ideals of scientific progress, equality, and emancipation from the terror of myth and superstition. However, they did not necessarily espouse a full-scale transfer of the structure of Western society to the new nation. Furthermore, their aim was not to represent themselves to the West but to explore their own society in moments of its major transformations. The West for them was never an ontological other against which they needed to posit an indigenous identity. They recorded lived history in alternately journalistic and symbolic registers, as they tried to make sense of their people's peculiar destiny.

In the early years of the republic, the critical efforts of intellectuals and writers focused on issues of deep cultural divisions in Turkish society. This concern is very much alive today. Therefore one cannot justifiably speak of a significant *thematic* divide between the novels of the early republic and those of Pamuk, Bilge Karasu, or Latife Tekin, who are seen as founders of a uniquely Turkish modern-postmodern idiom. Most Turkish critics identify this divide as the break from the realism of the Turkish novel toward the end of the 1970s, which is certainly visible in the formal properties of language and style. The tendency to use framed and interlocking stories, nonlinear narratives, seamless integration of real and fantastic sequences, and linguistic experimentation is much more pronounced in the work of Pamuk, Tekin, Nazlı Eray, Bilge Karasu, and Aslı Erdoğan than in that of their immediate predecessors, such as Tanpınar, Yaşar Kemal, and Adalet Ağaoğlu.

But I hope to show that the earlier novels, from the 1920s through the 1970s, with the exception of the so-called *köy edebiyatı* ("village literature"), represent such a diverse and complex triangulation of theme, form, and historical insight that the assertion of a genuine paradigm shift in the genre is problematic. It would be more correct to see the shift in the degree of emphasis that the different generations of writers have placed on such literary conventions as metafictions, intertextual references, embedded narratives, or the use of different levels of fictional reality. Such departures may be less visibly marked but are certainly traceable as early as the 1920s in the work of Halide Edib Adıvar and Yakup Kadri Karaosmanoğlu (we also need to remember that in the 1920s, Turkish literary criticism lacked the concepts and the vocabulary to identify these conventions). I am not trying to prove an integrated wholeness in the history of the modern Turkish novel. Rather my point is to show that the inherent generativity of the novel, its integration of other genres and styles, and its status as a nexus of cultural exchange between reader communities all allow for a dialogue across time. What the Turkish novel does today was immanent not only in the novels of the early Republican period but also in those of eighteenth-century Europe and the late-nineteenth-century Ottoman Empire, when with the growth of print culture the genre emerged as an institution that provided the means for readers to learn of their common experiences and to see themselves as members of an imagined community.

Today, Güntekin, Pamuk, and Yaşar Kemal are the three most widely read novelists in Turkey. In a sense, Güntekin and his contemporaries wrote the preamble to the modernist trends in the Turkish novel, with their insightful analyses of the complexity of their history and their moment in that history. Like their intellectual heirs, they saw their task as an attempt to understand the different ethnic, religious, and communal legacies that survived the Ottoman state. Like many modern Turks reassessing Turkey's transition from a multireligious, multiethnic, and multilingual state to nationhood based on unifying notions of language, culture, religion, and territory, Pamuk and other contemporary authors, explicitly or implicitly, express a strong unease with the rupture in the Ottoman Turkish cultural legacy that modernization and Mustafa Kemal Atatürk's reforms brought about. Concern for the preservation of a legitimizing cultural past appears in discourses ranging from nostalgia for all things Ottoman-Islamic to sharp criticism of state policies that suppress ethnic and religious diversity. This anxiety about the loss of inheritance is relativized by moderates, who argue that had the Turkish republic never come into existence, the question of cultural legacy or lack thereof could not have been posed in the first place. Therefore a critical understanding of modern Turkish literature needs to unfold along conceptual parameters, such as national and regional identities; the intimate relations among language, identity, and cultural memory; and the social responsibility of the writer in negotiating the encounter of different worlds and value systems. In these parameters, it is unfeasible to mark a distinct historical *coupure* in theme between the early Republican and the contemporary Turkish novel.

This study focuses on the modern Turkish novel as a body of texts that underwrite these conceptual categories and thus link the concerns of Turkish literature to those of other world literatures, while preserving the specificity of historical and political challenges facing Turkish society. The novel, as the modern *epos*, is closely linked to the foundational myths and ideologies of the nation as well as to their critique. It is the textual space where a symbolic exchange of societal values takes place and where official history is challenged by alternative scenarios and the recovery of suppressed memory. Although poetry had been the dominant literary genre of both Ottoman literature and the golden age of Arabic literature, prose became the leading idiom of modern literary revolutions in Turkey and the Arab countries. Theories of prose writing by both Turkish and Western critics and novelists therefore enable a new articulation of modern Turkish literary history that does justice to the range of complexities that underwrite both the cultural specificity of this history and its relation to contemporary literatures of what Milan Kundera calls the small nations, "secluded behind their inaccessible languages" (*Testaments* 193). The smallness of a nation is one not of scale but of destiny, the destiny of nations that have at some point or another "passed through the antechamber of death; always faced with the arrogant ignorance of large nations." Yet Kundera also points to the intensity of cultural life of these "small nations," where "the wealth in cultural events is on a 'human scale'; everyone can encompass that wealth, can participate in the totality of cultural life; this is why, in its best moments, a small nation can bring to mind life in an ancient Greek city" (192). In the spheres of Turkish culture today, journalists, teachers, preachers, *arabesk* singers, architects, painters, politicians, soccer fans, and readers from all walks of life provide the diversity of speech forms and cultural idioms that nourish the Turkish novel.

Although my investigation generally follows a chronological order, its double focus on the specificity of modern Turkish literature and on that literature's relation to other literatures produces a narrative that can switch between works that do not belong to the same period. The self-conscious concern of modern Turkish literature with the history of its social conditions and with the contingencies of its own thematic and formal development sets the parameters of my study and necessitates an interdisciplinary approach. "I am accustomed to consider literature a search for knowledge," writes Italo Calvino in *Six Memos for the Next Millennium*. "In order to move onto existential ground, I have to think of literature as extended to anthropology and ethnology and mythology" (26). Similarly, I see history, philosophy, and literature operating in contiguous fields of interest.

The chapters of this volume investigate thematic, formal, and historical paradigms in novels that display an unusual amalgam of forms and different degrees of mythic depth and historical interest. Much of this writing cannot be neatly classified in one category. A case in point is Pamuk's work, which is a compelling synthesis of concepts, forms, and literary legacies. A novel like his *My Name Is Red* can be read as detective fiction or a historico-philosophical treatise on representation. His *Black Book* has generated volumes of critical essays, which interpret it as a theory of the postmodern novel itself, a semiotic map, a cultural history of Istanbul, a picaresque novel, a detective novel, and an encyclopedic novel. Aslı Erdoğan's *Kırmızı Pelerinli Kent* ("The City with the Red Cape," trans. as *City in Crimson Cloak*) can be read as an autobiographical novel, a metafiction in which two authors compete for the end of the story, or an urban novel that offers a haunting portrayal of Rio de Janeiro. Bilge Karasu's *Night* is both a postmodern allegory of political persecution and a metafiction in which an author and editor comment on each other's work in footnotes.

Criticism is an open-ended, generative activity. The passage of time and contingencies of sociocultural histories enable readers conditioned by different histories to derive new implications from even the most overtreated texts. Reader-response theories and American New Criticism's notion of intentional fallacy have sufficiently underscored the point that authors are not the sole arbiters of the meaning of their work. Neither are the critics. The inferences I draw from reading the novels of this study can be contested, altered, revised. But scrutiny and reflection, conditioned by a wealth of recent and not so recent studies of the novel, necessitate a correction of fairly entrenched clichés about the nature of the Turkish novel, regardless of hermeneutic bias. Such stereotypical notions arise from an outdated conception of comparative literature that sees novels in terms of such binaries as Western-Eastern, high literary–popular, and romantic-realistic. In the framework of convenient binaries and periodizations, the Turkish novel is often marked as belated and imitative, which then leads to the notion that it is a translation, in the negative sense of lacking originality or creativity, of even plagiarizing.

An extremely exaggerated response to the charge of plagiarism is Jorge Luis Borges's enchanting short story–critical essay, "Pierre Menard, Author of the *Quixote*." Borges's narrator tells of a certain French writer, Pierre Menard, recently deceased, who aspired to rewrite Cervantes's *Don Quixote* as his own. Menard wanted his version to be an exact replica of the original. He succeeded so well in immersing himself in Cervantes's cultural milieu that the parts of the novel he was able to complete coincided with the original word for word. The narrator actually considers Menard's text superior to that of Cervantes, because Menard had to overcome the many obstacles posed to him by the great temporal gap. Furthermore, Menard (or the narrator/Borges) succeeds in overlaying his work with a new conceptual insight: his historical distance from the original *Quixote* imbues Cervantes's words with new meaning.

Borges's essay is a philosophical parable, a fiction, although, as in all his fictions, Borges makes references to real characters or things. But adaptations of fictional works are legion and legitimate. A real-life parallel to Borges's tale is the almost identical retelling of Heinrich von Kleist's *Michael Kohlhaas* (1810) in E. L. Doctorow's highly acclaimed *Ragtime* (1975). Borges's fictional essay anticipates postmodern theories of reader response, by which the act of reading constitutes a contract between writer and reader. The reception of a work and the meanings it generates are conditioned by different social and historical factors and lead to revisions of the original. A case in point in modern Turkish literature is the renaissance of Tanpınar's work. His novels and poetry have been reissued in high-quality editions, and his essays, interviews, reviews, and lectures have been collected and anthologized. What makes Tanpınar so relevant and present to today's readers is his reflective engagement with questions of Turkish identity and his deep knowledge and profound understanding of Ottoman-Islamic culture. These qualities were of import in his day, and his work was certainly respected in his lifetime. However, the growing preoccupation with the question of Turkish identity in the academic as well as the public sphere has endowed this work, not worn down by the baggage of modern identity politics, with the authority of critical arbitration.

What does it mean when a critic calls the Turkish novel belated or sees belatedness as its overarching theme? And what would the sentence be for this offense? What must the Turkish novel do to catch up? Some of the most compelling theories of the novel do not give a date for its birth; some register the date as the eighteenth century and the place of birth as Western Europe. Leslie Fiedler says Samuel Richardson is the inventor of the "true novel" (189). Of course, those who consider Miguel de Cervantes the first novelist will find Fiedler's assertion preposterous. Then there is Kundera, a major novelist and a decent literary critic himself, who sees the novel "taking flight" in François Rabelais's *Gargantua and Pantagruel,* a colossal folk epic written as a series of books between 1532 and 1542 (*Testaments* 3). Elsewhere, Kundera considers Laurence Sterne's *Tristram Shandy* (published 1759–67 in nine small volumes) and Denis Diderot's *Jacques le fataliste* (1796) "the two greatest novelistic works of the eighteenth century, two novels conceived as grand games" (*Art* 15). Mikhail Bakhtin, who has emerged as one of the most influential theorists of the novel in the last several decades, also sees in Rabelais's employment of diverse speech registers and pandemonium of narrative ploys the essential largesse of the novel as a genre. Both Bakhtin and Kundera endorse parody, paradox, and a finely orchestrated chaos as the strengths of the novel. *Don Quixote* (1605, 1615), considered one of the greatest novels of all time, incorporates parody, citation, and "grand games" as well.

Since *Gargantua and Pantagruel* and *Don Quixote* predate the great novels of the eighteenth century, does that make the eighteenth-century novels belated? Clearly, belatedness is not of much use as a critical category, unless we accept the eighteenth-century European novel as an absolute locus of reference. If we look for a historical coincidence, on the other hand, it is fair to assume that the rise of the modern novel accompanies that of the nation-state, since the novel has historically transformed the epic material linked to foundational myths into a coherent narrative of national concerns. Benedict Anderson contends that the novel, more than any other narrative form, endows a people with a sense of belonging to an "imagined community," his well-known (and worn) metaphor for the experience of affiliation with a nation.

The novel is already a belated form, separated by an enormous temporal gap from the original classical genres of epic, poetry, and drama. In *The Theory of the Novel,* one of the most important philosophical treatises on the development of the genre, Georg Lukács sees the novel as a Hegelian recollection of the lost epic unity of classical humanity with the world. In the modern world, "in which the extensive totality of life is no longer directly given, in which the immanence of meaning in life has become a problem, yet which still thinks in terms of totality" (56), the novel becomes "the epic of a world that has been abandoned by God" (88). It is only in memory and imagination that the protagonist of the modern novel can recapture the vanished connection of human life to its world.

The point on which most theories of the novel agree is not the date of its birth but rather its role as the symbolic denominator and archive of human experience, conditioned by history and culture. However, in the best and most enduring specimens of the genre, the historical viewpoint cannot be static; it must enter a dialectical relation with other times. Kundera writes:

> As a novelist, I have always felt myself to be within history, that is to say, partway along a road, in dialogue with those who preceded me and even perhaps (but less so) with those still to come. Of course, I am speaking of the history of the novel . . . and speaking of it such as I see it: it has nothing to do with Hegel's extrahuman reason; it is neither predetermined nor identical with the idea of progress; it is entirely human, made by men, by *some* men, and thus comparable to the development of the individual artist.   (*Testaments* 15–16)

Thus a novel can emerge in different places at different times and be produced by individual artists or by a community of artists in a shared tradition. It emerges when its time comes and "challenges the monopolies on representation sometimes claimed at the metropolitan center [centers identified by European literary histories]" (Lynch and Warner 5).

Clearly, a genre that has been variously transformed in time cannot be contained in preestablished or prescribed forms. Malcolm Bradbury asserts that in relation to poetry and drama,

> the novel is least susceptible to formal definition and characterization; it has no distinct typographical form, or context of performance, and a few recurring conventions. For this reason all theory of the novel has to be remarkably *loose* theory, and theory *about* looseness, for criticism has lost the disposition to see novels as formally tight, conventionalized, composed structures.   (10–11)

Bakhtin views the novel as a record of the meeting between cultures of class in a society that enables access to a diversity of voices. The novel offers an understanding of cultural specificities that have been obscured by some core methodology common to social sciences or historiography. Furthermore, for Bakhtin, the dialogic (or multivoiced) nature of the novel frees it from conventions prescribed by critics or externally imposed standards. In the narrative space of the novel, where diverse cultures meet, complex social allegiances and identifications emerge. In that context, novels shape popular fashion and taste and are shaped by them, as they circulate among a wide and varied readership and cross social boundaries in the nation.

One of the most important literary critical influences on the work of Bakhtin, Lukács, and Kundera came from German Romanticism—specifically, from the essays and fragments of the aesthetic philosophers of early Romanticism—a period known as the *Frühromantik*—whom Lukács calls "the first theoreticians of the novel" (*Theory* 74). Although the early Romantics did not always completely clarify their concept of the novel, they "drew a close connection between it and the concept of the Romantic; and rightly so, for the novel form is, like no other, an expression of . . . transcendental homelessness." Lukács's "*transzendentale Obdachlosigkeit*" refers to the homelessness of artistic creation, where the certainty of conception between "the form-giving subject and the world of created forms has been destroyed" (41) in the postepic age.

Friedrich Schlegel, the major theorist of this period, sought to reunite the fragmented world of artistic creation in the "new mythology" of "romantische Poesie." Schlegel defined "Romantic poesy" as a "progressive universal poesy" that incorporated a wealth of poetic utterances and forms, ranging from the poetic sigh of a child to the highest systems of art. It joined philosophy with rhetoric, poetry with prose, art with criticism and could not be "exhausted by any theory." The essential nature of Romantic poesy was a state of eternal "becoming" ("werden" [182]). The novel, which incorporated many other genres—poetry, novella, criticism, letters, diaries, among others—and represented its own ongoing transformation, coincided ideally with the concept of Romantic poesy, as it was both art and art criticism, both poetry and poetic reflexivity or the philosophy of poetry. Bakhtin corroborates Schlegel's notion of the novel's cross-generic quality in the development of its history:

> In its earliest stages, the novel and its preparatory genres had relied upon various literary forms of personal and social reality, and especially those of rhetoric (there is a theory that actually traces the novel back to rhetoric). And in later stages of its development the novel makes wide and substantial use of letters, diaries, confessions, the forms and methods of rhetoric associated with recently established courts and so forth. . . . [T]he novel often crosses the boundary of what we strictly call fictional literature—making use first of a moral confession, then of a philosophical tract, then of manifestos that are openly political, then degenerating into the raw spirituality of confession, a "cry of the soul" that has not yet found its formal contours. These phenomena are precisely what characterize the novel as a developing genre. (33)

The view of the modern novel as a revision of generic conventions or their reconfiguration also informs the analyses of the genre by many modern critics. In *Les règles de l'art* (*The Rules of Art*), Pierre Bourdieu develops a theory of the novel's aesthetic autonomy through the lens of Gustave Flaubert's characterization of his own work. Quoting Flaubert's indignation against being labeled a realist and his equally disapproving position toward "the false brand of idealism which is such a hollow mockery in the present age," Bourdieu demonstrates how Flaubert, like the Romantics before him and the high modernists after him, canceled established rules of division and perception by blending the poetic with the prosaic, the vulgar with the lyrical, concept with expression, and "subject" (innate creativity) with technique (92). In Schlegel's conception, such a work would incorporate the essence of Romantic poesy as "the mirror of the totality of its surrounding world" that "hovers in the middle between the representing subject and what is represented, free from all real and ideal interest on the wings of poetic reflection" (182). For Bourdieu, Flaubert invoked "the limits and the incompatibilities that ground the perceptual and the communicative order on the prohibited that is the sacrilege of the mixture of genres or the confusion of orders" (95) by trying to reconcile the "requirements and experiences ordinarily associated with opposing regions of the social space and the literary field" (94). To that end, Flaubert established the highest requirements of the poetic in "the art of the novel and the territory it explores, the prose of life" (Kundera, *Curtain* 90). Bourdieu's study makes a strong case for the intimate connections between art and the social contexts that play an important role in its formation and reception. Bourdieu establishes art's new autonomy as constitutive of a social structure where art comes into being.

In her theoretically sophisticated book on postmodernism in the Turkish novel, Yıldız Ecevit sees in the Turkish modernist-postmodernist forms of the novel the first encounter of Turkish literature with Romanticism and considers this encounter an exciting "revolution" in the realm of aesthetic creation (12). It is in the pioneering work of the early German Romantic critics Schlegel and Novalis (Friedrich von Hardenberg) that she locates the defining concepts of novelistic form that helped shape the modernist-postmodernist novel and that resound in the aesthetic of the modern Turkish novel (171–75).

The Romantic influence on modern literature in general is the subject of a great number of studies, since as Marc Redfield notes, "the texts we style romantic often provide a more rigorous critique of aesthetic-romantic ideology than texts from subsequent literary-historical periods, including our own" (179). But reading modern texts that exercise an *Ideologiekritik* ("critique of ideology") of our own institutions in a repeat performance of Romanticism's critical aesthetic runs the risk of overlooking historical conditions and contingencies. We can establish, however, that Romantic self-reflexivity, which arose from the ground of eighteenth-century critical philosophy and intimated the complicity of representational practices in ideology formation, has found its most explicit expression in our time.

Discerning theories of the novel have consistently commented on the inherent structural and thematic heterogeneity of the genre, which connects it to the ever-changing reality of the present. As Bakhtin notes, the novel "is, by its very nature, not canonic. It is plasticity itself. It is a genre that is ever questioning, ever examining itself and subjecting its established forms to review" (39). It should come as no surprise, therefore, that the novel of the late Ottoman period, which recorded the revolutionary changes in the fortunes of the empire in symbolic and interpretive registers, consecutively and simultaneously appeared as a translation-adaptation of the nineteenth-century European realistic novel; a pedagogical or political tool in novelistic form; and, as a result of the rise of nationalist consciousness, an expression of a search for identity—an attempt to forge a sense of Turkishness.

As I argue in the next chapter, early Turkish nationalism has its roots more in the literary than in the political sphere. Nevertheless, the short but productive formal history of the Turkish novel illustrates that this young genre of Turkish letters has never been an apology for an exclusionary notion of nationalism; rather it can be read as a dialogic narrative in the Bakhtinian sense, where voices across history and space are framed by stories. In this way, "contemporary reality and its concerns become the starting point and center of an artistic ideological thinking and evaluating of the past" (Bakhtin 29). Bakhtin's point applies to the early novels, which are seen as contributing to the foundational principles and ideologies of Turkish nationhood. The increasing critical interest in the genesis of the modern novel has helped emphasize the novel's cultural centrality not only in national consciousness but also as a "nexus of transnational exchange," since the novel is "neither a Western invention nor a Western franchise" (Lynch and Warner 4–5) but a narrative form that is always in progress, moving from its site of invention (however defined) to new boundaries, thereby transporting, transforming, and translating the form and idea of the original model.

In the light of the Romantic and modern critical reflections on the novel and the progressive inflections of its assumed original manifestation, we can reassess the genesis of the modern Turkish novel in a way that highlights both its universal interest and its cultural specificities. Through the lens of these alternately competing and complementary views of the art of the novel, we can now understand the early Republican novel as an aesthetic formal structure that tentatively negotiated a complex interaction of various genres, including fiction, history, memoir, and polemic. In this way, it sought to close various communication gaps between authorial and reader positions and to create a kind of a community forum, focused on the question of the nascent Turkish national identity. In *Cultural Institutions of the Novel*, the coeditors Deidre Lynch and Willliam B. Warner write that "[p]articipating in the social practice of novel reading can give readers the sense of participating in a nation that they imagine to be the product of consensus." Furthermore, echoing Bakhtin's notion of the novel's capacity for negotiating between classes, they maintain, "When novel reading traverses social boundaries within the nation, novels' popularity can seem an index of the nation's essential coherence" (4). Bakhtin validates the novel as a dialogic genre, since through its form and structure it links the low and high culture as well as the sacred and the profane. It is characterized by heteroglossia (*raznorečie*), which denotes the multiplicity of voices from the various ranks of the social milieu, different speech registers, idioms, generational languages, languages of the authorities and of bureaucracy, political slogans, and professional jargons. This internal stratification, in which various speech forms are registered, is "present in every language at any given moment of its historical existence" and "is the indispensable prerequisite of the novel as a genre" (263).

The study of influence characterizes much criticism on the Turkish novel, and the degree of this anxiety of influence becomes a determinant of aesthetic and critical worth—the greater the anxiety about Western or traditional influences on the work, the less its value. Critics who try to defend the late Ottoman Turkish novel from charges of imitation (of the high literary art of the European novel) point to its incorporation of indigenous elements of a long-standing literary practice, such as the *meddah* ("storyteller") tradition, folk tales, and heroic romances. Those who see the early examples of the Ottoman Turkish novel as a crude, even primitive, aesthetic endeavor that lacked originality of content and style attribute these faults to the absence of sociohistorical frameworks essential for the development of the novel form.[1] In a radical departure from similar views on the development of the novel from either the high literary or the folkloristic, Fiedler argues that the novel is related to nothing that precedes it, not to

> traditional High Literary Art (an art dependent on limited literacy) [or to] Folk Literary Art (an art dependent on mass illiteracy); since it is related not to such forms as Epic, on the one hand, or to Folk Ballad, on the other . . . but to much which follows: the comic strip, the comic book, cinema, TV.   (189)

Fiedler suggests that in our age the novel as a genre has been superseded by pop culture, which is another way of saying (without really saying it) that the novel is dead, an all too familiar lament in an age dominated by visual culture(s). On the other hand, Kundera defends his art eloquently when he asserts, "if the novel's *raison d'être* is to keep 'the world of life' under a permanent light and to protect us from 'forgetting of being,' is it not more than ever necessary today that the novel should exist?" (*Art* 17).

As an astute literary critic as well as a gifted poet and novelist, Tanpınar participates in these views and offers a culturally specific approach to the understanding of Turkish literature. He contends that the absence of a critical tradition in Turkish culture has delayed the realization of its literary potential. Instead of pointing to foreign influences as a marker of lack, critics and authors need to bring to light lost or erased indigenous cultural legacies. In such an undertaking, he states, one will always come across memories of other cultures. A lifelong student of Western and Eastern literatures, he sees the revivification of history's cultural assets essential not only for one's sense of identity but also for participation in and interaction with other cultures: "We shall enter the world concert with our national identity" (*Mücevherlerin Sırrı* 193).[2] Genuine criticism entails understanding the self in its relation to the other in the historical continuum.

Tanpınar offered this view in an interview in 1949, when Turkish prose was suffering from a lack of direction and a disorienting identity gap. His further comment, that the young generation of writers is unduly influenced by the outside and has not been able to define the angle from which it views the world, needs to be understood in that context. He does not in any way espouse a provincial or nationalist agenda in literature. He is concerned about what he perceives as a disorienting discontinuity in the tradition of prose literature. Writing almost half a century after Tanpınar, Kundera voices a similar concern:

The novel's spirit is the spirit of continuity: each work is an answer to the preceding ones, each work contains all the previous experience of the novel. But the spirit of our time is firmly focused on a present that . . . shoves the past off our horizon. . . . Within this system the novel is no longer a *work* (a thing made to last, to connect the past with the future) but one current event among many, a gesture with no tomorrow. (*Art* 18–19)

That one cannot speak of either a typology or a literary canon with respect to the modern Turkish novel should not be regarded as a critical problem. Attempts to define and establish a select canon of the Turkish novel remain contentious. But if we can distance ourselves from the contention and understand the genesis and status of the modern Turkish novel in the light of critical insights and astute aesthetic instincts that inform theories of the novel from Schlegel to Lukács, Bakhtin, and Tanpınar, we can read this important genre of Turkish letters not only as a seismograph of social and cultural shifts but also as a medium for transnational passages of lore. What makes the study of the modern Turkish novel valuable in a transnational context is reflected in Tanpınar's notion that in the literature of a people making a transition from one civilization to another there is always something exemplary and interesting for other nations (*Mücevherlerin Sırrı* 194). If the novel is a genre that is "ever examining itself and subjecting its established forms to review," as Bakhtin contends, then it is liberated from all constraints that would impede its "unique development" (39).

My analysis therefore circumvents issues of canonicity, authenticity, and influence that do not provide fruitful lines of investigation into the social, moral, and aesthetic concerns of the modern Turkish novel. Rather, the present study sees its subject emerge "in the zone of direct contact with *inconclusive present-day reality*" (Bakhtin 39; emphasis mine). Largely because of the historical upheavals that have accompanied its birth, the Turkish novel has been a forum where questions of national, religious, and ethnic identity resound beyond the borders of the literary text and national literary paradigms. Although my study conforms to a convenient typology of novel forms and periods (the early Republican period, the literature of social engagement, fictions of Istanbul, modernist-postmodernist trends), it does not identify major conceptual breaks in the development of the Turkish novel; it points to the consistency with which the novel reflects on what has unfolded in the social and cultural world outside it.

In the chapters of this volume, topics and conceptual frameworks are discussed through the lens of exemplary texts. Chapter 2, "Emergence of the Turkish Novel from the Spirit of Cultural Reform," is an overview of modern Turkish prose from the birth of the Ottoman Turkish novel, schooled in the tradition of the Western bourgeois novel of the nineteenth century, through its subsequent transformations, which parallel social transitions during the last days of the Ottoman Empire.

Chapter 3, "Growing Pains of the Nation," investigates a group of novels, written mostly during the early years of the republic. Güntekin's *Çalıkuşu* ("The Wren," trans. as *The Autobiography of a Turkish Girl*), a book that was instrumental in the decision of thousands of young Turkish women to seek teaching posts in Anatolia, and *Yeşil Gece* ("The Green Night"); Karaosmanoğlu's *Yaban* ("The Alien"); and Adıvar's *Ateşten Gömlek* ("Shirt of Fire," trans. both as *The Shirt of Flame* and as *The Daughter of Smyrna*), arguably the best novel of the Turkish War of Independence, all address the trials of a people who after the major trauma of the First World War are thrown into yet another battle, to reclaim their ancestral land from enemy invasion and devastation. Both *The Alien* and *The Green Night* show how the Turkish revolution failed to bring light to the vast stretches of Anatolia that remained submerged in the darkness of religious dogma and superstition. These novels foreshadow the challenges of transforming an Islamic society into a secular nation-state, intimate the power and wrath of repressed history, and witness how the Enlightenment idea of freeing human beings from fear through a disenchantment of the world has turned into a nightmare of the worst kind. Adıvar, on the other hand, reclaims the serenity of Islam and entertains the possibility of a harmonious coexistence of Islamic spirituality and art with Western ideals. This outlook is very much present in her autobiographical *Memoirs of Halidé Edib* and *The Turkish Ordeal*, both written originally in English. Two American publishers reissued different editions of *Memoirs* in 2003 and 2004, respectively.[3] I discuss the widely available *Memoirs* in this chapter to show how personal and collective histories intersect in the imaginative space of creative life writing. Fluent in Western languages, the writers of this period were also very prolific translators and thus instrumental, whether intentionally or not, in importing European cultural discourses into Turkish letters. During this period, political autobiographies also become what I call unofficial biographies of the nation.

Chapter 4, "Social Responsibility and the Aesthetic Imperative" reads selected fictions of the second half of the last century as poetic-critical interventions in the political, cultural, and philosophical debates around the dichotomies tradition and modernity, cosmopolitanism and regionalism, secular nationalism and religious nationalism, and women's rights and patriarchal practices. The chapter includes a brief discussion of the emergence of village literature. Anatolian life, hitherto treated by urban writers, is now claimed by its own children, such as Yaşar Kemal and Mahmut Makal, who write from the field. Kemal's work, which forgoes the tedious naturalism of the desolate Anatolian landscape and blends a rich literary mother lode of myth, dream, and memory with social issues and confrontational politics, has rightfully earned Kemal national and international recognition. His *İnce Memed* ("Slim Memed," trans. as *Memed, My Hawk*) bears testimony to his mythmaking power that has ensured Kemal's work an enduring and universal appeal. The book was recently reissued, with a new introduction by the author, in the series New York Review Books Classics.

The novels of Adalet Ağaoğlu and Bilge Karasu portray the darkest hours of the Turkish experiment with democracy between the two military coups—in 1972 and 1980, respectively—when the warring political parties, unstable coalition governments, terrorism, and a downward spiraling economy led to a virtual elimination of civil liberties, persecution and assassination of intellectuals, and an extended political stalemate. In *Üç Beş Kişi* ("A Handful of People," trans. as *Curfew*), Ağaoğlu's eloquent voice documents the lives of ordinary people lost at the crossroads of personal and historical destiny, and Karasu's haunting *Gece* (*Night*) bears witness to a traumatic time when countless intellectuals and writers were persecuted, incarcerated, and tortured.

As early as the 1960s, the poetic had begun to reveal patterns of social force. Literature came to function as an experiential index of the failure of political ethics. Faced with the threat of censorship, persecution, and imprisonment, writers began to speak in increasingly cryptic and allegorical voices, which demanded sophisticated strategies of reading and interpretation. Pamuk's *Kar* (*Snow*), his only political work on the challenges facing Turkish society today, documents—in the author's vintage literary games—the irreconcilable terms of secular and religious ideologies. The work of Ağaoğlu, Yaşar Kemal, Karasu, and Turkey's master humorist, Aziz Nesin, instructs the reader in the censor-resistant (allegorical) code. Reading becomes an act of conspiracy, where the reader sounds and activates the silences between covert levels of meaning. Nesin's *Sûrnamé*, translated as *Hayri the Barber Surnâmé*, a marvelous specimen of such conspiratorial writing, is a hilarious indictment of capital punishment, written as a parody of *surnâme*, a name given to books that chronicled major Ottoman festivities in which the public participated for forty days and forty nights.

Chapter 5, "Istanbul: City as Trope and Topos of Crossed Destinies," illustrates how Istanbul is not only the favored setting of Turkish stories but also a trope of East-West cultural encounters. Tanpınar, now widely regarded as the first writer to engage critically the question of modern Turkish identity, wrote several books in which Istanbul and its citizens become actors in search of an author to write them a destiny they can live with. Pamuk considers Tanpınar his literary mentor and the "greatest Turkish writer of the twentieth century" (*Öteki Renkler* 166).[4] Tanpınar's Istanbul is a melancholy landscape of lost or disappearing idioms of art, and the writer's vision is trained on the traces of the city's visual memory. Tanpınar's work has achieved the recognition it deserves not only as an extended meditation on cultural memory but also as an example of poetic and formal achievement. This chapter revisits Istanbul in his *Huzur* ("Peace," trans. as *A Mind at Peace*) and *Beş Şehir* ("Five Cities") and in Pamuk's *Kara Kitap* (*The Black Book*), his enduring tribute to Istanbul. The labyrinthine stretches of the city duplicate the complexities of its many histories and stories, and like Calvino's *Invisible Cities*, where all cities are projections of the dream of Venice and the novel becomes a commentary on the power of memory, *The Black Book*, an allegorical tale that references another (Şeyh Galip's *Beauty and Love*), turns the city into a maze of references, a palimpsest of memories, and a space of metaphysical dreams. In Yaşar Kemal's *Deniz Küstü* ("The Sea Is Offended," trans. as *The Sea-Crossed Fisherman*), the author paints a living, pulsating portrait of Istanbul's coastal villages and underbelly in a storytelling feat and feast of stunning poetry. At the same time, Kemal presents a frightening account of the environmental destruction in Istanbul's waters as a result of mismanaged and unchecked industrialization.

Chapter 6, "Scheherazade's Progeny: The Modern-Postmodern Will to Fiction," researches the international ties between Turkish writers such as

Pamuk, Latife Tekin, and Aslı Erdoğan and their literary relatives, Borges, Calvino, Kundera. Like Scheherazade, these high modernist narrators, exhausted by history and prophecies about the death of the novel, continue to invent to keep cultural demise at bay. In the texts analyzed here, the generativity of narrative operates at several levels. At the structural level, stories grow out of other stories, as in Pamuk's *Benim Adım Kırmızı* (*My Name Is Red*) and Latife Tekin's *Berci Kristin, Çöp Masalları* ("Berci Kristin: Tales of Garbage," trans. as *Berji Kristin: Tales from the Garbage Hills*). At the allegorical level, the doppelgänger motif forms the basis of self-reflection, as in Pamuk and in Erdoğan's *The City in Crimson Cloak*. At the level of language, words take on magical properties to illuminate the seamless integration of the real and the fantastic, characteristic of earlier pastoral and epic traditions, which were eclipsed by the mimetic constraints of nineteenth- and early-twentieth-century realism.

The afterword recapitulates reflections on the importance of criticism or secondary literature as constitutive of the second life of primary literature and suggests the possibilities of reading the exemplary texts of this study in a comparative context.

The selection of the seventeen books in this study (by a dozen authors) was based on their importance in terms of the categories I analyze, their linguistic and conceptual energy, and their freedom from derivative ideas and stilted literary parlor games. Pamuk certainly loves such games, perhaps too much, but he brings a great deal of encyclopedic and imaginative wealth into his prose, which ultimately redeems (most of) his stories. I decided on novels that linked cultural specificity to overarching human interests and themes. Such works resound beyond their borders, have universal appeal, and gain critical significance in the course of time. Another important criterion of selection was the availability of translations. Many important authors could not be represented in this study because of the lack of a translation in English—though a couple of novels not available in English are included, because they are indispensable to an understanding of the historical context of the modern Turkish novel.[5]

The books that have proved most effective in my courses in comparative literature are Pamuk's *The White Castle* and *My Name Is Red*, Nesin's *Surnâmé* (a perfect example of political satire and carnivalesque parody), Ağaoğlu's *Curfew*, Karasu's *Night*, and Kemal's *Memed, My Hawk* and *The Sea-Crossed Fisherman*. Tanpınar's *A Mind at Peace* should be a book of great interest to historians whose work involves, in his words, societies making momentous transitions from one form of civilization to another. Erdoğan's *The City in Crimson Cloak* promises to be an important and original addition to courses in travel literature, literary theory, and exile writing. For purposes of further research and for students and scholars in comparative literature, literary theory, and cultural studies, all these books will prove to be of interest.

Notes

1. There is much literature on this debate. A good overall view can be found in the first two chapters, "Türk Romanı ve Batılılaşma Sorunu" ("The Turkish Novel and the Problem of Westernization") and "Âşık Hikâyeleri, *Hasan Mellah* ve İlk Romanlarımız" ("Âşık Tales, *Hasan Mellah*, and Our First Novels") in Moran 1: 9–46. See also İnci.

2. All translations from Tanpınar's work are mine.

3. The first edition of *House with Wisteria: Memoirs of Halidé Edib* was by Leopolis Press in 2003. It retains the title of the original, *Mor Salkımlı Ev*, and is an affordable, high-quality paperback with an introduction by Sibel Erol. The 2004 edition is a hardcover from Gorgias Press and introduced by Hülya Adak, an Edib scholar. Adak also provides a bibliography. This edition is more expensive but contains many illustrations. I use the Gorgias edition in this book. The spelling of Turkish names in Edib's book was anglicized, since the typesetting technology that would have enabled the use of Turkish characters was not available at the time of her writing. Both recent English editions have retained this transliteration of Turkish words into English.

4. All translations from Pamuk's *Öteki Renkler* are mine.

5. Translations of earlier novels are out of print and hard to find, except in university libraries or through online booksellers. Pamuk's novels are readily available. *Memed, My Hawk* and its sequel, *They Burn the Thistles*, have just been reissued in the series New York Review Books Classics. Tanpınar's *A Mind at Peace* will be available shortly. Most of Aziz Nesin's work has been translated by Joseph Jacobson, a scholar of Turkish literature, and can be purchased easily through Amazon.com. Bilge Karasu's books can be obtained easily from Amazon.com or by special order. Nazlı Eray's *Orpheus* has just been issued by the University of Texas Press and is highly recommended reading. There is progress with regard to the translational undertaking of Turkish literary works. Walter Andrews currently heads a long-term, ongoing project of translation of Ottoman and Turkish works of fiction into English. Victoria Holbrook's translation of the eighteenth-century Ottoman poet Şeyh Galip's *Hüsn ü Aşk* as *Beauty and Love* was recently published by the Modern Language Association. See appendix A for a list of Turkish novels available in English translation.

CHAPTER 2

Emergence of the Turkish Novel from the Spirit of Cultural Reform

Awareness of being embedded in secular, serial time with
all its implications of continuity, yet of "forgetting" the
experience of this continuity—product of the ruptures of the
late eighteenth century—engenders the need for a narrative of
continuity.

—Benedict Anderson, *Imagined Communities*

The genesis of the Ottoman Turkish novel at the end of the nineteenth century is intimately linked to the ideas of freedom and the sovereignty of nations—the dream of freedom a response to absolute imperial authority seen as an impediment to all manner of human rights, the concept of sovereignty a consequence of the insurgent movements that resulted in the independence of the Balkan nations. Therefore it is impossible to isolate a discussion of the Turkish novel from its historical and sociocultural context.[1] Literary histories mostly link the emergence of the novel as a genre to the rise of the bourgeois class. One cannot speak in historical terms of the rise of a Western-type bourgeoisie in Ottoman society. On the other hand, the intellectual elite of Ottoman society at the end of the nineteenth century saw literature as a medium to marshal national energies for social mobilization. The emergence of the Ottoman Turkish novel coincided with a series of institutional and educational reforms known as the Tanzimat ("Reorganization"), intended to reduce the widening gap between the fortunes of the declining empire and the advancements of European nations. Through the founding of private newspapers and translation of Western political, cultural, and scientific works, a new cadre of intellectuals endeavored to inform the reading public of the state of the world beyond its borders. The thematics and aesthetics as well as the social imaginary of modern Turkish literature are strongly informed by the cultural developments that mark the end of the Ottoman Empire and the founding of the Turkish republic. Several important studies of this period are available in English or English translation for the interested reader.[2] The following outline presents a docent's tour of the historical context of Turkey's cultural transformation from a religious dynasty to a secular state in the context of what Emre Kongar has called an " 'induced acculturation' in social anthropological terms" (38).

Past the height of its age of conquest, when the Ottoman Empire ruled over the Middle East, the Balkans (and further west, to the gates of Vienna), and most of North Africa, the rigid and autocratic structure of this sultanate-caliphate began to slip into a steady decline. Among the many reasons for the final collapse of the empire are the deterioration of the armed forces, corruption in the palace, failure of the feudal classes to evolve into a bourgeoisie, inflation, and the steady loss of territories after the rising tide of nationalistic movements in the Balkans. As Bernard Lewis observed, "The decline of great empires has always been a subject of fascinated interest" (21), and the story of the Ottoman descent is no exception. However, the two events of interest in this case are the slow but steady disintegration of a multinational and multiethnic empire, whose unifying ideology nevertheless manifested itself in an emphatic practice of Islam in daily life, and the empire's reemergence as a secular modern nation from the remnants of its final decimation. Furthermore, this unique transformation was never sustained by a grassroots movement; rather, it was engineered by the elite and an intelligentsia that was composed of the military and civilian bureaucrats who participated in the revolutions that marked the twilight years of the empire. Kongar observes:

> The Turkish experience in social and cultural transformation is unique, not only because of its totality and success in an Islamic society, but also because of the synthesis it sought: an amalgamation of western and pre-Islamic Turkish cultures to replace the previously dominant Islamic culture. (19)

Since the Ottoman elite were inspired by the ideals of the French Revolution and those of the Enlightenment and attributed the decline of their land to its scientific and intellectual stagnation, their strongest impulse in the effort to salvage the empire was to import Western ideas and political practices. The culmination of long-standing reform projects was the Tanzimat Edict or the Gülhane Hatt-ı Şerif ("The Noble Script of Gülhane") of 1839, which declared such principles as the security of the life, honor, and property of subjects; abolition of tax farming and its replacement by an orderly system of taxation; regular and orderly recruitment into the army; and equality before the law for all subjects regardless of creed and status (Zürcher 53). The edict had the effect of solidifying the leadership of the elite, which in turn gave impetus to the idea of a constitutional state as the necessary remedy for the ailing empire. Because the disastrous trade policies of the regime had pushed the state to the brink of bankruptcy, the advocates of the constitution, known as the Young Ottomans, were able to force the hand of Sultan Abdülhamid II (1876–1909), whose accession to the throne had been steeped in palace intrigues. The sultan delivered his preaccession promise to proclaim the constitution. The stage was set for the first parliamentary elections in Ottoman (and Islamic) history. However, after two elections and two sessions of the parliament over a time period of a mere five months, the despotic and paranoid sultan, aided by the crises of the war with Russia (from April 1877 to January 1878) and the charges brought by the deputies against some ministers, shelved the constitution and put an end to all reform attempts for the next thirty years. Although Abdülhamid was able to stop the momentum of the reformist currents, the social and economic deterioration of the empire proved unstoppable, and another elite cadre of malcontents formed a secret organization in 1889, known as İttihat ve Terâkkî Cemiyeti ("Committee of Union and Progress"). This group was responsible for reigniting the reformist fires and paving the path to the restoration of the constitution.

The second coming of the constitutional regime was an event of momentous proportions that led the various constituencies of the empire to believe that freedom and equality for all were imminent. Indeed, the Young Turks of the Union and Progress group, eager to make up for lost time, experimented with all kinds of concepts and institutions borrowed from the West. However, as in the past, these reformist endeavors lacked political, social, and economic underpinnings, and members of the Union and Progress themselves were predictably divided along the lines of Liberals, who were well-educated and pro-West, and the Unionists, who, though they shared many of the political ideals of the Liberals, were members of the lower middle class that had suffered the consequences of the erosion of local trade and of the capitulations and treaties granting European powers privileges over

Ottoman citizens. The Unionists wanted to put an end to the power of the palace and of the old guard, ensure the progress of all the citizens of the state, and curb the European pressure that loomed over the empire. In addition to the inevitable factions that threatened the union of the Committee of Union and Progress, large territories of the empire were lost during the rule of the Young Turks. The steady erosion of land led to a significant homogenization of the empire and compromised the notion of Ottomanism that was a main tenet of the Unionist camp. Despite the numerous battles they had to fight at many fronts, the Unionists were able to carry out reforms that were to become the social foundation of the new nation-state that emerged in 1923 (Ahmad 40).

The trials of the Ottomans culminated in the First World War, which the empire entered on the side of Germany. At the end of the Great War, the Ottoman Empire lay in ruins, its allies destroyed, its provinces gone, its capital occupied by the victors, who proceeded to divide up the land among themselves. The Unionist leaders had fled to Europe, and the sultan and his court were willing to accept the terms of the Allies, as long as they were allowed to remain in power. However, the disagreements that arose among the Allies with regard to sharing the spoils of the war strengthened the position of the emerging nationalists under the leadership of Mustafa Kemal (Atatürk). Kemal was a Unionist who had remained independent of all political factions during the constitutional period and had attained prominence as an accomplished warrior and hero of the Dardanelles War. Denounced by the caliph sultan as heretics and outlaws, the nationalists waged a successful war of liberation, elected a new parliament based in Ankara, abolished the sultanate, and declared the Republic of Turkey on 29 October 1923. Throughout this ordeal, Mustafa Kemal and his followers had to show utmost care in dealing with the pull and power of Islam that was incarnated in the person of the Ottoman sultan. However, after the victory over the Allied powers, Mustafa Kemal launched a modernization-Westernization campaign that was meant to transform the new nation-state of Turkey into a member of the Western league.

The trials and tribulations of this adventure on the path to Turkish modernity continue to generate intense debate in the political, academic, and literary-artistic circles of modern Turkey. Novelists have invented multiple allegories to represent the sense of belatedness and incompleteness that haunts Turkish modernity. Tanpınar once observed that "[e]very history has its own fatality. The fatality of Turkish history is the awful thing we call belatedness" (*Mücerherlerin Sırrı* 138). Ernest Gellner, an astute philosopher of nationalism, provides an alternative insight into the problem in terms of the contiguity between political and cultural nationalism.

In "The Turkish Option in Comparative Perspective," Gellner, though no expert on Turkish politics by his own admission, offers a perceptive and convincing parable that explains in relative terms the Turkish dilemma. He sees the congruence between state and culture as the defining pattern of modern nationalism. Unlike in earlier societies, where culture marked status, in the modern world culture "marks the boundaries of political units and the kinds of pools within which individuals can move freely in what is inherently an unstable occupational structure" (240). Historical paths to the marriage of nation and culture in Europe have differed along different time zones and with respect to the relationship between the bride (high culture) and the groom (political situation). In the first of the three time zones of Europe (Spain, Portugal, England, and France), the strong political dynasties coincided more or less with the cultural domain; with the advent of nationalism, no engineering was needed to merge political and cultural maps. The only exception to this rule was the creation of the Republic of Ireland. In the second zone, a beautifully presented bride was ready, but there was no bridegroom. The culture of Italy and Germany had been established since the time of Dante and Goethe, but there was no political suitor. In the course of time, suitors were found in Prussia and Piedmont, and the marriage was arranged without too much trauma. But in the third zone, in Eastern Europe, neither the bride nor the groom was present, and the marriage that was supposed to be the foundation of nationalism had to be politically and culturally engineered.

In the Muslim world, a different scenario unfolds, for here nationalism and fundamentalism derive from the same source. In the transition from a stable agricultural society with no space for growth to a modern society, where agriculture is one occupation among others, growth is expected, and a unifying idiom of affiliation, "a semantic standardization" (241), is required. In Gellner's view, this transition has generally manifested itself in Europe as nationalism and in the Islamic world as fundamentalism, with the exception that in Europe, high culture for the most part has been divorced from religious doctrine, whereas in the Islamic world, high culture and religion have remained intimately linked. Gellner has no explanation for that close alliance.

The Turkish situation, which Gellner calls "profoundly eccentric" (242), challenges the narrative cohesion of this parable. During the great nationalist movements of Europe, the Ottomans had groomed the groom, but there was no bride. The groom was not a political entity in a real sense; he was a state elite that happened to speak Turkish, was in the past identified with Islam, did not have much interest in the Anatolian peasantry as a potential bride, and administered a religiously, linguistically, and ethnically diverse population. To find a way out of the decline of the state, the groom had to find a suitable cultural-ethnic bride. The Islamic choice was no longer viable, since religion had been too closely associated with the declining ancien régime. So the only available ethnic bride was the Anatolian peasantry, who wasn't quite sure what was happening to her and continued to think for some time about the union in religious rather than political terms.

Thus the Ottoman Turkish case differs in Gellner's parable from the European scenarios as well as from the Islamic one. For Gellner, the final act of the Turkish scenario was the emergence of a distinctively new political system. The Kemalists adopted Western models without subscribing to an overly determined political doctrine that would prove economically and politically unfeasible in the long run. What the elite cadres did was emulate those political principles, such as nationalism and constitutionalism, which they believed to be rightly or wrongly the reason for the success of Western societies. Gellner concludes that the basic problem in the adoption of Western sociopolitical systems lay in their implementation: political parties courting Islam would win the elections and betray the democratic principles that gave them a shot at power. Gellner's view is supported by the long history of military interventions on grounds that the ruling party had been fomenting religious sentiment. A major concern is this vicious circle that a generation of critics, no longer committed to Kemalist secularism, is trying to break by disassociating Islam from the ancien régime and trying to identify "out there in Anatolia" a more liberal, more pliable, "and perhaps more modernizable Islam" (244).

Although Gellner's analysis may be viewed with some skepticism by readers in search of more factual insights and a more positivist analysis, his parable sheds light on the opaque paradoxes of recent Turkish history and its parallels to the fortunes of modernity in other secular Islamic nations, such as Algeria, Tunisia, and Indonesia, where modernization projects have faced the challenge of accommodating Islam. Modern Algerian writers have been astute and passionate interpreters of their land's ongoing trauma of colonization, liberation, secularization, nation building, and terrorization by extremist branches of Islam. The family ties between some of the recent outstanding novels of political trauma that have come out of Algeria and the novels of the early Republican period in Turkey that foresaw the inevitable clash between Islam and modernity are worth noting. I pick up this thread in the next chapter.

The Context(s) of Cultural Nationalism

The long-standing reform movements of the late Ottoman Empire found their most persuasive and diverse modes of expression in the literary arena. As Lewis correctly noted:

> From about the middle of the century the spread of Western ideas and ac-
> climatization of Western political and social attitudes among the Turks was
> greatly accelerated by the rise of a new Turkish literature, differing both in
> form and content from classical Ottoman writings.   (136)

In particular, French literature replaced the Persian classics as a model of enlightened insight into human life. The French Revolution had left an indirect but enduring and powerful influence on the intellectual psyche of the Ottoman literati. The growth of print capitalism set up a grand bazaar that eventually became a site of exchange for the cultural producers of ideas and the consuming readers. Although the Sephardic Jews, who had fled the Spanish Inquisition and settled in the Ottoman Empire in 1493, brought the printing press with them to Istanbul and although the Armenians and Greeks had their own publishing houses in the empire, the printing of Arabic letters was legalized only in the early eighteenth century. After the Tanzimat period there was a visible increase in the number of publishing houses, and İbrahim Şinasi (1826–71), a French-educated Ottoman civil servant, poet, and dramatist who experienced the revolution of 1848 in Paris and was influenced by the ideas of the French intellectuals he befriended, founded the first Turkish newspaper, *Tasvir-i Efkâr* ("Description of Ideas") in 1862. When Şinasi, fearing official reprisal, fled to Paris in 1895, Namık Kemal, the patriotic poet and dramatist (1840–88), took over the editorship of the paper.

The young Ottoman elite saw as its mission the introduction of the ideas and ideals of the French Revolution and the Enlightenment to the reading public and identified two venues to that end: literature and the mass media of the time, journals and newspapers. These media became the forum for ideas of freedom and progress and for a shared sense of mission among their readership. Şemseddin Sami published the first Turkish novel, *Taaşşuk-ı Talât ve Fıtnat* ("The Love Story of Talat and Fitnat"), in 1872. What distinguished the writers of this period, like Şinasi, Namık Kemal, Sami, and Ahmet Mithat, from their predecessors was their use of a living, spoken Turkish that allowed their readership easy access into a world of ideas cast in terms of a familiar social imaginary. Furthermore, for these writers the pedagogical and social mandate of literature was inseparable from its artistic mission. In the foreword to one of his novels, Ahmet Mithat states that the novel is not merely an account of an amusing and strange event. In every case, such an event is linked to a branch of knowledge, to a philosophical concept, or to a geography or a chapter of history, with the result that the information provided on these subjects expands the knowledge of the reader (Moran 1: 19).

Berna Moran, who was a prominent literary critic and professor of English literature, relates how Namık Kemal and the Young Ottomans viewed newspapers and stories as a kind of open university that would spread the concepts of liberty, equality, and *fen* ("science" or "knowledge") among the people. Although Moran believed the Young Ottomans were naive to think that such intellectual capital could be imported into a different social and historical context, he praised their effort to keep in touch with the people by upholding the ideals of Islam, while injecting the ideas of the Enlightenment to combat widespread ignorance. In contrast, the Tanzimat elite, in Moran's view, erred by turning away from the people, ignoring the spiritual pull of Islam, and embracing the positivism, materialism, and Darwinism of the French intellectuals. In a society with a centuries-old, cemented Islamic base, this radical project of the intelligentsia was bound to generate a pronounced cultural duality. Today, debates around the origins, causes, and consequences of these bifurcated paths of the Ottoman heritage retain their currency and urgency, as they are intimately linked with the ever-contested issue of Turkish identity.

Lewis identifies 1859, the year İbrahim Şinasi published a lithographed book (*Tercüme-i-Manzume* ["Translation of Verses"]) of about a hundred verse translations from the French classics, as the birth date of the new Turkish literature under Western influence (439). The introduction of European literary conventions into Turkish literature was carried out in translation. At this time, the state had undertaken major steps toward training a cadre of bureaucrats in Western languages at the Tercüme Odası ("Translation Office") opened in 1833. The state trained this group (mostly in French) to serve as diplomats. This step was a novelty, as the Ottomans had until then used the services of the Christian dragomans in their dealings with the European states. When the Ottomans realized that they were losing ground to the Western powers not only in science, technology, and the arts but also in war and diplomacy, they decided that they needed to have their own representatives who could provide a firsthand understanding of the Western powers, which had become a serious threat to the empire. French textbooks were taught in military and medical schools. Since the Arabic script then in use captured the sounds of Turkish poorly and meaning often had to be derived from context, reading complex concepts in a Turkish using Arabic characters created confusion, so much so that the language of instruction at the School of Medicine, established in 1827, was French (Güvenç 262). Ultimately, during the course of his vast Westernization reforms, Atatürk undertook the most radical project of "translation," known as *harf devrimi* ("letter or alphabet reform"), by replacing the Arabic script with the Roman alphabet.

After the publication of Şinasi's translations from the French, the translation project, as an access route to Western civilization, branched out and formed the basis of the modern Turkish novel and drama. These genres served as cultural translators of Western idioms and European customs and, in a way, acclimatized readers and spectators to changes that were coming their way. Traditional literary criticism has tended to assign translations and adaptations a marginal status and considered a literature based on these low-status genres derivative and secondhand. Practically every work on Turkish literary history cites the birth of the Turkish novel from translation as an inauspicious beginning, an almost embarrassing fact that is best left unexamined or glossed over.

Any comparative study of literature would reveal the error of this view. Recent developments in literary history and literary theory have reclaimed the enormous influence of translation and translational activity and underscored their function in the formation of a national culture. In *The Experience of the Foreign*, Antoine Berman shows how the large-scale translation project of early German Romanticism, which realized the translation of major Western and Eastern classical works into German, aimed to expand and enrich the expressive capabilities of German. The language that translators create in making the unfamiliar familiar to the reader is contingent on the cultural capital of their language, and the labor of translation involves seeking and testing all the conceptual possibilities of one's language and reflecting on these. Ziya Gökalp (1876–1924), a prominent Turkish sociologist and critic writing in the early twentieth century, maintained that since the Turks were in the process of adopting Western civilization, they needed a new vocabulary to express Western concepts. In Gökalp's view, the way to a new language of concepts was through translation of the scientific, philosophical, and literary classics written in European languages:

> Through these translations, several new words and modes of expression will enter into the New Turkish in addition to several means of linguistic refinement, grammatical tools and organs, syntactical mechanisms and constructions, and new possibilities to express sentimental and symbolic meanings. Then, the New Turkish will become a vehicle to express the most complex ways of thinking.　　　　　　　　　　　　　　(*Turkish Nationalism* 296)

Translation also allows for inferences and interpretations influenced by new readings. Thus, in early German Romanticism, translation and criticism were considered creative activities that not only ensured the survival of the original work but also constituted a second-order art form themselves. The new generation of Ottoman writers, in their translations, mined the language of the people that had been neglected and dismissed by the practitioners of Ottoman poetry. Their investigations and reflections gave rise to a language that endowed readers with a sense of belonging to a larger culture that was no longer inaccessible to them. Since translation is the most direct route into the lives and realities of others, its pragmatic value for the Ottomans lay in its promise of clarifying and defining political strategy vis-à-vis the often unknown and unsympathetic Western other.

In a philosophical sense, understanding the other is the first prerequisite of self-understanding. As translation reinterprets texts for different audiences and for continued self-understanding and reflection, it generates the will for a conscious ownership of one's own language and heritage and for the future formation of communities. As Sandra Bermann observes:

> [L]anguage remains radically contingent upon specific local histories and contexts. . . . Cultural practices produce and sustain—and are in turn sustained by—the lexicon and syntax of a given language. Highly particularized cultural markers must therefore be taken into account in any linguistic interpretation— in principle, an infinite task and a necessarily self-reflective one.　　　(4)

In their translational and adaptational efforts, the early Ottoman novelists and writers made Western themes and forms familiar and naturalized them. At the same time, they reached beyond the confines of Ottoman court poetry and culture and reclaimed parts of the Turkish folk tradition. Gökalp argued that Turkish literature had to "go through an education in two schools of art for its development: One is folk literature and the other is Western literature" (298). Under the cultural influence of the Turkist movement, a neglected cultural past was reimagined, as evidenced in the emerging use of Turkish syllabic verse; in the revival of the fourteenth-century folk poet Yunus Emre's mystical lyrics; in critical interest in such popular writers as the seventeenth-century lyric poet Karacaoğlan and the travel writer Evliya Çelebi; and, most significant, in interest in the works of pre-Islamic Turkish literature, such as the epic of the Oghuz, one of the major branches of the Turkic peoples (Gökalp 299; Lewis 440). This tenth-century epic, known as *The Book of Dede Korkut*, presents a vast panorama of Turkish tribal life in action-packed detail. If one can speak of a Turkish national imagination, *Dede Korkut* is arguably the embodiment of its epic élan, for it represents a cultural synthesis, unique to its Anatolian background, whereby historical facts, real and imaginary persons, pastoral and social metaphors, elements of Greek mythology and Turkish *masal* ("fairy tale"), and men and women mix and mingle with natural ease.

Today, despite their ideological differences, most Turkish intellectuals see a synthesis of the usable capital of modernity with Anatolia's past and present cultures and a tolerance for and reconciliation of these in the national psyche as the only feasible solution to the trauma and turmoil a sociohistorically ungrounded project of modernity has brought in its wake. As Emre Kongar maintains, Turkey—a secular Islamic country, a cultural bridge between Eastern and Western civilizations, both a Middle Eastern and Mediterranean country, as well as a Balkan state strategically placed between various geographies and histories—stands a good chance of producing a new cultural synthesis for our times (61). However, the idea of incorporating Islam into the new cultural synthesis is a vexed issue for secular Turks, who have witnessed time and again how politics uses and abuses religion, how political parties with a strong religious agenda draw the votes of the poor and the underprivileged but do nothing to improve the lot of those who vote for them. On the other hand, there is a growing number of younger intellectuals who are critical of the systematic erasure of religious and ethnic differences in the name of national unity and the silencing of dissident voices. And there are respectable voices, those of prominent novelists, historians, and social scientists who claim that Kemalist secularism has demonized Islam, ignored its powerful spell on the masses, and disrespected this cultural heritage as atavistic and incommensurable with the welfare of the modern state. They advocate a reintroduction of Islamic practice into everyday life that would endow society with a sense of reconciliation and consolation. But they offer no clue as to how this integration can be accomplished. The idea may sound feasible at the level of discourse, but in terms of political reality none of its proponents has offered a viable process of implementing it.

The recent history of Turkish culture reveals that the demands of nationalism and democracy continually run the risk of aggravating ethnic and religious sentiment and that the inevitable necessity of transition to modern life wreaks havoc in traditional societies. It also suggests that the reforms or liberationist movements of yesteryear can calcify into reactionary or ideologically rigid views of today. Reformist missions may be caught in self-generated paradoxes. Even Atatürk, a single-minded architect of Westernization reforms, went in search of a distinctly Turkish mythopoeic prehistory, reconstituted from archaic, archival, or fictive fragments, while positing Western culture as the model that modern Turks should aspire to emulate. These paradoxes are unavoidable in any effort to seek continuity or unity in a history that has been disrupted. Benedict Anderson, for example, claims that the ruptures caused by the upheavals of the late eighteenth century led to a "forgetting" of being embedded in continuous time, and the loss of grounding in a historical continuum engendered "the need for a narrative of 'identity' " (205).

In the second half of the nineteenth century, the quest for this narrative of identity in Ottoman Turkish culture developed along diverging paths. The socially committed writers popularized reformist ideas and ideals against the intractability of conservative Islamic practices and institutions. Newspapers, journals, and novels became a vehicle for initiating social reforms. Kongar writes:

> The history of political struggles for freedom and constitutional government in the Ottoman Empire in the Nineteenth Century is the history of newspapers, journals, and literature, in the sense that they were either directly or indirectly attached to political organizations, or written and published by people who were fighting for political ideals. (48)

While Namık Kemal was promoting notions of freedom and fatherland through his newspaper editorials, novels, and plays, a few other writers and members of the Young Ottomans were concerned that Western culture, the source of such concepts as national identity, equality, and fraternity, would pose a serious threat to the formation of an Ottoman identity. Namık Kemal's patriotism implied a nascent form of nationalism, which found its full articulation later in the work of the sociologist Ziya Gökalp.

Nation, Language, and the Reformist Vision

Gökalp, arguably the most prominent champion of Turkish nationalism during the early years of the twentieth century, advanced his theories of Turkism in such journals as *Türk Yurdu* ("Turkish Homeland") and *Genç Kalemler* ("Young Pens"). Like so many Ottoman intellectuals, he was strongly influenced by French sources, and he underwrote his nationalism with sociological theories—particularly the positivist tenets of Emile Durkheim. He did not want to appear as a fanatic nationalist and so couched his formulations mostly in a conciliatory language and presented Turkism as an alternative to the divide between modernization movements in the Ottoman state, initiated by Sultan Selim III (1789–1807), and the Islamic revivalism. Gökalp was the first theorist of Turkish nationalism. However, he was not a politician either by vocation or by avocation and had no interest in the machinations of political power. He articulated a political sentiment but was not swayed to act on it. In fact, he modified his ideas of a Pan-Turkic dream by restating his position to conform to the unionist philosophy of the Union and Progress Party in power, which subscribed to the idea of unity among the different peoples of the Ottoman Empire. After a careful review of historical record, Gökalp reconstituted the information he gleaned in a triadic schema of Turkish identity. He concluded that Turks belonged to the Uralic-Altaic group of people, to the followers of Islam, and to Western internationality. "People cannot only live with one ideal," he wrote in *Turkish Nationalism and Western Civilization*, "as the ideal of nationality is imperative, the ideals of inter-community life, of international life, and inter-religious life are equally needed. With respect to ideals, we are pluralist" (103).

Today, Gökalp's legacy rests much more on his championship of the Turkish language than on his theories of Turkish nationalism. His commitment to the promotion of the accessibility of Turkish was not merely a linguistic and literary concern but a social and political one as well. Gökalp suggested, for example, that the Koran be read in Turkish so that the Turks could understand the meaning of their prayers and the command of God (301). For him, the religious rites and rituals that inspired the highest degree of rapture in the faithful were

> those sincere and silent supplications which are offered in the native tongue after the usual prayers [in Arabic]. . . . [T]he recital of the Birthday Poem [*Mevlid*] composed in Turkish is the ritual that gives the greatest . . . joy to the Turks. This ritual, which combines in itself poetry and music and dramatic events, became one of the most vital forms of ritual among the Turks in spite of the fact that it was a latter-day religious innovation.   (301)

Perhaps nothing binds people more intimately to missions, ideals, and ancient dreams than language. Anderson illustrates this point effectively when he states that for English speakers the mere nine words "Earth to earth, ashes to ashes, dust to dust" create an intimation of simultaneity across time. The power of this ritual chant from a centuries-old past derives only in part from the solemn meaning of its words; "it comes from an as-it-were ancestral 'Englishness'" (145). Likewise, Gökalp's oft-quoted lines from his poem "Turan" rang like a solemn prayer for many Turks, Ottomanist, nationalist, antinationalist, and even atheist alike: "Vatan ne Türkiye'dir Türklere, ne Türkistan / Vatan büyük ve müebbed bir ülkedir, Turan" (*Yeni Hayat* 119 ["Turan"]; "For the Turk, the homeland is neither Turkey nor Turkestan / that homeland is the vast and eternal land of Turan").

Atatürk shared Gökalp's passion for a Turkish language freed from the bondage of foreign influences; the idea of a mythical Turan and Pan-Turkism, however, was anathema to him. Throughout his political career, he remained a vehement opponent of all aspirations to reclaim any territory beyond the confines of the Anatolian homeland. As the political leader and policy maker of the new republic, he remained opposed to irredentist dreams. He showed no intention of salvaging lost lands but every intention of salvaging Turkish custom (culture) from Arab Islamic costume (forms of representation). He abolished all Islamic modes of headwear and attire and introduced the hat. He banned the wearing of religious vestments and paraphernalia for those not holding a religious office. Educated urban women began sporting Western fashions, but the veil and the wraps around women's bodies were not dispensed with that easily in the provinces. He categorically abolished the sharia (Islamic law), and a commission of lawyers adapted the Swiss civil code to Turkish society. A man of swift and decisive action, Atatürk proceeded to change the system of measurements, the calendar, and—most significant—the script. Feroz Ahmad considers the alphabet reform (or "letter revolution") as possibly the most "iconoclastic" (80) of Kemalist reforms. There were many official justifications for this reform, the most obvious being the aforementioned difficulty of the discrepancy between Arabic letters and Turkish sounds (or phonetic characteristics), which made reading difficult and was a major obstacle to literacy.

On 21 November 1928, the parliament passed the law introducing the Roman alphabet and announcing that all publications would use the new script as of the New Year. According to a 1927 census, less than nine percent of the population was literate. Atatürk, who believed that being literate was what made us human, saw to it that the government set up schools to teach the new script and urged his fellow countrymen to reach out and teach each and every citizen the new alphabet as their national duty (Ahmad 81). Atatürk himself went around the country teaching the new alphabet, on which he had worked with a committee of linguists. Beyond the official line, one of the major reasons behind the alphabet reform was a final symbolic disassociation from Islamic Arabic culture, a decisive step to urge the Turks to look westward. Predictably, these sweeping reforms met with overt and covert resistance, not only from within but also from other Muslim countries. Even some members of the elite were incensed by the interment of a culture that they saw as their rightful inheritance. A widely known anecdote recounts the distress of a noted intellectual who commented that the populace would not be able to read the writings on the tombstones. Halide Edib, a prominent author who participated on Atatürk's side in the revolutionary war, was skeptical if not outright critical of what she considered an unreflected acceptance of Western civilization.

The most radical break with the Islamic world and way of life came with the abolition of the caliphate, a move that created a great deal of anxiety, resistance, and resentment. The Ottoman sultan was also the caliph, head of Islam. The last sultan, Vahdettin, had been deported, but on 18 November 1922 the Grand National Assembly appointed a successor, Abdülmecid Efendi, as the caliph, thus separating the caliphate from the sultanate. The existence of the caliphate was an obstacle on the road to Atatürk's mission of absolute national sovereignty and independence. His determination to abolish the caliphate became even stronger when Indian

Muslim leaders implored the Turkish government to preserve it so as to command the esteem and confidence of the Muslim nations and endow the Turkish nation with a unique strength and privilege (Lewis 263). Atatürk was quite aware of the importance of the caliphate as a link to the Ottoman past and the Islamic world, and precisely for that reason he was intent on abolishing this last remnant of the old regime. By careful political planning and maneuver, he succeeded in having the Grand National Assembly declare the abolition of the caliphate and the deportation of all the members of the Ottoman dynasty from Turkey, on 3 March 1924.

The *Türk Devrimi* ("Turkish Revolution"), as the foundation of the nation and the attendant reform movements came to be called, was a revolution from above. In their range and ambition—from the alphabet reform to the changing of the system of measurements, secularization of education, bringing religious affairs under state control, the hat reform and Westernization of dress, and economic and agricultural reorganization—the reforms were invasive procedures. During the last years before its collapse, the Ottoman Empire was known as the sick man of Europe. The new republic started life with traces and memories of that sickness in the form of financial challenges, illiteracy, and deep division between a minority of educated civil servants, military officers, and intellectuals and a vast majority of impoverished and illiterate peasants and religious and otherwise deeply conservative forces whose loyalty was not to the nation but to the sultanate-caliphate and Islam. Atatürk had to resort to an aggressive and comprehensive treatment that the moment called for. He aimed at creating a totally new and Western society, "whereas the westernist movements prior to his time were geared to imitating Western societies (Kongar 29). However, somewhat ironically, Atatürk also had strong anti-imperialist views, derived from his understanding of Western civilization, that convinced him that the only way to be a part of the West was to be free from Western political and economic control and exploitation (29). His career as head of state was continually challenged by inside and outside powers. Nevertheless, since he had virtually absolute power as president, he could pass all the reform bills, and his opponents often found themselves facing a fait accompli.

The reforms were on paper and enforced by law, but in reality only a small elite cadre had embraced them. Atatürk needed another army to spread the gospel, to popularize the new reforms. This corps was formed by novelists, journalists, diplomats, and teachers. Many of them had been Atatürk's friends and allies during the War of Independence and had joined the nascent Republican movement early on. Their participation in the formation of the republic took them to the Anatolian hinterland, where they witnessed firsthand the trials, suffering, and ignorance of the peasantry. They experienced the cultural divide in their land in no uncertain terms and anticipated the trials that the young nation would be facing in the years to come. As I discuss in the next chapter, the work of the early Republican writers shows intimations of calamities that would return to haunt the new regime. Exhausted by two major wars and relieved to be finally free, the progeny of the Ottomans did not have the time, the chance, or the inclination to mourn the death of the empire. But the power of Islamic mentality, presumed buried in the rubble of the past, returned much sooner than expected. Güntekin's *Yeşil Gece* (1928; "The Green Night") and Karaosmanoğlu's *Yaban* (1932; "The Alien") envision the grave consequences of the return of the repressed with alarming clarity. The authors take a grim view of the antirational and potentially destructive character of an Islamic mentality that held backward Anatolian towns in its grip. But their portrayal of Muslim fanatics was far tamer than the reality of religious extremism that threatened the new republic only a decade after its declaration. *The Green Night* and *The Alien* respectively pre- and postdate the gruesome Kubilay incident.

On 23 December 1930, a mob led by a sheikh carrying a green flag surrounded the city hall in Menemen, near İzmir (Smyrna), demanding the restoration of the Islamic state and law and threatening to kill anyone resisting them. A twenty-four-year-old teacher by the name of Ahmet Kubilay, who was doing his military service in Menemen at the time, went unarmed to the scene of the demonstration and tried to calm the protesters. Seeing the young man in the uniform of the national army, the mob got violent, held him down, slowly decapitated him, and displayed his head on the pole with the green flag. This was a town liberated from the Greek invaders just a few years ago by young officers like Kubilay. The perpetrators were caught and punished, but needless to say this incident was a harbinger of things to come.

For the modern reader, the prescience of *The Green Night* and *The Alien* appears almost uncanny. History has a short memory, and although Kubilay has been mostly forgotten by history books, these novels remember the specter of his assassins. The early Republican novelists understood the tyranny of the forces of oppression, fear, and ignorance and also demonstrated the will to reimagine ways of confronting them. They believed that their fellow citizens and the following generations had the power to create a different society. Their writing anticipates the alternating periods of conflict and cautious reconciliation between Turkey's modernization forces and Islamic heritage.

Notes

1. For a very comprehensive study of the genesis of the Turkish novel, see Evin, whose study focuses on the late Ottoman and pre-Republican novelists and the sociohistorical context of the emergence of the Turkish novel.
2. In addition to the classic reference books used in this study (Bernard Lewis's *The Emergence of Modern Turkey*, Feroz Ahmad's *The Making of Modern Turkey*, and Eric J. Zürcher's revised edition of *Turkey: A Modern History*), Niyazi Berkes's *The Development of Secularism in Turkey* and Carter Vaughn Findley's comprehensive history *The Turks in World History* are highly recommended sources.

CHAPTER 3

Growing Pains of the Nation

Literature has a great part to play in solving the new tasks
imposed by the new life in every country. If literature is really
to fulfill this role, a role dictated by history, there must be, as
a natural prerequisite, a philosophical and political rebirth of
the writers who produce it.

—Georg Lukács, "Historical Truth in Fiction"

Not only must historical circumstance create a new existential
situation for a character in a novel, but history *itself* must be
understood and analyzed as an existential situation.

—Milan Kundera, *The Art of the Novel*

The novelists of the early Republican era were not an elite divorced
from the ranks of their fellow citizens. Though writers by avocation, by vocation they were teachers, journalists, politicians, translators, and diplomats. They had been witness to the long chain of calamities
that ravaged their land and were attuned to the silent distress of those who
lost their place in geography and their footing in history. A socially and historically engaged imagination that informed the work of these novelists
played a considerable role in the trials and travails of nation building. Like
Atatürk, prominent writers of the Republican era, such as Reşat Nuri Güntekin, Yakup Kadri Karaosmanoğlu, and the multitalented Halide Edib
Adıvar, advocated the ideals of progress, equal rights, and universal education. However, they were also guided by a visionary sensibility that anticipated the consequences of a hastened modernity. In Güntekin's *Yeşil Gece*
("The Green Night") and Karaosmanoğlu's *Yaban* ("The Alien"), selected
for discussion here, we see that repressed history—in this case, a long Islamic tradition demoted by Atatürk's ardently enforced reforms—returns
with a vengeance to stall Kemalist ideals at key junctures. What is interesting is that in both novels, the return of the repressed is not projected into

the future but happens in the present, before any possibility of secular nationalism's self-realization. Situated in a moment of great hope for an enlightened future, these works narrate an invisible history, one that no official historiography could afford to reveal.

Adıvar's work, on the other hand, does not share this grim view of a cultlike Islam but envisions the possibility of a serene and mystical Islam embracing the egalitarian sensibility of the enlightened West. Although Adıvar's vision for a progressive as well as an *avant la lettre* feminist Islam has provided the basis of some current sentiments that call for a full-fledged legitimization of the Islamic way in a secular state, it was Güntekin and Karaosmanoğlu's insight that proved to be prophetic, as modern Turkish society kept losing ground to political Islam.

One of the strengths of literature produced at critical historical moments is its ability and freedom to imagine alternative scenarios to a scripted or wished-for history. The literary imagination that informed the work of the early Republican authors, such as Güntekin and Karaosmanoğlu, foresaw the unfolding of history and a people's destiny in ways that did not agree with their own ideals and dreams for Turkey's future. Therefore, they saw it as their responsibility to point out that what had been forcibly removed from view, the entrenched religious sentiments that lay dormant beneath the surface of the fragile new secular institutions, were waiting for an opportunity to strike. The novelistic imagination of the early Republican writers foretells modern Turkey's long and arduous experiment with democracy and the trials of safeguarding the mandates of secularism against the offensive of political Islam.

The Formation of National Consciousness in the Early Republican Novel

Almost a century after the end of the Ottoman Empire and the Turkish War of Independence, the works of Adıvar, Güntekin, and Karaosmanoğlu, who witnessed the cataclysms and momentous transitions of their era, remain more popular than ever, despite the emergence of numerous talented writers in the contemporary Turkish literary scene. In his afterword to Adıvar's national romance *Ateşten Gömlek* ("Shirt of Fire"), Selim İleri makes an observation that I see as one index of the enduring legacy and popularity of these three novelists. "What I know about the trials of our recent history, I learned mostly from novels," İleri reflects. "History books, even memoirs and firsthand-witness accounts, were never sufficient" ("Bugüne Bir 'Ateş-ten Gömlek' " 229). The writers of this period belonged to a class we would today call public intellectuals. They were teachers, academics, writers, artists, or journalists; not bound by their vocation but active participants in sociopolitical life, they shared their expertise in the service of a wider public or to political and liberatory ends. The novels of the early Republican period reveal strong (auto)biographical strands, as they are situated at the crossroads of collective destiny and the life paths of individual authors or of their alter egos. This is especially true of Halide Edib Adıvar, whose life story parallels the adventures of her heroines as well as the fortunes of the times she has recorded with great critical insight. Because of these parallels, I read here what I consider to be her most accomplished novel, *Shirt of Fire*, in dialogue with *Memoirs of Halidé Edib*. Adıvar recently became the subject of many critical studies, not only because she was a reliable chronicler of the times but also because she is seen as the most important feminist political leader of her era and a trailblazer of Turkish feminisms.[1]

Halide Edib was born in 1882 into an aristocratic Ottoman Turkish family during the final years of the nineteenth century, as the Ottoman Empire began its final descent into historical obsolescence. Her mother died when Halide was a young girl, and she was raised by her father, grandmother, and first stepmother. She grew up amid different cultures—her grandmother's traditional Ottoman household, her father's Westernized world, and her stepmother's European books. She was tutored in Arabic and mathematics and went to a Greek neighborhood school. In 1901, she became the first Turkish graduate of the American College for Women in Istanbul. On graduation, she married her mathematics tutor, Salih Zeki, but they divorced after they had two children, since Zeki took a second wife. In 1917, Edib married Adnan Adıvar, a family doctor and a kindred intellectual and political figure. At the end of the First World War, Edib and Adıvar became active in Atatürk's guerrilla war against the sultan and the invading powers. With like-minded freedom fighters, they went to the Anatolian front to serve in the War of Independence. Edib witnessed firsthand, the ravages of this war and the sacrifices made in its name, as she served first as colonel and later as sergeant in the army. After the war, she and her husband had a falling out with Atatürk and went into exile. From 1926 to 1939, the two lived in France and the United Kingdom. They returned home from their self-chosen exile only after Atatürk's death in 1938. During their years away from Turkey, Halide Edib traveled widely and lectured in the United States (in 1931, she was a visiting professor of history at Barnard College). In 1935, she was invited to India to give a series of lectures. Her popularity in India rested to a great extent on the translation of her novel *Shirt of Fire* as *The Daughter of Smyrna*. The translation was a modified version of the original, as it was intended to promote anticolonial sentiment in India. After the Adıvars returned to Turkey, Halide Edib became a professor of English literature at the University of Istanbul. In 1950, she was elected to the parliament as member of the newly formed Democrat Party but resigned in 1954 after being disappointed by its politics. She never ran for political office again. She died in 1964 in Istanbul at the age of eighty.

Halide Edib's real life story comes very close to her imagined stories. Her early novels were inspired by her domestic troubles at home (when her husband, who was much older than she, announced that he was taking a new wife) and criticize women's lack of social status and rights. The female protagonists of these novels are usually women who, when they first walk into the space of the novel, don't turn heads, so to speak, but in the course of the story grow larger than life, inspiring love, jealousy, and deadly passions. Since the woman is the love object, the narrator is often a man (or one of the men) in love with or in awe of her. Usually he becomes aware of her presence through the comments or observations of those in his circle, and his initial secondhand impressions are negative. In time, the narrator discovers her attractive qualities lie in her understated but subtly powerful beauty, wisdom, intelligence, virtue, strength, and so on. A melodramatic atmosphere dominates these early tales, which also often focus on forbidden love leading to tragic consequences.[2]

Many of Edib's protagonists in these early novels are women who have succeeded in blending the best traits of Ottoman Islamic and Western womanhood in their persons, and they embody Edib's ideal of the Turkish woman of the time (critics have pointed out that these idealized women are often her alter egos). They are Western-educated, strong, self-possessed, and talented in languages, literature, and the arts but do not subscribe to Western materialistic values, maintaining instead a strong sense of modesty and respect for the spiritual side of life. The novelty of these early sentimental novels was, as Berna Moran observed, the creation of a new woman as the marker of reconciliation between conflicting representations of women (1: 156). The intellectual elite saw the Ottoman Islamic woman as submissive and ignorant, the product of a tradition-bound, backward society. The Westernized, modern woman, on the other hand, was regarded as someone who had lost her roots and moorings, suffering from the confusion of being caught between two alien worlds. Edib's idealized heroines negotiated these contrary universes with skill and grace, as they remained rooted in the comfortable zone of valued traditions while studying demanding subjects, mastering foreign languages, playing the piano, riding horses, engaging in sports, and even fighting alongside men in the battlefield. And they managed to hone and preserve their feminine charms (and seductiveness) during these complex negotiations.

From a literary critical viewpoint, Edib's early novels may not give the discerning reader much to reflect on. The sheer volume and wide range of her work, however, provide a rich resource for different modes of critical approach—in particular, for theories of autobiography and questions of cultural inheritance. Her prolific work, penned in English and Turkish, including twenty-one novels, four short-story collections, two dramas, four scholarly books, and a two-volume autobiography, reflects her various lives and careers as a freedom fighter, teacher, founder of a Montessori school for orphans in Jerusalem, novelist, critic, translator, and professor of English literature. Her life and work further embody an exemplary practice of cultural translation between the literary traditions of the East and the West. Unlike some of her contemporary writers, Halide Edib found much in the Ottoman Islamic culture that needed to be preserved and incorporated into the body of a tolerant nationalism. A multilingual writer, well versed in several Western as well as Islamic literatures, she published some of her most renowned books in English and then translated them into Turkish. In the (auto)biographical fictions of her more mature work, she creates a utopian selfhood through characters who actualize a world of ideals through its presence in themselves. Compassion; tolerance for other lives, cultures, and persuasions; and a sense of inclusive nationalism that accommodates different beliefs and histories are realized in Edib's own life experiences and are reflected in her characters. Her *Memoirs* bear witness to a long and unusual national history. Since she spent years away from her homeland, first teaching at outposts of the Ottoman Empire in Arab lands and later in exile in England and France, two great colonial powers, she developed, long before questions of postcolonialism, orientalism, and national, religious, ethnic identities were critically articulated, a keen sense of justice owed to those robbed of their history, heritage, and human rights. Her negotiations among languages and cultures naturally led to a peripatetic perspective that invested her work with the urgency to rethink nationalism not in terms of territorial, religious, linguistic, and ethnic unity but in terms of the possibility of finding alternative systems and syntheses that unequivocally tolerate diversity.

Memoirs of Halidé Edib and *The Shirt of Fire*: History Conjugated in the First Person

Memoirs of Halidé Edib, published in 1926 in London, tells of the final years of the Ottoman Empire, first in a third-person narrative, through the eyes of the child Halide, and later in the first-person narrative of the young woman novelist who served as a teacher-principal in the schools and orphanages at outposts of the empire. The thematic concern of the book revolves around the meeting of Halide's personal story with the historical destiny of a state in decline. At the structural and stylistic level, the device of using a child's voice during the early years of the narrator's life lends the book a simplicity and clarity that bring history into intimate contact with the reader.

In addition to representing an intersection of personal and collective history, these memoirs illustrate that the relation of women to the modern Turkish nation has never been an indirect or obscure one. Halide Edib was on active duty in the Turkish War of Independence, in which thousands of Turkish women participated behind the lines. The new republic granted women suffrage and equal rights in all spheres of public life. In keeping with Edib's vision, women came to play an increasingly important role in the sociopolitical and cultural life of the new nation. In many contemporary works of Turkish literature, they emerge as guardians of ancestral, community, and national memories, for their voices record remembrances vital to self-preservation in the present.

Halide Edib belongs to a generation of writers, including Güntekin and Karaosmanoğlu, who are credited with underwriting the educational policies of the new nation during the early years of the republic. Many writers of the early Republican period made note of the trenchant power of Islam that proliferated through saint cults. Their works stand as a symbolic warning against this obscurantist force that was poised to challenge and combat nationalism. Halide Edib, on the other hand, remained a firm believer in the possibility of reconciling the serene spiritualism of Islam with the progressive elements of an educational system based on the principles of Enlightenment humanism. The need for the comforting rituals of Islam within a vision of progressive education and women's freedom constitutes the major paradox of her work. The paradox operates in the belief that un-equivocal social freedom and equal educational and political rights for women are compatible with Islamic practice. At the level of personal faith or in a purely spiritual sense, this union is certainly possible—but not under the sharia.

Edib's memoir predates the postmodern consciousness of rhetorical strategies that dictate the shape of historiography. However, as a practice of memory that is informed by the specificities of a national history and that maps, in Michel de Certeau's elegant formulation " 'the multiple paths of the future' by combining antecedent and possible particularities" (82), *Memoirs* lends her autobiographical history the authority of tradition. As Certeau has observed, "we find a subtle alteration of 'authority' in every popular tradition," for memory hails from many different moments; makes possible alterations without being negated by them; and far from being a mere repository of the past, "it sustains itself by *believing* in the existence of possibilities and by vigilantly awaiting them, constantly on the watch for their appearance" (87).

Edib has harnessed the power of storytelling to reopen and continue received tradition and reimagine its potential within the sociocultural frameworks of impending history. Three generations later, Hélène Cixous imagines the role of women's writing in the purchase of historical agency in similar terms:

> As subject for history, woman always occurs simultaneously in several places. Woman un-thinks the unifying, regulating history that homogenizes and channels forces, herding contradictions into a single battlefield. In woman, personal history blends with the history of all women, as well as national and world history.   (882)

Although Cixous maintains that it is impossible to define a feminine practice of writing, she believes that it will be conceived by subjects of history that stand outside systems where master narratives dominate, by those who cannot be subjugated to the dictates of patriarchal political regimes. Where personal story blends with community history, as in Edib, the actors on destiny's stage are not the Napoleons, Atatürks, and Churchills of textbooks but rather the masses of unsung heroes and heroines whose individual and collective acts have ultimately led to seismic shifts in the course of time.

In "'Mor Salkımlı Ev'in Hikâyesi" ("The Story of *The House with Wisteria*"), a personal note appended to a Turkish edition of Edib's *Memoirs*, Selim İleri reiterates his position that history books are a far cry from recounting, expressing, and impressing on us the lived reality of human lives with all their joys and sorrows (300). Edib's work succeeds precisely where history textbooks fail. Her personal story, that of a young idealist writer and teacher of the Ottoman aristocracy, is interlinked with the history of the Young Turk revolution, one of the boldest and most peculiar events that marked the last years of the Ottoman Empire.

When the revolution finally took place in 1908, the despotic Sultan Abdülhamid was not deposed, strangely enough, but given another chance to reinstitute the constitutional regime he had abolished more than thirty years before. The series of uprisings that finally led to the 1908 revolution had started around 1906 in eastern Anatolia as a result of economic hardships. Soldiers and civil servants who had not been paid for months quit their jobs. Corrupt governors and other officials were fired, as discontent reached critical proportions. After eastern Anatolia and Syria, Thessaloniki, in today's Greece, was racked by a large-scale revolt of the Third Army Corps. Agents sent by the sultan to investigate the unrest came under violent attack. Finally the sultan, fearing for his life, agreed to reinstate the 1876 constitution. For a brief happy moment in its late history, the Ottoman Empire witnessed the coming together of its people in a collective celebration. The Young Turk leadership that took the power away from the sultan was to witness the decimation of the empire through several major wars. After the final defeat of the Ottomans in the First World War on the side of Germany, the Ottoman territory was divided among the victors and stripped of its sovereignty according to the terms of the Treaty of Mondros, signed 30 October 1918.

Memoirs covers highlights of this history until the onset of the First World War. Edib's account is prescient in its sense of unrest about the eradication of a cultural legacy that had sustained a people for centuries. It emphasizes the vital importance of maintaining and respecting the ethnic, religious, and linguistic differences that had constituted the foundation of a long-standing culture. Although Edib received a thoroughly American education in Istanbul, from a very early age she was exposed to both Western and Eastern cultures. Her personal experience of being caught between the otherworldly, religious, and tradition-bound world of her grandmother and the intellectual world of her father is the reason behind her lifelong endeavor to synthesize the tenets of (mystical) Islam with the principles of an enlightening and liberating education. There was both horror and comfort in her childhood experiences of religion, forged by the women in the family circle that included a half sister overly fond of tales about the torture of sinners in hell. The young Edib notices a melancholy trait in the Ottoman Turkish character: "All ceremonies in Turkey, even marriages and Bairams, tend to take on a sad and solemn tone; always the women with wet eyes and the men in softened silent mood. What makes other people rejoice makes the Turk sad" (Adıvar, *Memoirs* 88).[3] This remark follows a scene that describes the now forgotten festivity that accompanied a child's first day of school. Children would be dressed up in the finest silk and ride to school in carriages with pillows under their feet. At school they would kiss the hand of the teacher and were given sweets and money. This celebration was considered to be as momentous an event as a wedding and as expensive. In adherence to the strong sense of charity in Ottoman life, neighborhoods would pitch in so that children of the poor could participate in this ritual. This scene is one of the many in Edib's *Memoirs* that restore to memory a long-lost portrait of sociocultural history

In Edib's autobiographical narrative, two customs stand out as instances of everyday practices that resist amnesia. The first concerns the easy proximity of life and death, their intimacy, which is reflected in the fascination with cemeteries, incantations, and prayers for the souls of the departed. Communing with the dead through various rituals is a theme that runs like a thread through Edib's story and appears to be a practice much more common in the circles of women than in those of men. The young Halide, despite her intellectual father's strongly rationalistic upbringing, finds solace in the nightly prayers that her grandmother has taught her. She never goes to bed without saying them and is convinced they shield her from the many crises at the home front and in the larger world. She plays in cemeteries, where the cypress trees are believed to be reincarnations of the dead, and is told that although these cypresses look like trees during the day, at night they turn into ghosts who wear green turbans and haunt the neighborhoods. This intimacy with the dead allegorizes the resistance to forgetting, the comforting spell of the past, and the desire to preserve it.

The other cultural legacy lovingly recalled in Edib's memoir is the fabled Karagöz shadow play, a form of improvisational puppet theater accompanied by music and sound effects and performed by skilled puppeteers. These shows were a staple of Ramadan entertainment during the Ottoman years and represented a performance art that was socially engaged and often politically combative in intent. Since the play could be performed anywhere and did not have a written text, its political message was censor-resistant and eluded all manner of political or religious intrusion. The two protagonists of the play were Karagöz ("Black Eye") and Hacivat, and their entourage included members of all ethnic and religious groups living in the Ottoman Empire. The puppeteer had to be able to imitate different dialects, accents, and speech mannerisms. Hacivat was a caricature of the intellectual elite whose scholarly idiom went over the heads of the others. Karagöz, a street-smart wisecracker, was pushed around but was no pushover; he acted as a foil to Hacivat by repeating Hacivat's words as their homonyms, thus creating a semantics of nonsense to comic effect. This show fascinated Edib as a panorama of social groups that made up the Ottoman Turkish ethnic fabric.

What was the place and significance of nationalism on this map of various ethnicities in the aftermath of the Ottoman Empire, where there was not even a word for nationalism? The concept entered Ottoman consciousness with the nationalist struggles of its subject peoples, who one by one split from the empire, ending "for ever the 'Ottomanist' dream of the free, equal, and peaceful association of peoples in a common royalty to the dynastic sovereign of the multi-national, multi-denominational empire" (Lewis 218). The concept of "peoples" in the Ottoman Empire roughly corresponded to religious communities known as millets. These were legally recognized communities of specific denominations, such as Greek Christians, Armenian Christians, Jews, and Muslims. Turks, Arabs, and Kurds formed the Muslim millets. Greeks, Armenians, and Jews all constituted separate millets. In other words, the communities in the empire were recognized not as ethnic (or national) entities but only as people defined by religious persuasion. The idea of national affiliation superseded religious identification at a much later date but even then remained a relatively alien concept (Lewis 335).

The designations that separate people and provoke them to violence against one another confuse the child Halide, who "had not entered yet that narrow human path where religion and language as well as racial differences make human beings devour each other" (*Memoirs* 27). Although the Balkan Wars and the occupation of the Ottoman territories after the defeat of the First World War disabused Edib of her nostalgia for the multiethnic empire, where "simple peoples of Turkey" (272) lived in peaceful coexistence, and led her to embrace nationalism in the form of Turanism,[4] she remained a staunch opponent of exclusionist national sentiments. Her reflections on the as yet nebulous and problematic notion of nationalism take on the form of an attempt at self-understanding:

> The individual or the nation, in order to understand its fellow-men or its fellow-nations, in order to create beauty and to express its personality, must go deep down to the roots of its being and study itself sincerely. The process of this deep self-duty, as well as its results, is nationalism. I believe with all earnestness that such a national self-study and the exchange of its results, is the first and right step to international understanding and love of the peoples and nations. (325–26)

Thus Edib approaches the question of nationalism philosophically, assuming a hermeneutic position that predicates self-understanding on the understanding of the other. Both nationalism and internationalism, as she understands them, need to be based on a broad foundation of respect for and understanding of other peoples' lives, emotions, and identities, as reflected in a given national character. However, any form of nationalism that engages in the destruction of others for purposes of self-aggrandizement turns into chauvinism and imperialism. Chauvinistic and imperialistic nations

> have themselves suffered materially and morally more than the peoples whom they have tried to hurt. One must admit at the same time that chauvinism and materialism are not the only outcomes of nationalism. The internationalism of Soviet Russia has shown itself both chauvinistic and imperialistic in certain ways. (326)

Edib's self-searching reflections on the ethics of nationalism, national struggles, tolerance for other cultures and civilizations, and the paradox of war both as a necessary way to free a people and as an instrument of destruction of human lives and moral values continue in the second installment of her memoirs, *The Turkish Ordeal*. These probing questions emerge with tremendous force in *Shirt of Fire*.[5] A stylistically accomplished alternation of historical fact with fiction creates a formal space where pathos, national consciousness, and a sense of history and tragedy come together. The novel moves among the genres of romance, ballad, epistolary novel, memoir, and war biography. The story begins in the voice of the war veteran Peyami, who is awaiting surgery to have a bullet removed from his brain. A former diplomat, he was caught up in the liberationist fervor that infected many Turks after the defeat of the Ottoman Empire in the First World War and its subsequent occupation by the great powers. Forsaking his affluent lifestyle in an upscale neighborhood of enemy-occupied Istanbul and his snobbish mother and her friends, who were in awe of everything Western and welcomed the invaders with open arms, he followed his cousin Cemal and Cemal's friend İhsan, both officers of the nationalist guerrilla forces, to the battlefields of Anatolia. The story is told in flashback as Peyami, who has lost his legs in the war, lies in an unnamed hospital with only an orderly as company. He presents his story in journal entries, reconstructed from memories, dreams, and hallucinations, as he awaits an operation that he may not survive. At the center of his painful memories is Ayşe, a quintessential Halide Edib heroine, who is Cemal's sister and Peyami's country cousin. It turns out that Peyami's decision to leave for Europe as a young man had in part been prompted by his desire to escape an arranged marriage to this cousin, whom he had never met, until she came to her aunt's house in Istanbul after the invasion of İzmir and the brutal murders of her husband and young son by the enemy. Ayşe becomes for all those around her the walking symbol of a national trauma that began in İzmir and took the name of this city on the Aegean coast. Known as Güzel İzmir ("beautiful Smyrna"), the city is famous for its surrounding fertile lands, its harbor, its significance as a center of sea commerce, and its Turkish-Greek culture.

The invasion of İzmir slashed a deep wound in Turkish consciousness and left no doubt in many minds that this was the beginning of the end. The novel represents this historical context with great emotional power. İzmir, personified as a violated sacred and beautiful woman, sounds the war cry for liberation and reprisal. Ayşe, the widowed heroine who is literally and symbolically no longer whole, becomes an allegory of the violated, injured, and invaded motherland. In the eyes of the narrator, she is instantly transformed from the plain country girl he had always imagined her to be to a beautiful, urbane (it turns out she is fluent in French), and magnetic woman, who is also virtuous, fearless, and a skilled war nurse. She becomes the force that sends her brother, his officer friends, and the narrator to Anatolia to fight in the War of Independence.

It is to Edib's credit that this complete allegorization of Ayşe/İzmir and Ayşe's portrait as a vintage Edib heroine do not rob the character of her human dimensions. The narrator, who is deeply and secretly in love with Ayşe, reimagines her in all her history, as he witnesses the obsessive love his friend İhsan, a dashing officer and regional army commander, harbors for her. The narrator suspects that Ayşe is attracted to İhsan but admits that she remains an enigma for him and that he has never been able to find out what her real feelings toward İhsan were. Ayşe, the daughter of İzmir, as she comes to be known, is consumed by the desire to take back İzmir, and all her personal feelings and needs seem to have been buried with her husband and son. Her grief, her apparent will for self-sacrifice, and her silence and hesitation in the face of İhsan's febrile confession of love for her raise her character above a formulaic heroine type.

The hopeless love triangle of Peyami, Ayşe, and İhsan; the seemingly willed martyrdom of İhsan and Ayşe, who Peyami buries side by side; and the final tragedy of the now totally abandoned narrator waiting for death in a godforsaken, unnamed place constitute the romantic and melodramatic strands of the story and make for a gripping tale. However, it is the documentary and journalistic aspects of the novel, which have an imagistic quality to them, that lend the story its enduring power. One of the most memorable moments in the final days of the Ottoman Empire, which reversed the fortunes of the defeated Turks, was the meeting of Sultanahmet on 19 May 1919, the same day Mustafa Kemal landed in Samsun to campaign for a war of liberation and to organize the cadres of a national army. That day, thousands gathered at Sultanahmet Square and listened to Halide Edib address the crowd with great oratory skill. By all accounts, Edib did not have a prepared speech; but, seized by the overwhelming charge of public emotion, she improvised one and later put it in writing. Her famous line "nations are not our enemy, but governments are" (*Ateşten Gömlek* 219) characterizes her constant belief in the possibility of fraternity among all peoples. The emotional tenor of the Sultanahmet meeting, which is recreated in the novel, informs Edib's story and forms the steel of the novel's structural and thematic frame.

The immensity of human suffering, the poverty of the Anatolian people exacerbated a thousandfold by the liberation war, and the sacrifice of many a young and idealistic life are all depicted with a keen eye but without graphic detail. Of great historical interest is Edib's account of how a guerrilla army comes into being and how such an army, facing an invader far superior in numbers, arms, knowledge, and technology, can defeat the invader. It is a lesson in the methods of guerrilla warfare not taught at any military academy. Edib's narrator records in specific detail how Anatolian men, women, and children, and soldiers and civilian volunteers, perform miracles on a daily basis, tending to the wounded and saving lives in make-shift hospitals, feeding armies, transporting canons, delivering messages on foot, and gathering and directing intelligence, all under extreme conditions. In a simple yet eloquent statement, the narrator expresses an opinion that has proved to be true in so many instances where a powerful aggressor was defeated by the weaker but rightful owners of the territory invaded. Referring to the young warriors of a small army unit, Peyami reflects:

> The philosophy of their uprising was legitimate and clear. Certain outsiders had unjustly invaded their country in the name of a treaty and were robbing them blind. No matter how difficult it was to find supplies for warfare, to put up resistance, and to challenge and harm the enemy, they did it joyfully.   (70–71)

Clearly this message of a just and legitimate war of liberation resonated beyond the range of the Turkish revolutionary war, as evidenced in a poem with which students at the Aligarh Muslim University in India welcomed Halide Edib in 1935:

> For a long time your tales have been on our lips
> You remained unaware
> But you are no stranger to us.
> . . . .
> O but tell us, the wretched and the low, O great soul,
> How to remove the distinctions of colour and blood.
> O reveal to us the secrets of freedom
> How in the assembly is played the strain of liberty.
> . . . .
> Freedom, alas, is something that has eluded us.   (Haq lxxvii–lxxviii)

Surprisingly, this novel, so strongly defined by journalistic bravura and an infectious revolutionary spirit, ends on a note in the tradition of Romantic literature, especially the Romantic novella, where the whole story within the larger narrative frame turns out to be a dream, a phantasm, or a revelation by a phantom. Peyami dies during surgery (as he had expected), and the reader finds out from a conversation between two doctors in the epilogue that the main characters in Peyami's diary, Ayşe and İhsan, were figments of the patient's imagination. An investigation reveals that there was never a nurse by the name of Ayşe in any of the mobile medical units, nor was there ever a commanding officer called İhsan. The doctors conclude that the story was a hallucination caused by the bullet lodged in the patient's brain. In the book's afterword, Selim İleri interprets this device—closure in an epilogue told by a third-person narrator—as a sign that Edib could not resist writing off the unspeakable crimes perpetuated by the invaders as a nightmare that was over and would hopefully never reoccur ("Bugüne Bir 'Ateşten Gömlek'" 228). Judging from Edib's fondness for and knowledge of many literary traditions—Sufism, Hans Christian Andersen's fairy tales, Shakespeare's plays, Romanticism—it makes sense to read the ending more as a literary ploy in the romance or Romantic tradition than as an expression of the author's intention. In fact, this literary sleight of hand, which provides a sense of ambiguity, accentuates the poetic tenor of the novel and tempers its melodramatic tone.

As a metaphor, the shirt of fire or flame moves through different levels of signification. That a human being, injured by worldly transgressions, must go through the torment of fire or the purification by fire in order to be united with the divine is a concept common to both Christian and Islamic mysticism. To become a Sufi mystic, a dervish, one had to embrace asceticism and endure tests of physical endurance, such as eating a grain of iron and wearing a shirt of fire. In T. S. Eliot's *Four Quartets*, "the shirt of flame"— "Love is the unfamiliar name / Behind the hands that wove / The intolerable shirt of flame / Which human power cannot remove" (57 ["Little Gidding"])—similarly invokes the mystical notion of redemption by the tormenting fire of divine love. In Edib's novel, the fire literally burns the fallen young officer Ahmet Rıfkı, who could not afford even a shirt to wear under his uniform. Ayşe, İhsan, and the narrator, on the other hand, are condemned to wear symbolic shirts of fire, since it is not only the enemy forces that they are fighting in this war but also their pasts, human passions, and frailties. The gleam of the fiery metaphor is refracted through the narrative lens and captures the many registers of pain, desperation, and loss the nation suffered. As Halide Edib served in the ranks of the nationalist army during its Anatolian campaign and witnessed firsthand the astonishing efforts and sacrifices of the simple people in their freedom fight, this novel succeeds not only in terms of journalistic observation but also as a poetic biography of a nation in its struggle for liberation.

Beyond its metaphoric range, the book's title has an interesting personal history. In lieu of the usual acknowledgments, Edib opens the book with a letter to Yakup Kadri Karaosmanoğlu, who was also in Anatolia during the revolutionary war. She recalls that in a conversation between the two writers, Karaosmanoğlu mentioned he was planning to write a novel titled *Ateşten Gömlek*. She teased him in a friendly way by saying that she was also going to write a novel with that title. "Oh come on," Karaosmanoğlu replied, part in earnest, part jokingly, "is there no other title for a novel?" (Adıvar, "Yakup Kadri Bey'e" xiii–xiv). Edib goes on to say this title kept haunting her, and she would repeat it over and over as she thought about her experiences in Anatolia during the war years. Her letter, intended both as an apology and an expression of gratitude to Karaosmanoğlu, is also a brief account of how the novel came into being. She tells Karaosmanoğlu that she never dreamed of writing a novel of the Turkish revolutionary war while she was at the front, since witnessing an event of such magnitude was too overwhelming. But when she was back in Istanbul on leave, she was gripped once again by a writing fever, and her characters all took on a life of their own and persisted in calling their stories shirts of fire. She sees this novel, written with a "matchless passion," as her best work and dedicates it to the warriors of Sakarya, the battle that marked the definitive victory of the Turkish forces. "This book belongs to Sakarya," she writes. "It may be imperfect, but it is the best thing that my art could produce. One gives to those one loves most dearly only the best that one is able to create" (xv–xvi). She ends her letter with the hope that in fifty years, the two "Shirts of Fire," hers and Karaosmanoğlu's, will be sitting side by side on the shelf of a library:

> Maybe these two books, as in the fairy tales of Hans Andersen, will start speaking and reminisce about the past with each other. And who can tell how different from our own will be the shirt of fire the Turkish youth wear in that distant future? (xvi)

Yakup Kadri Karaosmanoğlu's *The Alien*

Karaosmanoğlu never wrote his "Shirt of Fire." However, ten years after the publication of Edib's novel, he published his novel of the Turkish War of Independence. Titled *Yaban* ("The Alien"),[6] it became an instant classic and was both acclaimed as the first truly original Turkish novel and harshly criticized as a one-sided, damning, and misguided representation of the Anatolian peasant. Like Edib, Yakup Kadri was born into an aristocratic family and exposed to Western ideas and education at an early age. Born in Cairo on 27 March 1889, he was a descendant of the Karaosmanoğlu family, who ruled from the end of the seventeenth century in the province of Saruhan (modern-day cities of Aydın and Manisa and their environs in the Aegean region). His father died when he was only six, and the family first moved to Manisa and later back to Egypt. He completed his secondary education at the French *Frères* school in Alexandria and entered the faculty of law after the family returned to Istanbul in 1908. He left the faculty in his third year to devote himself to full-time journalism and writing. He also taught literature and philosophy at the secondary school level. After the signing of the Treaty of Mondros, he committed himself fully to the revolutionary cause and went to Anatolia. When the first Turkish National Assembly convened, he was elected representative first from Mardin and later from Manisa.

The year *The Alien* was published, 1932, was a turning point in Karaosmanoğlu's career. That year, he began the publication of *Kadro* ("Cadre") magazine with a number of important writers, including Şevket Süreyya Aydemir, Vedat Nedim Tör, Burhan Asaf Belge, and İsmail Hüsrev Tökin, who believed that a revolutionary movement needed a revolutionary cadre and ideas to sustain it in the long run. *Kadro* was the first regularly published journal in the new republic. It aimed to inaugurate a culture of politically progressive and erudite journalism. The editors were strong apologists of Kemalist ideology, and the editorials aimed to define a course to implement the mandates of Kemalism in a socialist vein. The journal's leftist sympathies led to attacks on its supposedly hidden subversive agenda, and Karaosmanoğlu was exiled in 1934 as ambassador to Tirana, capital of Albania. After the forced departure of its editor in chief, the journal was closed down. He subsequently served as Turkish ambassador to Prague, The Hague, and Bern. On retiring from his enforced diplomatic career, he returned once more to politics and writing in Ankara. He resigned from the Republican Peoples Party in 1962, on the grounds that the party had betrayed Atatürk's ideals. He died 13 December 1974.

Karaosmanoğlu and Edib were contemporaries, and their lives and careers had much in common. Both were socially committed writers, and years spent in exile sensitized them to the complexities of issues concerning national, cultural, and religious identity. Both remained true to their respective ideological leanings. Karaosmanoğlu cherished the ideal of a socialist nation built on Kemalist principles. Despite his friendship with Edib, he did not share her faith in the peaceful coexistence of Islam with the principles of a modern secular state. The narrator of *The Alien* realizes, to his great chagrin, that for the Anatolian peasant, Turk and Muslim are opposing identities.

Edib's often nostalgic rhetoric about the unifying power of Islam could not have made much of an impression on Karaosmanoğlu's strong sense of realpolitik. Even though *Shirt of Fire* and *The Alien* share thematic concerns and may be sitting together on a library shelf, exchanging memories, as Edib imagined, they represent differing viewpoints of national mood and character.

Like Edib's *Shirt of Fire*, *The Alien* is a frame narrative, a journal kept by an officer, Ahmet Celâl, who was wounded in the First World War and retires to a small Anatolian village with his former orderly, Mehmet Ali, at the time the nationalist forces are gathering in Anatolia. Both novels present a narrative of remembrance. Both narrators are intellectuals who take refuge in Anatolia because of their deep disillusionment with their milieu, where an Istanbul elite, oblivious to the tragedy of the country, continues to support the enemy and the sultan's government in hopes of maintaining the status quo. Both narrators witness the hopeless conditions under which the nationalist forces fight, and they record these in detail. Both suffer the consequences of an ill-fated or unrequited love. Finally, Edib and Karaosmanoğlu, while writing a culturally specific period novel, underscore the universal relevance of the human tragedy of war and deracination by allusions to major works of Western literary tradition, ranging from the *Odyssey* and the Bible to Henry Wadsworth Longfellow's stories and Abbé Prévost's *Manon Lescaut*. Ultimately, however, the related narrative strands of the two stories produce different results; the novels diverge in tone, technique, and thesis. Because *The Alien* represents a political mood shift in the decade after the founding of the young Turkish nation, it offers a more critical insight into the conditions and limits of forging national consciousness.

In the light of the ever-deepening distrust between the West and the Muslim world and between secular and fundamentalist forces in Islamic countries, Karaosmanoğlu's representation of the cultural divide in Turkish society in *The Alien* has proved alarmingly prescient. As the author took great pains to write in a clear and colloquial language that resounds with poetic pathos, the novel still speaks to the history of Turkey's beleaguered modernity. After its publication, Karaosmanoğlu came under attack for representing the Anatolian peasant in the worst possible light. The negative reviews painted the author as a bureaucrat and a nationalist ideologue who held the uneducated and impoverished majority of the land in undisguised contempt. The criticism proved so harsh for Karaosmanoğlu that he felt the need to defend himself in the second edition of the book. Its introduction includes a short prose piece that the author wrote eleven years before the publication of the novel, at the time of the War of Independence. Composed as an apostrophe, "People of the Villages Burnt Down by the Barbarians" expresses in a highly emotional language the author's empathy for the endless trials and tragedies endured by the simple people of the Anatolian homeland.

As its reception history has shown, Karaosmanoğlu's novel was not a personal attack on the ignorance, obduracy, and lack of patriotism of the Anatolian peasant but a fictional investigation into the real and possible challenges and setbacks in the daunting task of building a nation from the divided, erased, and opposed cultures of a collapsed empire. Although *The Alien* has garnered much praise for its literary merits since the time of its first publication, there have also been dissenting voices that criticized its essayistic style for interrupting the story and fragmenting the structure of the novel (Moran 1: 201). Güntekin found the structure of the novel "most sloppy in terms of aesthetic rules," but he was overcome "by the power of exhilaration and pathos it awakened in [him]" (qtd. in Moran 1: 201–02).

These alleged stylistic shortcomings, however, are precisely what give *The Alien* the qualities that most theories of the novel uphold as the ideal of its formal autonomy. The inner turmoil of the protagonist reflects the chaos of the world around him. The ebb and flow of Ahmet Celâl's emotions, alternating between anger, pity, compassion, love, and sorrow, lead to no resolution and therefore defy narrative order and closure. The ambivalence of the authorial voice lends the novel a sensibility that transcends tendentiousness. The journal format juxtaposes different forms of discourse. It moves among a first-person narrative that reflects the inner thoughts and emotional state of the narrator; an ethnographic view of life in a small, backward Anatolian village during the War of Independence; the rhetorical apostrophe to the peasant and the intellectual; and progress reports on the war in the form of hearsay, rumor, and telegrams, which add another dimension of journalistic metalanguage to the narrative. Berna Moran correctly points to the shift in the tone of the novel between the first and the second parts of the story, when the focus moves from Ahmet Celâl's self-referential musings to the looming reality of the battle a stone's throw away (1: 202). In fact, as the village that Ahmet Celâl lives in is occupied by the enemy, and he is under virtual house arrest, he writes:

> I want most of all that the rest of this [the record of the last phases of the war] be read. Because the stories of this Anatolian battle, this great tragedy called the fight for freedom that will not be told by any history, are written in this

journal. . . . This is no longer my story. Even my own experiences are told, as
if they were another's.   (211)

The transparent thesis of *The Alien* concerns the social and cultural
abyss that has existed between the elite and the masses since the last centuries of Ottoman rule. Although Karaosmanoğlu quite clearly focuses on
this long-standing cultural divide, which has been an important concern of
modern Turkish literature, the novel owes its enduring currency to a profound understanding of the role of novels in safeguarding memories of
events that history may forget or fail to record in their specificity. Ahmet
Celâl's fictional journal becomes a metonymy for the biography of a momentous war of liberation. Georg Lukács sees "the biographical form" as a
structural device that contains "the discrete, unlimited nature of the material of the novel," as opposed to the "continuum-like infinity of the material
of the epic." Even though the scope of the world of experience and of any
history is limited by the perception of the novel's protagonist and his reflections on the way to self-recognition, the heterogeneity of events and characters achieves a continuum and unity in the protagonist's view and becomes
contiguous with the problems that his life story symbolizes (*Theory* 81).
What the reviews of *The Alien* that predominantly focused on its message
missed is Karaosmanoğlu's subtle yet masterful use of rhetorical forms and
tropes that resist reductive interpretation and transform each reading into a
renewed challenge of understanding. As Milan Kundera put it simply, the
"novel says to the reader: 'Things are not as simple as you think' " (*Art* 18).

The story's frame is composed of an italicized preface that explains
how a commission, sent to investigate the war damage in the areas surrounding Ankara after the victory of the battle of Sakarya against the Greek
army, found among ruins and human bones a tattered journal. When one
of the commission members asks the villagers, who are scurrying around to
find scraps of food in burnt fields, who the owner of the journal was, they
shrug and say they don't know. Irritated by their lack of concern, the inter-
rogator asks how it is possible that they wouldn't know anything about the
fate of a man who had lived with them for years, one villager answers,
"Well, he was an alien like you" (28). This is the story of that alien, the
name the villagers gave Ahmet Celâl and all those like him, the educated
cadre of soldiers, civil servants, and teachers who saw themselves as Turks.
The thematic focus of the novel not only reflects the gap that separated the
Ottoman Turkish elite and the educated class from the great majority of the

land's superstitious, unschooled, and religious masses but also that majority's reaction to the nationalist struggle.

Ahmet Celâl is a Westernized intellectual and a veteran of the First World War, where he lost more than an arm. His disability prevents him from joining the nationalist army. Crippled in body and spirit and unable to suffer the humiliation of living in enemy-occupied Istanbul, Celâl seeks refuge among the simple peasants. He wants to live like the village folk, become one of them, enter the fold. Quickly disabused of this notion, he realizes that he can never be like these peasants; he'll forever remain an alien to them, and they to him. His orderly tells him that the peasants find it odd that he combs his hair every day, like a woman. Because he has books and reads every night, they think he is an evil sorcerer. He cannot win them over with money or good advice. For these villagers, Mustafa Kemal is a heathen at war with the holy caliph (sultan). Since the sultan supports the Allied powers, the villagers are on the side of the enemy. They believe (or were led to believe) that the invading armies are not the enemy but saints with green turbans sent by a queen called Europe to save them from Mustafa Kemal's gangs. After Europe's soldiers defeat Kemal and his gangsters, she will convert to Islam and rule over the land (presumably with the caliph) happily ever after. Ironically, the supposedly devout peasants embrace a heathen queen (because she has been won over to Islam) and consider their own liberators the enemy. When the retreating enemy army enters the village, they welcome the soldiers with open arms, only to be raped, swindled, and burned by them later on. Even then they forgive the enemy and condemn Ahmet Celâl and all that he represents, including reason, justice, and compassion for one's compatriots.

Can the Anatolian peasant, poor and pure of heart, be as evil as portrayed here? Karaosmanoğlu paints a very convincing portrait of a dark time and place, forgotten ironically by both God and the Enlightenment. We never see these peasants practice the five pillars of Islam; they don't pray, fast, or give alms. They do everything to abet the real infidel enemy, hide deserters, abuse their mothers and women. The agha ("landowner") confiscates Mehmet Ali's inherited land, leaving his widowed mother without any source of income. Every character is either crippled or blind or suffers from an incurable disease. Even the landscape and the water are described as ailing. The stream is likened to smelly, oozing pus, the hills to tumors. The disease that afflicts people and nature becomes an allegory for the state of the republic in the tenth year of its existence. What was driven underground (saint worship, superstition, the power of religious hojas and sheikhs) festered just beneath the surface of the new order (secularization, the alphabet revolution, Westernization reforms). Various allusions and symbols find their way into the pages of the journal and call for a broad interpretive engagement with the text. As Moran points out, references to the Bible abound. Mustafa Kemal emerges as an allegorical version of Jesus, trying to save those following the enemy. The nonbelievers who betray Kemal and his followers and "worship" the caliph resist all redemption (1: 207). Like the biblical Jesus, who compared himself with a shepherd, the narrator compares Kemal with a shepherd looking to gather his flock. "Where is the shepherd?" Ahmet Celâl asks. "The shepherd is calling from the top of Ankara's jutted rock, trying to gather his flock. Hail the holy shepherd; may your battles be blessed! I wonder if I will one day be among the flock you gather?" (146). Writing a decade after the final victory of the War of Independence, Karaosmanoğlu makes it clear that a sense of national affiliation and a consciousness of national identity had not taken hold in the distant provinces. The political and cultural revolution had never been a grassroots movement, and by now the author-narrator had witnessed the divisions in the ranks of power, the loss of revolutionary fervor, and the invincible grip of religious fear reasserting its presence among the disenfranchised and downtrodden masses.

But is the narrator laying all the blame for a country's tragic fate on the crooked shoulders of the unpatriotic, obdurate, and superstitious Anatolian peasant, who symbolizes the other of reason and progress? Even a cursory reading of the novel does not support that charge. The author's use of self-reflective monologue and apostrophe problematizes and challenges the notion that the novel is an uncritical proponent of Kemalist ideology or a demeaning portrayal of the Turkish peasant. There are at least five people in the village whom Ahmet Celâl loves and cares for. One is his former orderly, who invited him to the village to live with his family. The others are a naive young man deserted by his wife and gone mad; a war veteran; a little shepherd boy; and Emine, a beautiful young orphaned girl who becomes his love interest and who is sold as a bride to the midgetlike brother of Ahmet Celâl's orderly. Ahmet Celâl feels great admiration for the villagers at work in the fields. A detailed journal entry, accompanied by editorial remarks that eulogize the sacrifice and valor of the impoverished Anatolian peasant, reads:

You big, strange turtles [emaciated peasants carrying ammunition wrapped in their blankets in rickety carts to which they seem glued like turtles to their shells] who walk in sorrow on the endless Anatolian roads. . . . On this extraordinary battlefield, you carry, among the tattered worldly belongings of the Turkish peasant, the stuff of legend. From a distance you remind me of mythical animals.   (105)

The journal records many acts of heroism with compassion, such as the heartbreaking story of the little shepherd boy Hasan, who refuses to let enemy soldiers take a single one of his sheep and is beaten to death by them.

Of greater critical significance than the positive or negative emotional reactions of the protagonist, however, is his interrogation of the enlightened Turkish intellectual by apostrophe. Ahmet Celâl addresses himself and the class (or mentality) he represents by asking why he or they failed to reach out to their own people, to enlighten them, to improve their lot:

You are responsible for this [abandonment of the peasant to poverty, illness, and ignorance], O Turkish intellectual! What have you done for this devastated land and these impoverished human masses? For years and centuries you have bled them dry, disposed of what remained of them, and now you justify your right to be disgusted by them.   (147)

This is no mere realistic novel, one long on description and short on historical analysis. The narrator observes, for example, that it is an illusion to think of education in the abstract as a panacea for the ills of society. Education cannot have any redeeming power on the masses, if it is not woven tightly into the cultural fabric of society: "Education, training, model behavior are all temporary. As long as the environment doesn't change, human beings cannot change" (40). This ironic distance the narrator achieves when he steps out of the continuum of the story line and poses questions that offer no facile answers lends the novel a skillful combination of literary technique and critical reflection.

One of the reviews of the novel that appeared in the *Rheinisch-Westphalische Zeitung* after the book was issued in German translation, praises the story as achieving great drama in its simplicity and "in abiding by the timeless principle of all literature, awakening pity and fear" (Karaosmanoğlu 288 ["Alman Basın'ında 'Yaban'"]). In a similar vein, Güntekin notes in his review that Karaosmanoğlu succeeds as a great tragedian, because the reader is gripped by the sorrow of the inexplicable that tragedy has traditionally represented. Güntekin calls the novel a masterpiece of Turkish literature that "every Turk needs to memorize" (Rev. 264). Clearly he sees in this novel a valorization and continuation of his own views on the trials of nation building, represented most notably in his *Yeşil Gece* ("The Green Night") and *The Autobiography of a Turkish Girl*. Like *The Alien*, *The Green Night*, which precedes its metaphoric sequel, *The Alien*, by a decade, represents a prophetic view of the resurgence of repressed religious orthodoxy.

Reşat Nuri Güntekin's *The Autobiography of a Turkish Girl*

> O Lord, what miracles can love and compassion perform!
> —Reşat Nuri Güntekin,
> *The Autobiography of a Turkish Girl*

The youngest of the three major novelists of the early Republican period, Reşat Nuri Güntekin was born in 1889 in Istanbul. Half a century after his death, his books are still widely read, and their author remains a symbol of tolerance, idealism, and hope for the possibility of a harmonious society based on shared goals of education. Güntekin, an educator himself, dedicated his life and art to teaching tolerance. It would be hard to find a Turkish woman who has not read his most popular novel, *Çalıkuşu* (*The Autobiography of a Turkish Girl*), which is still reprinted in great numbers and has been filmed and made into a television series. Even critics who underestimate Güntekin's work as overly sentimental concede that he has touched a nerve in the nation's psyche and that, more than any other Turkish writer, he has succeeded in mapping the complex emotional landscape of his people. Time and again, readers young and old express their enthusiasm in finding themselves in Güntekin's insightfully drawn characters. His good old-fashioned novels or well-told tales have a strong but never pedantic social tenor.

After completing a degree in literature at the Dar-ül-fünûn ("House of Knowledge"), later the University of Istanbul, Güntekin worked as a teacher until 1931 and was superintendent of schools from 1931 to 1939. In 1939, he was elected to the Turkish Grand National Assembly as parliament representative from the Province of Çanakkale. After the Second World War, he was appointed Turkish representative to UNESCO in Paris. He died 7 December 1956 in London, where he was undergoing medical treatment.

Besides twenty novels, several short-story volumes, and numerous essays, he translated several French classics into Turkish as part of the Major Works of Western and Eastern Literature Translation Project undertaken by the Ministry of Education.

Güntekin achieved considerable fame at the age of thirty-three, when in 1922 *The Autobiography of a Turkish Girl* was serialized in the newspaper *Vatan* ("Motherland"). Although until the publication of *The Green Night,* in 1928, his novels emphasized the sentimental and the adventurous, they still represented in a historical-critical vein the social trials and tribulations of building a new nation. In his later novels, Güntekin's youthful optimism and faith in the power of education to free people from the grip of superstition and religious dogma gradually yielded to a sorrowful view of the moral fragility that had marred social life and of the waning of the young nation's ideals. However, even in the most despondent instances of his tales, the clarity of his language and his total lack of literary pretension allow the reader to participate in a social and communal act of reading and potentially become part of the response to the crisis the author depicts. Ahmet Hamdi Tanpınar, among others, has pointed to the exalting tenor of Güntekin's prose: "He strove for a pure and unadulterated humanity, he left in the heart of Turkish a deeply felt tremor of love and compassion" (qtd. in Naci 11). Güntekin's English translator, Wyndham Deedes, notes that *The Autobiography of a Turkish Girl* "revolutionized the novel in Turkey and made him [Güntekin] the most widely-read Turkish novelist" (vii).

In his foreword to *Afternoon Sun* (*Akşam Güneşi*), one of Güntekin's two novels he translated into English, Deedes explains why he came to be interested in the Turkish author's work. He read three books by Güntekin and, to his great surprise, was fascinated by them, since he "never read modern fiction" (v). Like so many of Güntekin's Turkish readers—both his contemporaries and more recent ones—who see their lives reflected in his novels, Deedes found parallels between his own life and the lives of the characters in the novelist's work:

> [I]n reading Güntekin's books, I have relived some of my own life. Take the hero of this novel [*The Afternoon Sun*], Nazmi Bey: how well I know the type! I had one such as my colleague during the two years I spent in Tripoli in Africa. He too had been a member of a "band" in Macedonia. . . . Then the old Gendarmerie sergeant in this tale; I was a Gendarmerie officer myself. . . . And as with persons, so with places; as I read I see them all again in my mind's eye. (vi)

In the finely wrought observations of time, place, and human lives that draw readers into specific or multiple forms of identification and in the simple grandeur of Güntekin's language lie the major determinants of his unabated appeal. Even though the historical context of *The Autobiography of a Turkish Girl* is outside the horizon of experience of today's reading public, the story overcomes temporal distance by encouraging the reader to understand the present in its relation to the past.

How have the novels of Güntekin and of the early Republican writers survived their historical specificity and become classics? In terms of reader reception theory or reception aesthetics, classical is not an immanent quality of a work of art but rather an attribute that emerges in the dialogue between the work and its reader in the course of time. The reader cannot locate anything inherently classical in the work. However, if the work imagines as yet unknown experiences, anticipates unforeseen problems, or responds to newly emerging questions, it maintains an ongoing engagement with the reader, irrespective of the time of its production. Hans Robert Jauss, one of the leading theorists of reception aesthetics, contends that for a work of art to claim classical status, it must

> displace the insight that classical art at the time of its production did not yet appear "classical": rather, it could open up new ways of seeing things and perform new experiences that only in historical distance—in the recognition of what is now familiar—give rise to the appearance that a timeless truth expresses itself in the work of art. (31)

Fethi Naci, a Turkish critic and author of a book-length study of Güntekin's novels, judges them to be classical representatives of the Turkish novel, despite his often harsh criticism of what he considers the novelist's sentimentalism and ideological naïveté: "The more I read of Reşat Nuri, the more I discovered in him a splendor that has rarely been noticed." In Naci's view, Güntekin is an "exemplary" writer, because he

> has owned up to the responsibility of maintaining the ethical values of the Turkish people, approaches social realism critically, has a genuine affection for all the peoples of Turkey, and opposes all kinds of discrimination based on language, religion, and ethnic origin. (19)

For Naci, Güntekin's exemplary status and enduring popularity since the early 1920s constitute the terms that define the classical.

In some ways, *The Autobiography of a Turkish Girl* is a classic in the genre of Louisa May Alcott's *Little Women*. Both are realistic stories of interesting young women set against the backdrop of a major war; both books draw the reader into strong identification with the characters; and both novels forgo all literary affectation (and invention), adhering instead to a straightforward narration that appeals to the lay reader. Readers' reviews of *The Autobiography* and *Little Women* on Turkish and American booksellers' Web pages, respectively, express almost identical sentiments. Such remarks are typical: "I thought reading a classic would be boring, but I couldn't put the book down," "This book taught me to love novels," and "The book teaches moral behavior." One Turkish reader calls *The Autobiography* "Güntekin's greatest gift to Turks."[7] Readers, Turkish and American, find in these books their heroes, their goals, and maybe that elusive courage to face life's challenges. In terms of setting a trend for young readers, *The Autobiography* may also be compared, albeit in an inverse fashion, with Johann Wolfgang von Goethe's *The Sorrows of Young Werther*. *Sorrows* is the tragic-ironic story of Werther, a youth desperately in love with a married woman. The pain of this star-crossed love drives him to suicide. Although the tone of Goethe's tale is more ironic, even comic, than tragic, the book triggered an alarming trend of suicides among despondent young men in love, whose bodies were fished out of rivers with a copy of the book in their pocket. Güntekin's book proved to inspire hope rather than despair, as his numerous young women readers went to remote corners of Anatolia to educate the poor and disenfranchised children of the young nation.

Çalıkuşu is the nickname of a spunky orphaned girl, Feride, whose aunt takes her in and sees to it that she gets a good education at the Notre Dame de Sion, a French convent school for girls in Istanbul. A troublemaker yet an immensely lovable and smart character, the tomboyish Feride falls in love with her cousin Kâmran, while still at school. She gets engaged to him after graduating but runs away from home the night before her wedding. Her decision to leave is occasioned by a visit from a woman who tells her that she was Kâmran's lover during the time he was a student in Switzerland. Now all alone in the world and without any means of support, Feride applies to the Ministry of Education for a teaching job and asks to be assigned to the most remote and desolate provinces. Her experiences in many one-room, run-down village schools that until her arrival had only a one-course curriculum—religion—are so disastrous as to break the will of the most idealistic teacher. Feride is a real trooper, but she is constantly harassed by religious villagers and has to keep moving from village to village. She remains true to her ideals against all odds.

Compassionate to a fault, Feride adopts one of her students, an angelic little girl by the name of Munise (the name means "good-natured"), who was abused by a heartless stepmother. As a single mother, Feride is pursued by a horde of single and married men and faces the additional problem of defending herself from these seducers. She agrees to marry an old doctor, a father figure, who takes her in with the child. The story is explicit that this marriage is a marriage in name only. In a narrative somewhat overburdened by coincidence, the adoptive child dies and the doctor is diagnosed with cancer. Knowing his days are numbered, the doctor secretly contacts Kâmran, sends him Feride's diary (which is a testimony both to her love for Kâmran and to her chastity), and makes him promise that he will marry Feride when she is widowed. After the good doctor's death, Feride and Kâmran are reunited (coincidentally he is also widowed and has a child) and presumably live happily ever after. It is not clear if Feride will resume her teaching career.

No summary of the story can do justice to the emotional resonance of the book, nor can it explain its enduring appeal to the reader, because the tale is much greater than the sum of its parts. Although the historical moment of its production had much to do with the success of the book, its continued success is indebted to strong characterization, masterful language, and a heartbreakingly realistic portrayal of a bleak and desolate Anatolia. Most important, however, the book was instrumental in legitimizing and valorizing teaching as a desirable profession for educated women and allowed them to venture out of Istanbul into the provinces in pursuit of an ideal.

Like Karaosmanoğlu's *The Alien*, Feride's story tells of the great cultural divide that has persisted since the nineteenth century until the present between a minority of educated, often Western-trained urban elites and the majority of Anatolians, schooled or misschooled (since most had no knowledge of Arabic, nor were they literate in Turkish) in Koran courses only. Like the modern Peace Corps volunteers, the young Turkish women who followed Feride's lead (without her happy ending) to take up teaching posts in remote corners of Anatolia went to a foreign country in a frighteningly real sense. Many were resented and hated by the religious clergy and the conservative townspeople of the provinces. Often they were driven away by hostility and resentment. There is an anecdote of a young woman who approached Güntekin during one of his Anatolian trips as a superintendent of the Ministry of Education; she told him that his novel was responsible for her ending up in the school from hell that he had come to inspect. However, against all odds, many an idealistic teacher persevered and stayed the course.

Nowadays, in the eyes of the women of the educational corps, Feride may seem an outdated figure. One critic who admits to admiring the timeless qualities that the character represents and upholds—pride, fearlessness, honesty, diligence, love, and compassion—also claims that today's woman would find nothing in Feride's life to identify with. This critic does not believe that in the increasingly conservative climate of today's educational system, any teacher can manage to appear so "cute." Feride, as the always "protected" child of the elite, represents a "hypothesis" that is alien to the reality of contemporary social problems. Instead, the characters who speak to women today are those who have been abused, forgotten, exploited, and even wasted by men or by the system (Köksal 102). Such devaluation of Güntekin's (and some of his contemporaries') work is common currency among critics who expect novelists to write as social analysts, to offer socioeconomic studies to explain the acts of their characters, or to help make social policy.

If literature is to offer any moral guidance, it cannot do this by proselytizing but by awakening a sense of awe, wonder, and fear, as its classical role mandates. Humanity needs artists to depict its life without illusions, and literature continues to redefine the ways we see ourselves. Güntekin offers no illusions about idealistic teachers transforming the Anatolian schoolroom into a safe place for learning and for eliminating or even alleviating the entrenched poverty, fear, and ignorance of the peasants. The ignorance, torpor, and lack of moral fortitude Feride continually confronts are tempered by her expansive tolerance—and by the author's implicit understanding of the historical determinants of group dynamics that emerge here as collective resignation, suspicion, and fear.

Furthermore, Güntekin manages to open the borders of the modern Turkish novel, which until then was set within the city limits of Istanbul, to the vast scenes and populations of the Anatolian mainland. His memorable depiction of Zeyniler Köyü ("the village of Zeyniler") in *The Autobiography* turns this typically desolate Anatolian piece of land and its impoverished people, whose major preoccupation is the afterlife, into a major character of the novel. He treats these people with a certain amount of levity but sees little hope for their self-emancipation. Ultimately, it is the aesthetic appeal of Güntekin's promotion of tolerance and compassion that strikes a moral chord. In the context of its time, Feride's story offered a guardedly optimistic view of a brighter future, a future that the elite, who had embraced the mission to better the lives of their less fortunate compatriots, were willing to work hard to realize.

The idea of a young woman with a fighting spirit who goes to Anatolia at the height of the War of Independence resonated with a public that needed heroes and heroines to map the road to a new, free, and enlightened land. As one writer mentioned in his memoirs, there was a copy of the novel in the sack of every soldier sent to the front in the war. Güntekin "not only managed to save our cities under occupation, but he almost declared the founding of the republic and sent Feride to Anatolia as the representative of Turkish reforms." At the time of the novel's publication, the Turkish homeland was under enemy occupation, the republic had not yet been founded, and the Kemalist reforms were far from being realized. Nurullah Aytaç, a gifted author and critic, found the idea of Feride's going to İzmir as a teacher, as if the city had already been liberated, "the most beautiful of dreams" (48).

Güntekin foresaw not only the triumph of the struggle for liberation and the foundation of the new nation but also the frightening consequences of the cultural divide that persists to this day. At the time of the novel's publication, not many writers or thinkers shared his sense of the limitations of any reform movement in the face of an all-powerful and intransigent Islamic way of life, fueled by the relentless poverty and ignorance that kept the Turkish peasant in its grip. *The Autobiography* and the decidedly more political *The Green Night* charted the path not only to Karaosmanoğlu's *The Alien* but also to the socially engaged literature of the 1960s and 1970s. Critics charge Güntekin with a reductionism that saw religion at the root of all the social and cultural ills of Turkish society. But the compassionate vision of the novelist and his commitment, both in life and in art, to his people's common humanity, despite all cultural, religious, and class differences, belie any charge of reductionist vision or ideological bias. In reference to *The Autobiography,* Tanpınar observed, "That was an easy and beautiful language. It was an amiable agreement on values. It was a concept of responsibility that made good without shaking our world" (qtd. in Aytaç 48). In their secular perspective and commitment to humanist ends, both Güntekin and Karaosmanoğlu voiced Enlightenment ideals not in the form of abstraction but in characters who struggled to bring the school to the unschooled. The passion and dignity with which these characters approach their mission are tangible markers of enlightened reason.

The Green Night: The Chronicle of a Calamity Foretold

The Green Night is Güntekin's story of the eclipse of reason at the height of religious fanaticism. The "green" in the title refers to the color traditionally associated with Islam, as it was considered the color of the Prophet, Muhammad. In the novel, allusions to the "green flag" and the "green army" underscore the militant power of religious righteousness, ever ready to overcome its opponents: the "educational army" and its warrior teachers, soldiers in the war for national liberation, and proponents of secularism. Watching in horror an obscene play performed by two hojas (teachers of a madrassa, a religious school) impersonating a coquettish woman and her lecherous pursuer, as an audience of students screams with pleasure at the obscenity, the protagonist, Şahin, a devout student at the madrassa, asks himself, "Are these the students in search of divine mysteries under the heavenly roof of the madrassa? Are these the volunteers of the green army, who, following the green flag, would one day invade the four corners of the world?" (25). The novelist's vision of the ubiquitous darkness of the green night finds expression in Şahin's internal monologue:

> The green night of the madrassa has not only managed to cast darkness on this institution but has spread it all over the land. How could it have been otherwise? Until now, those who guided our minds and consciences had all been trained in these madrassas. What could these men give to this land save darkness? . . .
>
> Yes, this poor country had been living for centuries in a green night.
> People saw the world only through this darkness.   (43)

Like Feride, the heroine of *The Autobiography of a Turkish Girl*, Şahin Efendi is a young and idealistic teacher who requests a position in a backward, poor, forgotten village run by opportunistic and cunning religious fanatics. Şahin himself is the son of a man who wanted to raise the boy as a faithful servant of the green army. Şahin begins his education in the madrassa. A gifted and intellectually curious student, this would-be green army soldier has a change of heart, drops out of the madrassa before graduation, and applies to the Darülmuallimi ("Teachers College") to train as an elementary school teacher. To his great surprise, he passes the entrance examination with flying colors. Once at the college, he witnesses the tension and partisan struggle between the fez wearers (the Westernized) and the turban wearers (madrassa graduates). The headwear serves as a semiotic marker of the competing forces of Ottoman history, of the irresolvable antagonism between the intellectual elite and those who are products of the madrassa. Today, the fez-turban divide has become the open head–headscarf divide among women. Ironically, it is the total lack of a genuinely spiritual experience at the madrassa that erodes Şahin's faith and his belief in the mission of the green army.

Unlike Feride, who takes a leap of faith by enlisting in the educational corps, a leap prompted by a lover's betrayal and the necessity to escape desire and memory, Şahin decides to teach as a conscious and premeditated flight from what he sees as the antirationalism and futility of his Islamic upbringing. Unlike Feride, he comes not from the ranks of the urban elite but from a world of green flag bearers. Güntekin's critique of the anesthetization and provocation of the masses by religion unfolds through a narrative that recounts Şahin's humanistic self-education. The more Şahin studies history and the history of religion, the more questioning and skeptical he becomes of the religious ambition for eternal life. He comes to see religion as an inevitably divisive and corrupt institution that has strayed far from its original mission of piety, compassion, and consolation:

> There is not much else to see in history than deities. All the religions had different gods, prophets, and rituals; their adherents regarded their idols as the true ones and the others' gods and prophets as the false ones. Does it not follow then that they were all products of human imagination? Human inventions? And if this is the case, isn't it necessary to give up hope for eternal life?   (33–34)

Thus the one-time recruit of the green army emerges from his Nietzschean meditations with a new mission. Over the years and during the course of his self-education, this easygoing, tolerant, laid-back, pious young student of religion acquires a new countenance, "that of a fiery proselyte, burning with the divine fire of teaching what he saw as a new religion" (47–48). Şahin accepts a position as the principal of an elementary school in the village of Sarıova. His life as an educator in the conservative village becomes an ongoing struggle against the forces of ignorance, represented by the religious leaders who wage a ruthless war against the idealistic young principal and other dedicated teachers of the school. The ploys of the village leaders to break the will of the teachers are abetted by the superstitions and fears deeply embedded in the lives and minds of villagers. Their strategies of resistance against Şahin's attempts to improve the school and their attempts to defame Şahin and other teachers are all too familiar tactics of corrupt politics anywhere. The village leaders burn a shrine and blame the arson on one of the teachers and try to assassinate him. When Şahin tries to have a new school built, the workers he hires are told that they'll be attacked by the spirits of the holy saints, so they leave the job. Prostitutes are hired to seduce Şahin, so he'll be caught and charged with adultery. All these attempts are foiled by chance or help from the few honest officials who support Şahin.

For his part, Şahin tries to free the little boys from the large turbans they have to wear, stop fathers from taking their sons out of the school, and instill a sense of national unity in people who can see themselves only as a religious community. With the outbreak of the First World War, the powerful village leaders either escape or collaborate with the enemy. Şahin stays in the village to help the people and the national army. Many of his close friends and colleagues are killed by the Greeks, and he is exiled to a Greek island. After the victory of the Turkish army, he returns to Sarıova only to find that the former religious heads and enemy collaborators, now beardless and in Western garb, are in positions of power once again. Even though all his dreams for his people are now realized—the caliphate is abolished, the shrines and madrassas are closed, the religious fanatics are gone—Şahin sees that he must keep moving, since his old enemies are now his new enemies and just as powerful as before. This time, they wear the mask of modern reformers and try to expose him as an old-regime sympathizer. Realizing that he can no longer win against the power of corruption and resume his teaching career, Şahin decides to leave Sarıova. At a crossroads, he opts, symbolically, for the middle road, "If I follow the one in the middle, it will take me to the birthplace of victory and revolution. There, they'll listen to my woes" (249–50). Thus, in the words of one critic, Şahin becomes "the first middle-of-the-road follower (advocate) in Turkish literature" (Naci 118).

Güntekin implicitly admits to the impossibility of reversing the deadly consequences of religious intolerance and ignorance extending into the eternity of the "green night." At the close of the novel, Şahin remarks, "It is very true that the thing called revolution cannot happen overnight" (249). In this respect, Güntekin foresaw what Atatürk did not want to or could not believe would come to pass. In a conversation Atatürk had with small-business owners on 16 March 1923 in Adana, he told them that the evil minds that had consistently misled our innocent people had done so in the guise of religion and the sharia. "Read our history and listen to it, and you'll see that the evil that has devastated, imprisoned, and demolished our people has always been the curse and cowardice masquerading as religion," Atatürk told the listeners (qtd. in Naci 119). Nevertheless, Atatürk, cognizant of his position as the leader of a predominantly Islamic and deeply religious people, was always careful not to condemn religion publicly. However, he often emphasized how religion became a tool of exploitation and oppression in the service of vested interests. The post-Atatürk era in Turkey has seen numerous instances of political parties' drawing on religious rhetoric in campaigns for office and confronting the established judicial system by appeals to Islamic law. Like all opportunists, power brokers with religious masks can effortlessly switch roles as political winds change.

Güntekin's tale of the unstoppable threat of green armies charging toward "four corners of the world" (45) may be read as a chronicle of a calamity foretold. It heralds the coming of the reign of fundamentalist religions in most parts of the world, including the United States. It also depicts the endless possibilities of torture; exploitation; oppression of women, children, and the poor; and the imprisonment and killing of intellectuals and artists. In an age that has witnessed the meteoric rise of militant Islam, *The Green Night* proves to be a work of astounding prescience. If it had been available in translation, it could have shared the acclaim of such contemporary novels from the Muslim world as Yasmina Khadra's *The Swallows of Kabul* (2004; *Hirondelles de Kaboul* [Khadra is the pseudonym of the Algerian army officer Mohammed Moulessehoul, writing in France]), Assia Djebar's *Algerian White* (2000; *Blanc de l'Algérie*), Tahar Djaout's *The Last Summer of Reason* (2003; *Le dernier été de la raison*), and Azar Nafisi's *Reading* Lolita *in Teheran* (2003).

These novels speak eloquently of the destruction perpetuated by Islamic fundamentalists, ayatollahs, and the Taliban in modern Muslim nations and attempt to comprehend the enormity of trauma that imprisons people when the lights of reason, conscience, and human compassion go out. In *Swallows of Kabul*, Mohsen and Zunaira are an educated middle-class couple from Kabul who have been dismissed from their respective jobs by the Taliban. Zunaira's words of lament are uncannily reminiscent of the images in *The Alien* and *The Green Night*. A thirty-two-year-old former magistrate, she cannot stand wearing the burka and refuses to leave the couple's apartment. When her husband urges her to take a walk with him, she replies:

> I refuse to wear the burqa. Of all the burdens they've put on us, that's the most degrading. . . . It cancels my face and takes away my identity and turns me into an object. . . . If I put that damned veil on, I'm neither a human being nor an animal, I'm just an affront, a disgrace, a blemish that has to be hidden. That's too hard to deal with. Especially for someone who was a lawyer, who worked for women's rights. (77–78)

Khadra's depiction of Kabul under the Taliban, a devastated city of "skeletal facades," "beaten tracks scraped by clogs and sandals" (11), "the antechamber to the great beyond," and "a puritanical ordeal" (10), recall the Anatolian villages in *The Green Night* and *The Alien* and especially the Zeyniler village in *The Autobiography of a Turkish Girl*.

In *The Last Summer of Reason*, the protagonist, Boualem Yekker, lives in a world besieged by Islamic extremists who have taken full control of daily life, the situation of Algeria during the 1990s. This is a world where the last breath has gone out of reason and where hundreds of writers, teachers, and thinkers are killed on a daily basis. Yekker is abandoned by his family for not giving up his convictions and terrorized by the fundamentalists (who actually assassinated the author in May 1993 for his views). The incomplete book manuscript was found among Djaout's papers after his death. The atmosphere of horrific repression and fear that permeates the book reflects the author's own situation. The fundamentalist assassins claimed that they killed him because his pen was becoming too powerful a sword. Compared with the febrile tone of these best-selling authors who took a stand against highly politicized and militant Islam, *The Green Night* speaks with a voice tempered by a greater critical distance to its subject matter but with no less apprehension or anxiety.

Güntekin and Karaosmanoğlu's misgivings about the success of progressive reforms in an environment of entrenched Islamic beliefs have drawn criticism from certain quarters, including critics of the Enlightenment and Turkish intellectuals who believe in the possibility of peaceful coexistence between a benevolent Islam and the mandates of progress and modernity. I read Güntekin and Karaosmanoğlu as sincere adherents of the Enlightenment ideals of tolerance, scientific progress, and universal humanism. The sense of disillusionment that informs *The Alien* and *The Green Night* arises from an awareness of the relative absence of these ideals in Ottoman Islamic culture.

Paradoxically, in our age, the ideals of the Enlightenment are questioned and critiqued by various philosophical and political constituencies, including postmodernist and postcolonial theorists. Specificities of race, class, gender, and their sum total identity challenge Enlightenment's universalist values. The original text that generated this critique of the Enlightenment is *Die Dialektik der Aufklärung* (*The Dialectic of the Enlightenment*), by Max Horkheimer and Theodor Adorno, two leading German philosophers of the twentieth century. Writing from the United States at the height of the Nazi reign in Europe, Horkheimer and Adorno fervently argued that the Enlightenment ideal of reason as the supreme faculty governing justice, freedom, and morality yielded, in time, to the will of unchecked progress and cultivated the authoritarian aspect of instrumental rationality. The fractured myths of liberal humanism and universalism reemerged in practice as forms of persecution, racism, and ultranationalism. In an ironic rereading of the dialectic turn of history, Horkheimer and Adorno see the transformation of the ideals of reason, knowledge, and humanism into their own opposites and into a "massive betrayal of the masses" (41). The inflammatory tone of their argument needs to be understood in the context of an age when a generation of Europeans lay prostrate in the face of raging fascism. Times of extreme crisis and trauma generate phantom scapegoats whose relation to the problems at hand is often inscrutable.

In the continually paradoxical fortunes of Turkish social and cultural life, the role of early Republican writers in addressing issues of nation building has undergone conflicting interpretations. Although Halide Edib's many novels about independent women figures have been criticized as formulaic and sentimental, her *Shirt of Fire* is considered one of the best fictional accounts of the War of Independence. *Memoirs of Halidé Edib* is acclaimed and reclaimed as a significant social and literary document of the momentous times it depicts. Although in the eyes of readers committed to secularism in a strict sense, Edib's efforts to reconcile Islamic values with a Westernized Turkish national ethos may appear somewhat naive, her vision of a serene and benevolent Islam has struck a chord among those who wish to make a place for faith in the quest for Turkish modernity. Her current iconic status as a leading Turkish feminist has made her life and work the subject of scholarly study both in Turkey and in English-speaking countries. *Halide's*

Gift, a novel by Francesca Kazan loosely based on Edib's *Memoirs,* was a best seller in Turkish translation. Well-written and informed by its author's genuine interest in Edib, Kazan's intriguing novel provides further access to Edib's work for the English-speaking reader.

On the other hand, in their belief in the paralyzing effect of religion on poor, uneducated, and disenfranchised masses, Karaosmanoğlu and Güntekin emerge as the more realistic and visionary writers from a political and sociocultural viewpoint. Their vision is cautionary and corrective rather than confrontational in the assessment of the respective roles of religion, secularism, and modernization in the labors of nation building. Thomas de Zengotita, an anthropologist and contributing editor of *Harper's Magazine,* argues that "in spite of all the undeniable gains we owe to identity politics, . . . progressive politics is still, *as a matter of fact rather than rhetoric,* based on Enlightenment principles and has been all along" (37). Zengotita takes issue with postmodern (and implicitly with postcolonial) critics who read into Enlightenment's abstractions—"(natural law, state of nature, etc.), to whose authority the Enlightenment appealed for leverage out of the Middle Ages"—imperial ambitions and justification of the Western domination of the rest of the world (39). He maintains that the principles of the Enlightenment still hold universally and cites a long list of concrete forms of identification in the notion of humanism that connect each one of us to others. Like the philosopher Jürgen Habermas, a firm believer in the universality of Enlightenment ideals, Zengotita considers these ideals the only framework in which a genuine critique of power and domination can be articulated. "A commitment to universal rationality in spite of the differences," Zengotita maintains, is "a commitment that is natural in the Enlightenment sense" (40).

This kind of commitment is evident in the works and careers of all the early Republican writers discussed here. In the final analysis, however, Güntekin and Karaosmanoğlu, astute students of French thought, follow more consistently than Edib in the footsteps of Jean-Jacques Rousseau, Michel de Montaigne, and Voltaire and pick up the pen to combat superstition, irrationalism, and oppressive religious practices, which they see as endemic to regimes of tyranny. After all, the Enlightenment was a movement that aimed to free human beings from ignorance, superstition, and fear. It placed the control of one's life not in the hands of some deity but in the faculties of reason and understanding. It validated human agency against arbitrary readings of heavenly signs and messages by self-appointed representatives of God on earth.

In a speech made on 30 August 1925 (the anniversary of the victory of Sakarya), Atatürk stated that "it was a disgrace for a modern society to ask for help from the dead" (Naci 119). In *The Alien* and *The Green Night*, Güntekin and Karaosmanoğlu embody this sentiment in their protagonists, who struggle to free the villagers from the hold of saint cults, soothsayers, corrupt religious men, ruthless landlords, and all kinds of opportunists who, behind a mask of religion and tradition, keep the masses in fear and any possibility of reform at bay. Interestingly, their artistic vision had a wide range, encompassing not only the near future but also the dialectic turn of history that ensued thereafter. On 3 March 1924, the law to merge school systems (religious schools and schools proper) went into effect, the madrassas were closed, and a major step was taken toward the secularization of the educational system. The religious schools were history. The irony, of course, is that history never dies, and its ghosts return in an uncanny (both strange and familiar in the Freudian sense) way. İmam Hatip lycées (religious secondary schools) have been very heavily enrolled in the last few decades and are ubiquitous. Most Anatolian villages still lack schools but enjoy an abundance of large and small mosques. It is not surprising, then, that so many readers and critics marvel at the timeliness and relevance of the historiesstories Güntekin and Karaosmanoğlu tell in *The Alien* and *The Green Night*.

Notes

1. For a concise account of Adıvar's importance in modern scholarship on autobiography, see Adak and the bibliography in Adıvar's *Memoirs*.
2. *Raik'in Annesi* (1909; "Raik's Mother"), *Seviyye Talip* (1912), *Handan* (1912), *Son Eseri* (1913; "Her Last Work") belong to this category. See Adak ix–x; Moran 1: 153–55.
3. Edib's English in this passage sounds antiquated and lacks the ironic as well as the solemn tone of the passage in the Turkish version of *The House with Wisteria*. I translate this passage: "Marriage, holidays, even starting school, in short, all the occasions that are cause for great joy and celebration in other lands become for us occasions of mourning. Women unfailingly cry; men assume a pose of fearful reverence. Yes, all that gives others joy gives us sadness" (*Mor Salkımlı Ev* 70).
4. Turanism is a late-nineteenth- and early-twentieth-century movement to unite politically and culturally all the Turkic peoples living in Turkey and across Eurasia.
5. There are two translations of *Ateşten Gömlek*: *The Shirt of Flame* and *The Daughter of Smyrna: A Story of the Rise of Modern Turkey, on the Ashes of the Ottoman Empire—The Turk's Revolt against Western Domination, His Thrilling Adventures, Sufferings and Sacrifices in the Cause of National Honour and Independence*. The second translation is actually more of an adaptation (as is clear from the elaborate subtitle) to serve the cause of

"the anticolonial struggle in India" (Adak xv). Since both translations are long out of print, I use the Turkish text in my analysis.

6. *Yaban* can be translated as "the alien," "the stranger," "foreign," "the wild, the desert," and "the world of strangers." The novel treats all these themes both literally and metaphorically. *Yaban* was translated into German as *Der Fremdling* and into French as *L'étranger* ("the stranger" in both cases). I prefer "the alien," as it better reflects the protagonist's perception of himself in the story.

7. Web-page reader reviews underscore the popular appeal of certain books that draw critical interest in time. The reviews usually have little critical value, but they are a sure and encouraging proof of the formation of reader communities. I was surprised by the large number of these sites in Turkey and the willingness of lay readers and seasoned critics to comment on books. Another surprise was the enduring popularity of Edib, Karosmanoğlu, and Güntekin and the great number of unfavorable reviews of Pamuk (although this was not all that surprising). Among the sites I checked (for this rather unscientific survey) were the Turkish sites www.yenisayfa.com and www.kitap.antoloji .com and the American amazon.com.

Social Responsibilit
and the Aesthetic Imperativ

> All things considered, the novelist cannot separate himself
> from social problems, even if he wanted to. However, this is
> an issue not of influence but of cognizance. The novelist's
> choice to interpret his own time or to reinterpret the past is a
> reflected choice, since his objective is to investigate and reveal
> the inner dynamic of an age.
> —Ahmet Oktay, *Romanımıza Ne Oldu?*
> ("What Happened to Our Novel?")

> Despite its recent emergence and brief existence, our literature
> is predominantly realistic. But its realism only inhabits the
> outer shell of life. . . . It has not been fostered by the great
> insights based on the needs and inclinations of classes and
> generations. . . . The main reason for this is the lack of any
> sustained discussion on these issues among ourselves.
> —Ahmet Hamdi Tanpınar,
> *Mücevherlerin Sırrı* ("The Secret of Jewels")

Writing in 1940, when the young Turkish nation was anxiously watching the advance of Hitler's armies through Europe and exploring strategies to avoid a conflict it could not afford to engage in, Tanpınar possibly wanted his contemporaries to move beyond a realism that aspired to portray lived history to a critical examination of national, generational, and social identities. He valorizes works that transcend writers' subjective impressions, to reflect on larger social and philosophical concerns. These writings may not live in memory, but they make up an anonymous literature of ideas and issues that nourish literature per se. He laments the absence of critics and philosophers in public life who would have been catalysts in the emergence of a genuine critical realism. He singles out Karaosmanoğlu's *The Alien* as the only truly accomplished Turkish novel of reflective, philosophical realism (*Mücevherlerin Sırrı* 183). Contrary to Tanpınar's desire for a more reflective literature, however, the 1950s and the early 1960s witnessed a progressive growth in novels that moved away from the critical writing of the early Republican authors and indulged in an often jarring naturalism that depicted, in monotonous detail, the utter misery of Turkish village life. There are, of course, notable and poignantly beautiful novels and short stories that were exceptions to this trend.

Although a writer like Güntekin, who had traveled widely in Anatolia as a superintendent of schools, portrayed rural life and its trials in an intimate and empathetic way, the changed political climate, resulting from Turkey's first experiment with democracy, now impelled art to intervene in the social and public sphere in a more challenging way. Literature needed to hold up a mirror to the increasingly distorted face of social reality. The writer felt the need to raise public consciousness about how and why the fortunes of a nation, founded in an auspicious moment, buoyed up by progressive reforms, and spared the ravages of the Second World War through matchless diplomacy, were beginning to decline so soon. One clear cause was the perpetually poverty- and ignorance-stricken existence of the rural masses that the reforms had not reached or could not have much affected, if they had. The birth of what came to be known as village literature, from a committed, socially engaged literary consciousness, happened soon after the end of the Second World War, which also marked the institution of a multiparty regime in Turkey. The first products of this literary trend issued from the pens of graduates and teachers of the *köy enstitüleri* ("village institutes"). In order to understand better the conditions of the rise of village literature, its place in modern Turkish literary history, and its gradual displacement by a more sophisticated literature of social commitment, readers need a brief detour through recent history.

Since the first reform attempts undertaken in the Tanzimat era to ease the mounting political tensions within the borders of the Ottoman state, the great majority of the population that clung to the bosom of Islam viewed all modernization efforts of the state with apathy or suspicion or both. Even if these social reforms had been welcomed and had succeeded in their mission, they could not have prevented the political and economic catastrophes that culminated in the First World War. The bankruptcy of the state and the enemy occupation of the Ottoman territories overstretched the will and energy of Anatolian peasants, who had lost their lives in wars and what little they possessed in taxes. Devastated by constant poverty and warfare, they remained at best indifferent to enemy occupation and at worst supported it, as portrayed in the stories of Güntekin and Karaosmanoğlu. When a small cadre of military officers and teachers tried to enlist the peasants, they faced resistance, suspicion, and outright hostility. In the end, it was the landed gentry that supported the nationalist forces, since they feared losing their lands to the enemy if the war was lost. However, as soon as the victory was won, these landlords wanted their loans back with interest, so to speak. They were compensated for their financial contributions to the War of Independence with several seats in the National Assembly. As a result, this land aristocracy, which for ages had ruled over Anatolia in the manner of feudal lords, formed a strong conservative wing in the assembly.

When Atatürk began the challenging task of instituting modernization reforms, he was aware that these had to be implemented in all sectors of Turkish society. For the reforms to break through the resistance of the rural populations and the religious forces, a certain amount of consensus had to be reached between the urban intellectuals and the educated nationalist military officers, on the one hand, and the rural masses and religious leaders, on the other. The first step in building a bridge between the divided cultures of the land would be the institution of a progressive, universal educational system. Atatürk and his able ministers proceeded methodically and passionately to implement this goal. In November 1929, the National Schools project was launched, and Atatürk urged the literate population to "[t]each the new Turkish alphabet to every citizen, to every woman, man, porter, and boatman" and to make this task a national priority, in order that "our nation . . . take its place by the side of the civilised world" (Ahmad 81). However, despite the government's best efforts and the radical increase in literacy on the whole, the project of taking elementary education to the villages suffered major setbacks. There were obvious reasons for this failure.

First, the economic conditions essential for the realization of universal education were not in place. In the closed and static village economy, a peasant who needed the combined efforts of every member of his family and his ox for minimal subsistence could not afford to give up working hands and therefore would be reluctant to send his children to school. An eternity of economic stagnation had instilled in the peasantry a sense of fatalism, fear, and suspicion that resisted all modernization efforts. A second significant hurdle on the path to universal education was the difficulty of finding teachers willing to serve in the backward villages of Anatolia (the trend set by Güntekin's popular heroine Feride was an exception). Atatürk was not oblivious to the economic causes of the peasantry's resistance to mandatory elementary education. However, each time he introduced a land reform bill that aimed at ameliorating the peasants' plight, the conservative wing of the assembly made sure it would be defeated. So Atatürk took another tack and appointed an educational commission to investigate the causes behind the frustrating failure of taking elementary education to the villages. The commission's report recommended that aspiring teachers be recruited among the village youth and be trained not in the cities but in their own milieu, be taught about the reforms and their mission, and also be made aware of the practical applications of their curriculum, so that they would become not only village schoolteachers but also community aides and leaders. Acting on the findings and the recommendation of the commission, the government decided to set up the village institutes in 1940.

The village institutes enjoyed great protection and power under the auspices of the National Defense Law. However, they faced fierce opposition from the conservative wing from the very beginning. Despite the one-party rule and the lack of an institutionalized opposition, when the bill had to be voted on in the Turkish Grand National Assembly, a great number of the deputies were absent. The idea of not only teaching the Anatolian peasants to read and write but also educating them in such areas as husbandry, health care, and child rearing was threatening to many powerful conservative groups. Furthermore, even some supporters of equal universal education suspected that the sole ruling party was trying to recruit idealistic youths in order to turn them into its own unquestioning followers. The opposition accused the institutes of propagating communism's goals. Under increasing criticism and open attack, the institutes strayed from their original goals, coeducational training was ended, and fieldwork was replaced by theoretical courses.[1] The Demokrat Partisi ("Democrat Party"), which won the election of 1950 and was the first opposition party of the republic to come to power, closed them down for good. During its ten-year reign, this party, which started life with the best of democratic intentions, realized that its ticket to eternal power (and possibly eternal life) would be issued by the religious right. It began an unapologetic campaign to exploit religion for political gains. The corruption that infected the Democrat Party and led many of its idealistic members to quit (including Karaosmanoğlu and Halide Edib) came to an end with the military coup of 1960, but the architecture of religious revival remains its legacy.

Although the laudable project of village institutes buckled under conservative forces, its short life span produced a fair number of enlightened village teachers. The institutes had managed, despite all odds, to send a ripple effect across the vast Anatolian terrain. Teachers became agents in the ongoing struggle against village landlords and religious leaders, often in the service of those leaders. Had this institution survived the political assaults it suffered, it could have changed the fortunes of the Anatolian peasantry in the long run.[2] The village institutes also produced prominent writers, among them Fakir Baykurt (1929–99), Talip Apaydın (1926–), and Mahmut Makal (1933–), who began their writing careers with the essays, stories, and poems they published in the periodicals of the village institutes. Wyndham Deedes, Güntekin's translator, also undertook the translation of Makal's work into English. *A Village in Anatolia* (1954) is actually a two-part book that consists of the main chapters of Makal's *Bizim Köy* (1950; "Our Village"), an autobiographical ethnography, and *Köyümden* (1952; "From My Village"). The publisher's note explains that in the interest of avoiding "misunderstandings which might arise in the minds of readers unfamiliar with Turkey" (viii), the English editor added a commentary to the text and omitted certain passages. I am not sure that the omissions were necessary; nevertheless, the translation retains the poetic spirit of Makal's writing.

Mahmut Makal's *Our Village*: A Literary Autoethnography

Born in 1933 in Demirci, a village of the Niğde province, Mahmut Makal is a native son of the Anatolian hinterland. He graduated from the İvriz Village Institute and became a village schoolteacher. His first book, *Our Village*, is based on the notebooks written during his years in that post. In its tragicomic moments and memorable scenes, this lyric memoir cum ethnography communicates the stark isolation of teachers who had no support from the government in the challenges they faced. Makal went on to become an accomplished writer and journalist, after serving time in prison for publishing *Our Village* and being banned from teaching again. However, like the village institutes whose life was cut short but whose legacy remained strong, the influence of Makal's first book survived the regimes that tried to silence Makal. *Our Village* became an unlikely best seller when it was published in 1950. It enjoyed numerous reprints; was translated into English, German, French, Bulgarian, Russian, Italian, Rumanian, and Hebrew in short order; and garnered critical praise in every country where it was published. Bernard Lewis has called the book "a most remarkable human document from a graduate of these [village] institutes" (478n).

The universal acclaim of *Our Village* is neither fortuitous nor undeserved. Its translatability alone points to an element that struck a chord with an international reading public that probably had little knowledge and understanding of Turkish society. Its aesthetic appeal lies, to a great extent, in the poetic blending of the genres that defy categorization and prevent the story from slipping into a tedious social documentary, a self-centered autobiography, or a narrowly focused ethnography. The book masterfully appropriates aspects of genres such as memoir, ethnography, political tract, and metafiction and manages to present this literary concoction with irony and humor. Literary autobiographies and poetic autoethnographies have become the focus of critical analysis in the poststructuralist camp, where literature is no longer seen as a necessarily rarefied and aesthetically pleasing form of human expression but one signifying system among others— language, signs, customs, social practices, folklore. *Our Village* has been read variously as a socialist manifesto, an ethnography by a native anthropologist, and an invective against the ruling powers. The book may have had its greatest influence on the budding socialist sentiment among the intelligentsia that saw in it a concretization of Marxist-Leninist thought. Content alone, and a specific historical and political one at that, does not ensure any book a long shelf life. Makal's topic—Turkish village life in the first half of the twentieth century—may be time-bound and culturally specific. However, its effortlessly moving (in both senses of the word) language and style, authenticity of dialogue, and cultural acuity lend it an aesthetic edge that many other books of village life lacked.

Our Village does not define itself in terms of a specific genre. There is no subtitle, such as "Memoir," "Tales from the Village," or "The Biography of a Place." In 1973, twenty-three years after the first publication of the novel, Makal added a postscript as a prefatory frame to its tenth edition. "The Story of This Book" relates his persecution by the Democrat Party regime after the book appeared. Predictably, the government saw the book as a defamation of national character and a threat to its image in the world. Ironically, the issues Makal touched on in an evenhanded and slightly sardonic manner became aggravated during the Democrat Party rule. In this sense, his story proved prescient. Instead of heeding the sincere voice of a visionary author and taking measures against the further descent of Anatolian peasantry into serfdom, apathy, and fear, the rulers did precisely the opposite: they locked the disenfranchised rural poor more securely in the prison of religious superstition.

A memorable scene from the book shows how the Democrat Party during its first years in opposition (1946–50) played the religion card to secure the rural vote in the coming elections. In 1949, two hours of optional religious instruction on Saturday afternoons (in the fourth and fifth grades) was introduced into elementary schools for pupils whose parents requested it. In 1950, religious education in the fourth and fifth grades became mandatory. The villagers, as the narrator remarks, heard about the introduction of religious instruction before him and began relentlessly pursuing him to find out when he would start giving religion courses. For a long time, they had been trying to convince him to drop the curriculum and have him team-teach with the village hoja to ensure that their children got full and proper religious training. Finally, the religion textbooks arrived. One day the narrator invited all the adults to a reading of this textbook, which represented a rather secularized version of Islam. The villagers enjoyed the recitation but complained that the textbook did not teach *namaz* (ritual prayer performed five times daily). Nevertheless, they were enchanted by the story of a miracle in the book, where the Prophet transforms famine into abundance. They chimed in, "Thank goodness, you Demirkırats [a corruption of the word *democrat* that means 'iron stallion'] deliver everything you promise. This year you brought religion lessons, next year you'll come to power and bring back that real Muslim script and the fez" (*Bizim Köy* 147; *Village* 106).[3] The villagers were completely on target, leading the narrator to muse in an apostrophe to the reader, "You see what means the opposition leaders employ to move and win! They have already made good use of this strategy. If they promise that they'll drop everything from the curriculum save religion, they'll pave the way to power with one leap" (147; 106).

Our Village is divided into four nonchronological chapters, composed of observations and impressions of everyday practices, from a keen political and philosophical perspective. Within the covers of this slim book, Makal manages to portray with stunning clarity the grip of sheikhs on the population, the silencing of women, the isolation of villages from the rest of the world, and the dissemination of superstition and rumor. These reflections are not mere snapshots but insightful tableaux of social disconsolation. Episodes are related with metaphoric and ironic punch. In a section entitled

"An Epidemic of Sheikhs," the narrator matter-of-factly reports that in the eleven villages he visited in September 1947, the smallest number of sheikhs lived in the village of Hicip; a little over fifty (111; 86). Villagers believe in the omnipotence of these sheikhs, who don't even know what sect they are from and can never show proof of the miracles they performed. Listening to the villagers' litanies about miracles and how sheikh so-and-so can make riches pour from heaven with one prayer, the narrator, suffering from sheikh fatigue, cannot help but mock the peasants, who "never question why they are never free of poverty in that case" (115; 90).

The invisibility and silencing of women has gone to such absurd lengths that the narrator cannot resist portraying his encounters with students' mothers with a touch of sarcasm (well, maybe sarcasm laced with compassion). Since women literally cannot open their mouths in the company of men, relatives, and older women, mothers who come to the narrator to explain their children's illness or to ask that their children be excused from class, must resort to gestures: "They tell me all their troubles with signs and head movements. If someone unaware of these traditions were to see them, he would think the poor things were born deaf and dumb" (90; 69). In a gruesome episode, a woman gapes at a wedding crowd. Her husband sees her gaping, runs to get his ax, and cripples her. It does not matter that the mouth, which involuntarily opened, is shut again when he returns to attack her. When the narrator censures the brutality of the husband, the husband retorts, "What do you mean, it's a disgrace? For her or for me? She needs to be aware of her unworthiness" (90; 69).

Makal's faith in the power of books to transform, heal, and redeem remains strong. Makal remarks:

> The peasant is not a scholar, but he is wise. I know very well that he is capable of interpreting what he hears by far better than the so-called intellectuals. The problem is to put the right kind of publications into the hands of the peasant. When are we ever going to seriously deal with an issue as important as peasant education? (144; 103–04)

He emphasizes the instructive power of fables on the village folk. He starts a tradition of reading a newspaper article, story, or fable in the village community room in winter days, when there is no school, and encourages his listeners to comment on the readings. Slowly the villagers get addicted to the pleasure of listening to texts read aloud. They become particularly enchanted with *Fables of La Fontaine*, rendered in the poet Orhan Veli Kanık's verse translation. Kanık's powerful language and skillful use of familiar idioms leads them to appropriate the tales to fit their own lives and experiences. One of the fables proves to be so popular, the narrator ends up reading it fifty times. "The mountain that gave birth," an expression already familiar to many, becomes a catchword due to Kanık's wonderful translation. At the first meeting, one of the young villagers quips, "A simile is never wrong. That mountain really reflects our situation." The narrator is about to ask what the connection is, when the youth continues:

> People expect the mountain to give birth to a city, judging only from the noise it makes. Aren't we just like that? You've read us all those things about how things will be this way or that. As we listened, we thought all these things would come true. What was done? We were told a school would be built. We waited, and nothing happened. . . . We know what you are going through here. . . . They say it will be built, ten, twenty years pass. Just words! At least that mountain brought forth a mouse, ours, nothing.　(156; 113)

The book ends with a strangely sad fairy tale (or anti–fairy tale)— omitted from the English version—about a poor teacher who spends his life trying to bring light to dark times and lives unhappily ever after (but still never gives up his dream). Like the Anatolian *aşık*s ("bards"), who refer to themselves at the end of their songs, Makal concludes this haunting tale with an allegory of himself. Such judiciously employed literary forms— satire, anti–fairy tale, folktale, *aşık*'s voice—as well as intertextual references transform what is essentially a documentary narrative into a work of poetic resonance. When on his return from a visit to his own village, Makal sees the village school brought down by strong rains and beyond any possibility of restoration, he finds solace in Sait Faik's (Sait Faik Abasıyanık's) lines from a story (149). In response to those who attacked *The Alien* for belittling the Anatolian peasant, Makal emphatically reaffirms Yakup Kadri Karaosmanoğlu's insights into the realities of village life. People who only want to see an idealized picture of "pastoral" Anatolia "know nothing about this land. Until we fully embrace the realities of this country, let us at least stop claiming to know our villages and speaking on their behalf" (48; 37). Faced with the desolation of the Anatolian heartland, he writes, "Yakup Kadri's voice, shouting the verses, 'Oh sorrowful land / pity on those who do not know how to love thee,' rings in my ears" (35; 25). Makal lends to lived experience the insight of careful observation and the soulful creativity of the storyteller's art. Ultimately, in this poetic ethnography, life and drama, fact and fiction emerge interlinked in their contiguous fates.

Our Village ushered in a literary trend that generated a host of village novels. Unfortunately, most of these works emphasized documentary and ethnographic forms of writing without the poetry and philosophical insight that informs Makal's narrative. What began as a sincere attempt to represent the concerns of the neglected and disenfranchised village populations by their own writers (as opposed to Istanbul authors' viewing the villages from their comfortable urban dwellings) and to hold up a mirror to social realities often censored in books usually turned into a repetitive litany marked more by self-pity than by corrective insight. Granted, the genre encouraged a search for social and political facts and validated the efforts of progressive and enlightened voices in the fight against a regime that exploited the poor, hypnotized them with religious rhetoric, and sabotaged secular and universal education. Nevertheless, the practice of tendentious literature is aesthetically risky business. When writing turns into whining, it oppresses imagination and inventiveness and reduces experience to an eternal recurrence of misery. There is an element of truth in José Ortega y Gasset's words, "Las artes se vengan de todo el que quiere ser con ellas más artista, haciendo que su obra no llegue siquiera a ser artística" (126; "the arts take their revenge on those who are not content with being mere artists by ensuring that their work does not succeed even aesthetically").

Another factor that contributed to the waning popularity of village literature as well as overtly tendentious literature was the obsessive tendency of many representatives of these trends to write in an artificially pure Turkish, which came to be associated with leftist politics. This style not only compromised the readers' pleasure of the text but also created a linguistic barrier to understanding. What had begun in line with Atatürk's attempts to purify Turkish of its heavy Arabic and Persian baggage through the coinage of Turkish neologisms went overboard starting in the 1960s, and written Turkish became, in most instances, "as unintelligible to the mass of the people as 'high Ottoman' had been" (Mango 122). A detailed discussion of the long history of the Turkish language reform and of the debates on forging a Turkish *bilim dili* ("scientific language") are beyond the scope of this study. However, it is important to point out that the confusion created

by this over-the-top Turkification of language hampered writers and re-
duced reader interest. The most accomplished novelists of the current Turkish literary scene owe their success and popularity to their usage of a more
accessible, balanced, and colloquial language. They have also made the rea-
sonable choice of preserving Arabic words that have been totally assimilated
in spoken Turkish and denote concepts difficult to render in artificially created neologisms. On the other hand, authors such as Makal, Yaşar Kemal,
Fakir Baykurt, and Kemal Tahir have integrated the dialogic richness of
Anatolian regional idioms into their writing. Like Makal, Yaşar Kemal, another gifted bard of Anatolia, stayed clear of the wooden aesthetic of village
literature, while maintaining a genuine attachment to his Anatolian roots
and the magic of poetic imagination. Little wonder that his work continues
to be widely read, translated, and analyzed by Turkish and international
scholars.

Yaşar Kemal's *Memed, My Hawk*

> [W]hen people find themselves cornered, when they feel the
> pain of death in their heart, they tend to create a world of
> myth in which they try to take refuge.
>
> —Yaşar Kemal, Introduction to
> *Memed, My Hawk*

At the tender age of twenty-five, Yaşar Kemal began writing the saga of one
the best-known characters of the modern Turkish novel, *İnce Memed*. His
protagonist, Memed, was twenty-one at the time. When Kemal was finished with the fourth and final volume of Memed's story, he was over sixty
and Memed only twenty-five (Introd. viii). *Memed, My Hawk* was first serialized in the daily newspaper *Cumhuriyet*, between 1953 and 1954, and was
later published as a book. The novel was an instant success and has been
translated into forty languages. Despite the success of Kemal's numerous
other books, which have received national and international awards, including Germany's Friedenpreis des deutschen Buchhandels ("Peace Prize of the
German Book Trade") in 1997, the popular and critical appeal of *Memed,
My Hawk* remains unsurpassed. It is a testimony to the enduring popularity
of the novel that New York Review Books recently reissued the novel and its
first sequel, *İnce Memed II* (translated as *They Burn the Thistles*) in its Classics series.

Yaşar Kemal was born Kemal Sadık Gökçeli in 1923 in Hemite (now Gökçeadam) in the province of Adana. His father was a farmer, and the family had been uprooted from its original home in northeastern Anatolia because of war and occupation. As a young child, Kemal lost an eye in an accident. When he was five years old, he witnessed the murder of his father, who was praying in a mosque. The incident left him traumatized for a long time. He had to leave middle school short of graduation and worked at many jobs, ardently reading and learning along the way. He was only seventeen when arrested, for the first time, for his political activities. Throughout his life and career, he had many brushes with the law and endured jail sentences because of his political beliefs, but his resolve to speak out for his people and for what he believed never wavered. In 1951 he came to Istanbul and after many hardships landed a job as a reporter at *Cumhuriyet*. He gained recognition for his reportages and short stories during his time there. After the publication of *Memed, My Hawk*, he became a household name. Other novels followed in quick succession. His reception in the West was enthusiastic, as his lyrical and passionate tales gave voice to a little-known geography that intrigued readers, and his deep respect for nature and empowerment of simple folk resounded beyond regional and national borders. Furthermore, the ready availability of his works in translation in many languages figures as a factor in his international fame. That his late wife, Thilda Kemal, was an able translator of his novels and made it her life's mission to render his poetic voice in English certainly helped.

In the introduction written for the recently reissued *Memed, My Hawk*, Kemal offers a retrospective view of the lifelong political and poetic sensibilities that underwrote his most celebrated work. He traces the roots of his creative interests to the Kurdish epics and hero stories he listened to at home; to the Turkish epics he heard in the Turcoman village near the Mediterranean shore, where he was born; and to the works of Anton Chekhov and Stendhal he read in the Adana Library, where he worked as a young man. He identifies the defining impulses of his work in his intimacy with nature, his faith in the redeeming power of myth, and his attraction to characters who are committed (ix–xiii). The word Kemal has used to describe the characters that draw him is *mecbur* (a loanword from Arabic), which means "obliged" or "compelled." For him, *mecbur* suggests a belief so strong that the character who has it cannot act against it. In this context, Kemal mentions the story of the sheikh of Sakarya, a *mecbur*, who is a prototype of Memed. The young sheikh, a warrior who defied the Ottoman sultan Murad IV, turned

down the sultan's offer of riches and the rank of vizier and was then captured and killed by the sultan's forces. When the sultan's grand vizier and
commander in chief had met the sheikh in the mountains of Sakarya to offer him the sultan's gifts and ask him to join the Ottoman army, which was
marching on Baghdad in 1538, the sheikh refused despite the threats to his
life and the lives of his men, because his mission was from God, and he was
"committed to that alone" (ix).

In his excellent study of *Memed, My Hawk*, Berna Moran attributes
the poetic achievement of the novel in part to Kemal's creative reworking
of the theme of the noble bandit (2: 101–21). Moran analyzes the composition of *Memed* against the British historian Eric Hobsbawm's *Bandits*,
which identifies nine characteristics common to the noble bandit type portrayed in novels, stories, and poems from all over the world. In summary,
the noble or kindhearted bandit in fiction is someone who takes to the
mountains not because of a crime he committed but because of an injustice
he suffered. He rights wrongs. His mission is to take from the rich and give
to the poor and to rectify the wrongs inflicted on the innocent. He kills
only in self-defense or to avenge the wronged. At least in theory, he is elusive and cannot be caught. He is beloved and supported by the people, and
if he returns to society alive, he'll be revered. He'll be killed only by the actions of betrayers, because honest people will not turn against him. The
noble bandit is never an enemy of the king or emperor, because these figures represent justice; his enemies are the feudal lords who exploit and per-
secute his people (Hobsbawm 35–36). Moran maintains that although
Memed partakes in these universal features of banditry tales (such as those
of Robin Hood, Billy the Kid, and Jesse James), structurally it adheres to
the plot development in traditional Turkish bandit legends. In fact, legends of Köroğlu, Yalnız Efe, and Çakıcı Efe appear as embedded or framed
narratives in Memed's story.

Memed, a gentle lad with an adventurous spirit, lives with his old
mother in an impoverished small village whose inhabitants are treated as
virtual slaves by the ruthless and greedy landowner Abdi Agha. The agha
claims two-thirds of the crop the villagers produce, so that every year the
famished villagers, who run out of food before the end of the winter, come
to the agha's door, asking for a loan. The vicious cycle of debt and hunger is
perpetuated by this feudal form of land ownership. Memed runs away from
home and is taken in by a kind father figure, but he returns after a while to

protect his mother from the agha and endures the vengeful abuse of this villain. Although Memed and his childhood sweetheart, Hatçe, are betrothed, the agha interferes and tries to force Hatçe into marriage with his own nephew. Memed and Hatçe elope but are caught, and in the confrontation that ensues Memed wounds the agha and kills his nephew. Hatçe is caught and imprisoned on false charges of murder, and Memed takes to the mountains. The agha takes his revenge by having Memed's mother murdered. He also sends his men after Memed. Memed escapes all the traps set by the enemy and even frees Hatçe from the prison in an act of daredeviltry.

There are two kinds of brigand bands in the mountains: the murderous ones, in the service of landowners, and those who are the noble bandit types, taking from the rich and giving to the poor. The first group Memed joins turns out to be the first kind, thieves and assassins. He leaves them to form a band of three, he and two trustworthy friends. Although his reasons for becoming an outlaw were personal, his life on the run turns him into a rebel with a cause. Through his eyes the author displays a brutal feudal system of ownership, where the hardworking peasants are kept in perpetual poverty and fear. Memed becomes the legend that people would have created, had he not existed. In the end, Hatçe is killed in an armed encounter, leaving him with their infant son. A peasant woman who had lost her son to another brutal landlord and had joined the couple in the mountains takes the child to raise him as her own. Memed returns to the village, as he has a final matter to settle. He kills the agha, rides into the village to tell the villagers that he made good on his promise, and disappears, never to be seen again (until the sequel).

In his analysis of the novel (2: 101–21), Moran claims that because of its structural affinity to Turkish legends of noble banditry, *Memed, My Hawk* is more firmly rooted in local traditions than in the universal thematics of bandit legends. The Turkish legends, Moran argues, have a four-part structure. The first part depicts the conditions of oppression and exploitation that lead to the protagonist's rebellion against the existing order. In *Memed*, Abdi Agha, who owns the five villages where the peasants work the land, exploits them ruthlessly, taking away the little they have, causing misery, hunger, and abject poverty. In the second part, the protagonist becomes an outlaw, after a loved one, a parent, sibling, spouse, or betrothed is persecuted or tortured by the feudal lord or the landlord. Memed's mother is killed and his betrothed, Hatçe, is forcefully separated from him, to be given to Abdi Agha's nephew in marriage. The third part is an account of the good deeds of the bandit, who helps the impoverished peasants and delivers justice. Memed gives the villagers their land back and kills the ruthless Abdi Agha. The fourth part recounts the final station of the outlaw's adventures. Either he returns home a hero or disappears, never to be heard from again. At the close of the novel, we read, "No news of Slim Memed was ever heard again. No sign or trace of him was ever found" (370).

Writing for the reader of the 1950s, Kemal had to go beyond traditional molds; he re-created the legend of the noble bandit in the context of the contemporary social climate and superimposed poetic and conceptual innovations on the basic plot structure. Moran notes that by adding a love story to the bandit legend, Kemal weds the legend to the romance tradition of Anatolian bards. By portraying Abdi Agha as a tyrant who lets the peasant hunger and Memed as the figure who gives back to the peasant what is rightfully his, Kemal establishes the symbolic dichotomy of lack and abundance. The final scenes of the book, which portray the villagers' feasts before the onset of the plowing season, conjure up images of abundance rites and endow Memed with the stature of a savior. Unlike the noble bandit in Hobsbawm's study, who does not aim to change the existing order, Memed emerges as a "utopian revolutionary," whose struggle implicates existing economic conditions in the ever worsening misery of rural life (2: 113). In Moran's view, the novel succeeds because it incorporates in the person of the protagonist the stuff of myths and dreams. Memed becomes a legend, as he comes to embody the universally revered acts of rightful revenge, saving the imprisoned lover, freeing people from a monster, and bringing abundance and wealth to the community. These deeds exemplify moral values that literature has traditionally aspired to inculcate. By fusing them with a keen insight into peasant psychology and character, Kemal has produced a work of lasting appeal that has captivated countless readers and was made into a film (2: 120).

But there are other, thematically and structurally less tangible elements in Kemal's novel that exert a powerful pull on the reader. Critics have pointed to a quality of freshness that never becomes old. Each reading leads to an insight that gives a deeper understanding of the human condition, of the prison of social relations, and of the redeeming power of imagination. Memed's message does not outlive its historical necessity; even though it is a forceful indictment of feudal practices and their persistence in a given time and place, it is not specific to that time and place. Its purchase does not rest on a thesis. Kemal has empathy for the peasants but does not idealize them. Just as in *The Alien* and *Our Village* the peasants believed the sheikhs to have superhuman powers, now they exalt Memed to the status of a saint who can perform miracles. But they are ready to turn against him when they find out that he was unable to kill Abdi Agha the first time around. They are not happy with the prospect of an amnesty that would save Memed and his family from hunger and danger and allow him to return to his village, because they fear Abdi Agha would come back to the village too: "What is this amnesty? If a brigand's a brigand, his place is on the mountain" (362).

In the displeasure of the peasants lies a great irony. Memed becomes an outlaw to protect his people from the terror of the landowner and a social order that is bound to lead to their deracination and destruction. His commitment, however, condemns him to an exile from which the people he tries to save refuse to save him. Although the novel celebrates the nobility of its protagonist, it also underlines the great toll displacement and deracination exact. I think this last aspect is yet another feature of the novel that resounds in today's world, where millions have been uprooted by famine, ethnic violence, and political persecution.

In his retrospective look at *Memed, My Hawk*, Kemal reflects on how his work in general addresses present-day issues. These reflections provide another point of entry into his creative work. One of his greatest concerns is the human destruction of nature. "Confronted with the massacre of nature, that great scourge of our age, the dangers of which we have not yet been able to adequately understand, we will create myths of fear as our ancestors did," he states (Introduction xii). Beyond its generic identity as the story of the noble bandit, *Memed, My Hawk* asserts the inviolability of the bond between man and nature. Memed is a skinny, short lad whose physical development was probably arrested by poverty and poor nutrition. Yet at one point we read that his physique is the product of the earth that bore him: "One grows up, matures, according to one's soil. Memed grew on barren soil. His appearance was that of an oak, short and gnarled" (*Memed* 51). True to the Romantic tradition, nature is anthropomorphized and joins the cast of characters as a living entity. Like Abdi Agha, who comes to symbolize hunger and poverty for the villagers, the thistle fields represent barrenness and starvation. At the close of the novel, after Memed kills the agha with three bullets to the chest and restores the fields to the peasants, the peasants initiate a ritual of burning the thistle fields before plowing. When the fire devours the thistles, these "seem to shriek as they burn" (371).

Kemal believes that "[e]ven the smallest particle of nature has an identity, a unique personality." He feels the word "personality" is not quite what he wants to say, yet he "cannot find the right name for this. One day humanity, scientists, writers will find it" (Introduction xii–xiii). (Rhetoric provides us with a term, *prosopopoeia*, a trope that personifies a nonhuman entity, mostly an element of nature.) In fairy tales, nature and animals speak the same language as human beings, and the otherness of nature is overcome in poeticized language. In *Memed, My Hawk*, Kemal includes the fascinating story of Lame Ali, the reader of tracks who, against his will, is forced to follow the trail of the eloped lovers. For Ali, the soil reveals its signs and script, as it does to a scientist, poet, or nature philosopher, and nothing can stop him from reading the text of the earth until it divulges the presence of what is sought: "It's enough for him if there is a trail to follow. . . . When it comes to tracking, nothing else matters" (*Memed* 90). As Ali makes out the imprint of a sandal in the ground, he can tell that the "sandals have been newly sewn" and that the "hairs on the leather are still long. Surely that's the skin of a bull calf that died last winter" (91).

As in Romantic fairy tales or novellas, nature is inscribed with human history and can communicate it to those who can decode its language. One reason that the *Märchen* ("fairy tale") emerged as a predominant genre in German Romanticism lay in the Romantic conception of language as an all-encompassing, even ontological ground of experience that determined our reality. Nature as the real object of subjective perception also resided in language and was, furthermore, seen as the reflection of the self. Therefore, the fairy tales are inhabited not only by human beings but also by speaking animals and nature. Romantic idealism, which strove to mend the split between the subject and the world, saw in dream, imagination, and poetic language the possibility for the recovery of the lost subject-object unity. In the poetic idiom of *Memed, My Hawk*, sustained by fable and fabulation, the human and natural worlds are seamlessly integrated.

Another point Kemal highlights is the consolation that myths, legends, and stories offer humanity in its darkest hours: "By creating myths, by conjuring up worlds of dreams, one can withstand the great suffering of the world and attain love, friendship, beauty, and even, perhaps, immortality" (Introduction xi). Despite appearances, then, Kemal's "myths" are not about heroes: "I have never believed in heroes. Even in those novels in which I focus on revolt I have tried to highlight the fact that those we call heroes are in effect instruments wielded by people" (x). Granted that the truth of a work of art is not necessarily in the artist's intent, it is fair to assume that the major focus of *Memed, My Hawk* is not the character Memed—whether immortal hero or accidental savior—but a social imaginary that taps into a mythopoeic reserve to communicate the hope of freedom to the downtrodden. Folk heroes, idols, saviors all belong to the "authors" who create them, to the people who will them to life. Kemal's narrator reflects:

> No matter how limited a man's field of vision, his imagination knows no bounds. A man who has never been outside his village in Deyirmenoluk can still create a whole imaginary world that may reach as far as the stars. Without travelling, a man can penetrate to the other end of the world.   (*Memed* 77)

The power to imagine, in turn, derives from collective memory. "Bandits," as Eric Hobsbawm concludes, "belong to remembered history, as distinct from the official history of books." Hobsbawm lets Ivan Olbracht, "who has written better about it [the bandit legend] than almost anyone else," (115) have the last word on the topic: "Man is filled with a strange, stubborn urge to remember . . . and in addition he carries within himself the wish to have what he cannot have—if only in the form of a fairly tale" (115).

Kemal's faith in the redemptive power of imagination to sustain the will to live and overcome the burden of history has not always been well received by critics who take issue with his poeticization of genuine and deep-seated social and economic ills. While Moran praises *Memed, My Hawk*, he believes that the second and third *Memed* sequels, though retaining their poetic strength, no longer adhere to the conventions of the noble bandit genre. In *Memed, My Hawk*, by killing Abdi Agha, Memed not only revenged the deaths of his mother and Hatçe but also delivered justice to the villagers who had no one else to turn to. The death of the incorrigible tyrant symbolized the triumph of good over evil and abundance over destitution. In the sequels, Memed continues to kill landlords, but new ones replace them. Although Memed realizes that killing the landlords is no solution and cannot change the system, he sees no other way out. As the sequels can no longer represent the righting of wrongs or the victory of good against evil or abundance against lack, they become arbitrary forms of punishment with no redeeming value (Moran 2: 120–21). In the long run, the steady rehearsal of killing the bad guys fails to deliver either moral elation or catharsis.

Kemal Tahir (1910–73), one of the most vocal voices of Turkish literature of commitment, struck out hard against what he considered the glorification of petty criminals who perpetuated the evils of the system. Many bandits were also active in the service of the landlords, who used them to terrorize and silence the peasants whose lands the landlords had confiscated. In a hilarious parody of *Memed, My Hawk, Rahmet Yolları Kesti* (1957; "Mercy Blocked the Road"), Tahir subverts the myth of the bandit through political humor as well as a social psychological portrayal of the Anatolian peasants' need for bandits. The parody starts with the double entendre of the title: *rahmet* means both "God's mercy" and "rain." In Tahir's tale, a mean agha hires the brigand İskender, who has seen better days, to rob Kasım Dede, a filthy-rich, old villager. İskender, though impoverished, is unwilling to take the job but gives in to nostalgia, as he remembers his days of glorious banditry. With the help of two friends, he manages to rob the old man and his young wife, but on the way back they get caught in a storm. The avenging rain (or mercy) forces them to burn some of the booty for heat, and because they are drenched, they have to change clothes and wear the robbed wife's fancy robes. Laden with booty bags, clad in feminine apparel, replete with fancy underwear, and totally flustered by the torrent, they emerge as grotesquely comic characters rather than heroic bandits, when the gendarmes and a group of villagers catch up with them.

Tahir took an unequivocal position against the mythologization of the bandit figure not only among the gullible peasants but also among the Romantic leftists. He emphasized that an institutionalization of bandit worship or banditry as a panacea for economic disenfranchisement would only lead to a distorted view of real social grievances. He also tried to bring to public consciousness the victimization of the bandits themselves and the gravity of the socioeconomic context that necessitates their desperate acts. Although Tahir's book in no way lessened the popularity of *Memed, My Hawk*, its achievement both as a village novel of critical realism and as a memorable social satire cannot be disputed. In a later novel, *The Sea-Crossed Fisherman* (see chapter 5 in this volume), Yaşar Kemal wrote his own, updated parody of bandit glorification; this time, however, it is not the peasants who are dazzled and bamboozled by the exploits of glorified bandits but Istanbul's sensation-hungry denizens, whom the media is only too happy to accommodate by turning petty criminals into larger-than-life heroes.

Seeing History through *Snow*:
Orhan Pamuk's Political Vision

Yaşar Kemal was a perpetual contender for the Nobel Prize in Literature. He had taken the Turkish novel beyond Istanbul's metropolitan center; interwoven its texture with Anatolian ballads, legends, songs, and colors; and developed a poetic prose of epic grandeur. Yet the coveted prize eluded him. After a lot of speculation on the part of the Turkish literati and press, Orhan Pamuk finally became the first Turkish Nobel laureate, beating the competition of such names as Philip Roth, Mario Vargas Llosa, and Milan Kundera. In recent years, Pamuk's name began to circulate in the rumor mill as a sure winner, since he had garnered major international prizes and had become a celebrity in the European literary scene. Furthermore, Pamuk, buoyed by fame and riches (and certainly by a good dose of conviction), stood up to what is known as *derin devlet* (literally, "deep state"), a powerful cadre of high-ranking officials and members of the military who see themselves as guardians of the secular state. He made public statements about Turkish responsibility in the massacres of ethnic Armenians during the First World War and in the crushing of Kurdish separatist uprisings. In an interview in a Swiss newspaper, Pamuk was quoted as saying that thousands of Kurds and a million Armenians were killed in Turkish territories, yet he was the only one to openly talk about it.

The official Turkish line is that neither the Armenian massacre nor the suppression of Kurdish riots can be termed genocide. Turkey does not dispute the killing of Armenians but rejects charges of a genocidal strategy, claiming that in the clashes that witnessed the fall of the Ottoman Empire many ethnic Turks were also killed during uprisings and reciprocal attacks. As for the Turkish-Kurdish struggle, it assumed the character of a civil war in the 1990s. Not one to shy away from highly charged and divisive issues, Pamuk plunged into the fray and got in trouble with the law: he was charged with insulting the state. When "the affair Pamuk" became a cause célèbre, charges were quickly dropped on a technicality.

Yaşar Kemal, an ethnic Kurd, also spoke out against the state-led oppression of Turkey's Kurdish minority on many occasions, and he was often put on trial. Today, Kemal and Pamuk are the two internationally renowned Turkish novelists. In different yet complementary ways, both have rejuvenated the modern Turkish novel with visionary energy. Their works are widely read and translated. Though both have engaged in political discourse, they remain first and foremost artists of the word. Yet their life stories could not be more different. Whereas Kemal is a child of Anatolian plains, comes from very modest circumstances, and is self-educated, Pamuk is the son of a wealthy Istanbul family, went to prestigious schools, and has enjoyed the luxury of not having to hold a day job.

Born in 1952 in Istanbul, Pamuk has rarely left his hometown for long, except for a stint at the International Writing Program at the University of Iowa and for short-term visiting appointments at Columbia University. He graduated from the American High School, Robert Kolej of Istanbul, studied architecture for a while at the Istanbul Technical University, but dropped out to devote himself to writing full-time. His first novel, *Cevdet Bey ve Oğulları* (1982; "Cevdet Bey and His Sons"), a multigenerational novel of an Istanbul family, was an instant literary success in Turkey. With the translation of *Beyaz Kale* (1985; "The White Castle") into English, French, and German and with the translation into major languages of his subsequent novels and the memoir *Istanbul: Hatıralar ve Bir Şehir* (2003; *Istanbul: Memories and the City*), Pamuk became an internationally recognized name. Unlike the work of many modern Turkish novelists, his fiction has never been overtly political. Rather, his political sensibilities are couched in philosophical terms and exoticized and estranged from real-life settings. I use *exoticize* here in the sense of displacing a thing, event, or concept to a distant or mythical time or place.

Snow, a postmodernist allegory of the sociocultural imbroglio contemporary Turkish society is caught in, is Pamuk's first self-consciously political novel and arguably his conceptually most sophisticated work to date. Although Pamuk began writing *Snow* long before the fanatical arm of political Islam struck the United States in the form of hijacked commercial airplanes crashing into the World Trade Center, with the release of the novel in English translation in the United States, he became the unofficial interpreter of Islam for the American public. The German Book Trade awarded its prestigious Peace Prize for 2005 to Pamuk, honoring him as an author committed to a concept of culture based on knowledge and respect for others and one who writes from a space where Europe and Islamic Turkey can coexist. As mentioned earlier, Kemal was the first Turkish writer to be honored with this prize.

Ironically, many secular intellectual Turks are irritated by Pamuk's oppositional stance to what Pamuk sees as an intolerant secularist state and its Jacobin advocates from his very privileged space as the freelancer son of a wealthy Istanbul family. In *Snow*, however, he does not lend credence to those who see him as a champion of modern Islam or who condemn him as an agent provocateur against the republic and the Kemalist reforms. In fact, he marshals his impressive erudition and literary skill to craft a historically informed and aesthetically performed commentary on the fortunes of a land entangled in the thorny ramifications of its past and the pressures of conforming to the dictates of modernity. Like most of his previous novels, *Snow* is a metafiction, a text that reflects on the act of (re)constructing a story from fragments of other stories, evidentiary documents, eyewitness accounts, tapes, videos, notebooks, and other traces of memory. At the level of thematics and symbolism, *Snow* becomes a fictional vehicle in pursuit of a people's identity in the complex web of history and modernity and an allegorical account of a fateful search.

The original title, *Kar*, carries a heavy symbolic cargo. The story takes place in the distant border city of Kars, whose name is supposed to come from *Kar-su* ("snow water"). In addition to this cognate pair, the consonant *k* in the title and in the protagonist's name, Ka (his real name is Kerim Alakuşoğlu, but instead he uses an acronym-pseudonym, the first letter of his given and family names, in school and in his published poetry books), not only form another set of cognates but also recall Kafka's protagonist, K, in *The Castle*, the parable of a man's search for truth doomed to failure in the prison of a frightening state apparatus. Ka is a forty-two-year-old, never-married writer from Istanbul who lived in political exile in Germany for twelve years. He never learned German during this time but continued to write in Turkish, so as not to be exiled from his mother tongue. On his return to Turkey, he goes to Kars, a provincial town on the Russian border, which he briefly visited twenty years before, to report on the upcoming municipal elections there and a wave of mysterious suicides among young women. The suicide theme is ripped from headlines and thus interlinks the fictional theme with lived history. Batman, a city in eastern Anatolia, where Kurdish resistance, political Islam, and state intervention were locked in an ongoing struggle, was the site of an epidemic of suicides by young women. These women, who were forced into marriages that they did not want or who were terrorized by fathers and husbands, began killing themselves in spates. In an effort to curb publicity, which might lead to copycat suicides, the government asked the help of the clergy, but that move backfired.

Pamuk's analysis of complex and paradoxical affiliations, disaffiliations, and conflicts among a host of ethnic and religious groups is strongly informed by two books, which he chose as the two best books of the year in the *Times Literary Supplement*'s "International Books of the Year": Müjgân Halis's *Batman'da Kadınlar Ölüyor* ("Women Are Dying in Batman") and Ruşen Çakır's *Derin Hizbullah* ("Deep Hizbullah"), an account of the atrocities of Hizbullah in Batman. Although Pamuk makes a serious effort to get into the minds of Islamists in *Snow* and has been criticized for his apparent sympathy for them, his words in the 7 December 2001 issue of the *Times Literary Supplement* belie that charge. We need to keep in mind, however, that these words were written in the aftermath of September 11, which may have given him pause. Referring to Çakır as "a courageous and brilliant journalist and expert on Islamic movements," he tells how Çakır

> demonstrates that the nihilism and paranoia described by Dostoevsky in *The Devils* are no longer characteristic of Stalinist left-wing organizations but live on in Islamic organizations which operate as small, independent cells, and are more inclined to kill their own members on suspicion of being agents of the State than supporters of secularism.   ("International Books")

Read against Pamuk's concerted effort to gain insight into the Islamists' psychology in *Snow*, the intensity of these words comes as a surprise. Although his narrator does not play the blame game and describes the bloody acts of both the Islamists and the secularists in an almost noncommittal tone and with a certain amount of levity, he does describe the acts in gory detail. In other words, he neither censures nor censors. In *Snow*, the real culprit that reveals itself in the undertone and the subtext is the state.

Ka accepts a temporary assignment from the secular and left-leaning Istanbul daily *Cumhuriyet* to report on the politically charged events in Kars. He also has a private agenda: to see İpek ("Silk"), his university classmate, for whom he still holds a torch. He has learned that İpek is separated from her husband, Muhtar, also a former acquaintance of his. Muhtar is running for mayor. This election is one of the many threads in the narrative that are part of the Islamist-secularist debate. Muhtar is a secularist turned Islamist (a born-again Muslim, if you will), whom İpek leaves because he has forced her to cover herself and become the dutiful Muslim wife.

As a journalist, Ka has the opportunity to listen to the divergent and contentious views of many citizens of this historical border town, a place desolate and broken, replete with memories of glory and atrocity, with remnants of Armenian and Russian occupation, and with the early laurels of the nation's Westernization efforts. By transposing the setting from the sunny and hot southern city of Batman, with its Arabic culture, to Kars, situated at the northeastern tip of the country, a city known for the snowstorms that blanket it for days at end, Pamuk infuses the story with an eerily muffled quality. The city's geography and landmarks reveal almost nothing of an Islamic Arabic climate or history; rather, they evoke memories of the culture Russians brought to Kars and that "fit perfectly with the Republic's west-ernizing project" (*Snow* 20). The secular ex-mayor Muzaffer Bey, a relic of the old Republican days, tells how the people of Kars once enjoyed sports, music, festivities, and theater performances, how young girls rode their bi-cycles to school in short-sleeved dresses without being bothered, and how lycée students came to school gliding on their ice skates. When in the late 1940s a theater group came to town to perform a revolutionary play, in which a young woman who has spent her life in a black scarf finally takes it off and burns it, not a single black scarf could be found in town, and the of-ficials had to order it from Erzurum by phone. Muzaffer Bey laments:

> Now the streets of Kars are filled with young women in head scarves of every kind. . . . Because they've been barred from classes for flaunting this symbol of political Islam, they've begun committing suicide.   (21)

The ironies of Kars history represent in microcosm those of Turkish history. The seemingly harmonious coexistence of multiple cultures, languages, religions, and ethnicities in the Ottoman state is now transformed, as Ka experiences first-hand, into irreducible differences whose terms are no longer negotiable, as the conflicting groups proliferate (secular Turks, Islamist Turks, Kurd nationalists, Marxist Kurds, Islamist Kurds) and move to even further poles.

  There is also no agreement about the reason for the wave of suicides: the Islamists claim pious girls kill themselves because they are forbidden to wear the head scarves in schools, whereas others maintain the girls commit suicide to escape patriarchal oppression sanctioned by Islam. As conflicts escalate, they take on a murderous aspect and lead to bloodshed. On his very first day in Kars, Ka witnesses the assassination of an old secularist educator, the director of the Institute of Pedagogy, by a young fanatic, who after a long debate with the director at a café shoots him in cold blood because the director would not let covered young women in the class. A whole chapter (chapter 5) is a taped account of the conversation between the director and the assassin. The old educator speaks in a tone that is patient, rational, tolerant, and respectful of

Muslim modesty, whereas the young man's argument and tone escalate to a level of irrational rage that precedes his killing of the school official. True to the structural premise of the book, which is predicated on a reconstruction of the past, the narrator tells us that his record of the conversation comes from the tape in a listening device that MİT (*Millî İstihbarat Teşkilâtı* ["National Investigation Agency"]) officials planted on the director, who had been getting death threats from the "turbanists." The assassin, who had a Muslim radio program in the town of Tokat and who had read about the school's ban on head scarves, traveled to Kars for the sole purpose of killing the director.

Ka tries to understand each viewpoint and the reasons that drive people to acts of self-destruction and violence. He visits an Islamic sheikh who holds a lot of young people in his power and is eerily reminiscent of the sheikhs in Karaosmanoğlu's *The Alien*. Ka allows Lâcivert ("Navy Blue"), a young and charismatic Islamic radical, to engage him in lengthy debates. Blue is worshipped by his many followers and is lover to both secular İpek and her born-again Muslim sister Kadife ("Velvet"), who is the poster child of covered young women. Blue and Kadife bear no resemblance to stereotypical images of fanatical Muslim youth. Blue's "eyes were deep blue—almost midnight blue—a color you never saw in a Turk. He was brown-haired and beard-less . . . he had an aquiline nose and breathtakingly pale skin. He was extraordinarily handsome, but his gracefulness was born of self-confidence" (72). Blue is a walking paradox or the allegory of paradox, in that he identifies with terrorist Islam, although he hasn't killed a soul. He shares some of Pamuk's publicly stated views but takes them to their extreme, where they buckle under the weight of their illogic. He becomes the very personification of the political contradictions that haunt Turkish modernity. He tells Ka that he did not come to Kars for political reasons but to try to stop the suicide epidemic. He is caught in a dilemma. Suicide is a sin in Islam. If the covered girls are killing themselves because the head scarf is banned, then they are committing a sin. Blue confesses that one girl killed herself over a love affair, but if this were known, the boys in the religious high school would be infuriated. He warns Ka about writing anything concerning the suicides either in the Turkish or in the European press.

Like many fanatics, Blue is adept at spinning conspiracy theories that justify acts of violence against the presumed perpetrator. Referring to the institute director's murder, he claims, "First they used this poor director to enforce their cruel measures, and then they incited some madman to kill him so as to pin the blame on the Muslims" (76). Serdar Bey, the editor of the *Border City Gazette*, who habitually prints news before it actually happens, has his counter-conspiracy theory, "This is the work of the international Islamist movement that wants to turn Turkey into another Iran" (27). On the other hand, Blue—an Islamist, a self-styled terrorist, and a womanizer—seems to share Pamuk's sorrow about the cultural amnesia modern Turks are suffering from. Out of the blue, Blue tells Ka the story of Rüstem and his son, Suhrab, from the poet Firdevsi's *Shehname*, not to show what it means to him

> but to point out that it's forgotten. . . . [B]ecause we've fallen under the spell of the West, we've forgotten our own stories. They've removed all the old stories from our children's textbooks. These days, you can't find a single bookseller who stocks the *Shehname* in all of Istanbul. How do you explain this?   (78)

As a reflective and poetic soul, Ka is confronted by more questions at every turn, and his tolerance and compassion paralyze him in his search for answers. He continues to pursue İpek, trying to convince her to marry him and go to Germany. His self-guilt as a middle-class citizen who saw in Islam the dope of the duped and missed his chance as a young man to understand his people leads him to the flitting image of Islam as the answer, a memory that must be captured and pressed into the service of a nation's salvation. For the first time after a long dry spell, he feels inspired to write poetry after a meeting with three Islamist young men who refuse to believe that Muslim girls would commit suicide. He hears "the call from inside him: the call he heard only at moments of inspiration . . . the sound of his muse" (86). Ironically, the muse appears after Ka, who admits to sometimes being an atheist, listens to Mesut's fanatical attacks on atheists, who should not be buried in the same cemeteries with Muslims. A character right out of Güntekin's *Green Night*, Mesut rages, "It's not just the torment of having to lie beside the godless till the Judgment Day; the worst horror would be to rise up on Judgment Day only to find oneself face-to-face with a luckless atheist" (85). But this same Mesut becomes totally disillusioned after joining a small activist Islamist group in Erzurum. After four years of activism, he quits the movement.

At a visually structural level, the narrative is held together by the three intersecting poles of the snowflake; at the points of each pole, opposing characters, ideologies, feelings, and styles are juxtaposed in a series of nineteen poems that Ka writes in Kars but never publishes. One of the thematic lines that parallels this structural movement is the narrator's (the third-person narrator, a close friend of Ka's, turns out to be Orhan, another Pamuk double or Pamuk himself) ongoing search for the lost poems. We assume that the narrator hopes to publish them posthumously. His detective work writes a text of reconstructed memory, since, in his search for the missing poems and Ka's unidentified assassin(s), he interprets the clues in the diagram of the snowflake he finds in one of Ka's notebooks in Frankfurt. Ka had registered moments of epiphany in everyday life in Kars through the poems he wrote in a green notebook. The reader wonders why none of these poems are in the novel. At the thematic level of the plot, this omission is probably warranted, since the narrator never finds the book of poems, just as Ka's search for selfhood, community, and love remains unfulfilled. With the elision of poetic solace from its pages, *Snow* becomes the epic story of a world abandoned by God. Early on in the book, İpek sums up the situation tersely for Ka; "the men give themselves to religion, and the women kill themselves" (35).

In mourning the loss of an idealized past of Islamic brotherhood, the Islamists defy the secular state that has deprived them of their mooring. İpek's ex-husband speaks for a lot of young men in search of a sense of belonging, who once looked for answers in leftist movements, when he declares to Ka that he has found a community among the Islamists, because they are "modest, gentle, understanding. Unlike westernized Turks, they don't instinctively despise the common people; they're compassionate and wounded themselves" (60). But unlike the Marxist activists of the 1960s, who believed that the historical dialectic would redeem the misery of the present, they do not want to comprehend their fate in order to transcend it and fight for a different future. Instead they regress into a state of nostalgia for a world ruled by fatwa. They reject the idea of freedom, because the only freedom for them is to be a Muslim, that is, to be part of a community of Muslims. The narrator comments:

> As Ka knew from the beginning, in this part of the world faith in God was not something achieved by thinking sublime thoughts and stretching one's creative powers to their outer limits; nor was it something one could do alone; above all it meant joining a mosque, becoming part of a community.   (60–61)

Nietzsche and Dostoevsky showed us that resistance to joining the tribe and transcending herd mentality exact an unbearable toll on frail souls. It is almost as if Dostoevsky's "The Grand Inquisitor" in *The Brothers Karama-zov* walked over the Russian border into Kars and after surveying the land-scape repeated the words he said to Christ: "Did you forget that peace and even death are dearer to man than free choice in the knowledge of good and evil? There is nothing more seductive for man than the freedom of his con-science but there is nothing more tormenting either" (254). The Grand In-quisitor blames Christ for thinking man is strong enough to decide for himself what is good and evil. There are "three powers, only three powers on earth, capable of conquering and holding forever the conscience of these feeble rebels, for their own happiness—these powers are miracle, mystery, and authority" (255).

These powers hold sway in Kars, as the residents, no matter where their affiliations lie—and these shift in the course of time, along with their identities—come under the regime of these forces. This becomes evident in the two climaxes of the story, which are staged as plays at the Kars National Theater, where illusion and reality tangle in a deathly dance. The first play is *Vatan Yahut Türban* ("My Fatherland or My Head Scarf"), a crude prop-aganda vehicle from the 1940s, which Sunay Zaim, the staunchly secular, Kemalist director of a touring theater company, chooses to stage, knowing it will provoke the students of the religious school to a riot. Its title is a clear reference to the patriotic poet Namık Kemal's famous theater piece *Vatan Yahut Silistre* ("Motherland or Silistre"). Namık Kemal's play related the story of a young woman who in 1853, at the time of the Crimean War, dressed up as a soldier and fought by her beloved's side. The play stirred up strong feelings of nationalism and liberty at the time and, despite the sim-plicity of its plot, attracted much attention at home and abroad. It was first translated into Russian and later into other languages. Kemal faced political censure and was exiled to Cyprus.

Pamuk's allusion clearly marks *My Fatherland or My Head Scarf* as a pa-thetic parody of Kemal's much-acclaimed, emotionally stirring piece. Taking advantage of the fact that Kars is snowed in and inaccessible to outside inter-vention, Sunay Zaim assumes the power of the state when he enlists the help of the military in staging a coup in the guise of a theatrical performance—in response to the shooting of the institute director. The simple plot is summa-rized in five episodes: a woman covered in black is walking on the street and appears troubled; she takes off her scarf and proclaims her independence; her family, fiancé, and several bearded Muslim men demand she cover herself, but she burns the scarf; the religious fanatics are outraged; just as they are

dragging the woman away to kill her, the soldiers of the Republic rush in
and save her (146–47). Although the play gives rise to loud shouts of
protest from the religious school students, as planned, and nobody can hear
the actors on stage because of the commotion, the spectators can follow the
action because of the simplicity of the story and the mimelike nature of the
performance. So when real soldiers come on the stage as actors, no one ex-
pects the carnage that follows.

The soldiers start shooting real bullets, which kill, among others,
Necip, a mild-mannered Muslim youth, whom Ka befriended and who aspired to write the first Islamist science fiction and publish it in one of the
major Istanbul newspapers and "not in a paper that sells seventy-five
copies" (103). Necip and his doppelgänger, Fazıl, who are both in love with
Kadife, are another set of the doubles of the story. Necip is the gentler and
more introspective of the two; he struggles with the possibility that the
atheists may be right, that the suffering endured in this world may be in
vain, if there is no God to redeem it in the afterworld. Like most names in
Pamuk's novels, Necip and Fazıl have a referential significance. Necip Fazıl
Kısakürek (1905–83) was a controversial poet often jailed for his openly Islamic voice and harsh attacks on secularist reforms. Like many characters in
Snow, Kısakürek was a person of contradictions. He completed his secondary education in British and French schools, studied philosophy at the Dar-
ül-fünûn and in France. He continued to live the bohemian lifestyle he
adopted in Paris in Istanbul, until he found Islamic mysticism. A gifted poet
and thinker, he became an outspoken proponent of a return to Islamic
statehood.

The second play performed by the touring theater is also inspired by
another, this time *The Spanish Tragedy*, by Thomas Kyd. The structure of
this play is much more complicated. It is the story of a senseless blood feud
in a backward and impoverished unnamed small town. It is constantly interrupted by plays within the play (reminiscent of Pamuk's own novelistic
ploys); soliloquies on the glory of the French Revolution, cooking, table
manners, city traffic, scenes from Shakespeare, Hugo, and Brecht; and anecdotes about Atatürk. None of these vignettes explain the bloody actions
that make up the plot of the play.

During his investigation into Ka's life, the narrator learns from Mesut,
one of the former students of the religious school (the one who would not
share cemetery space with the atheists), that Zaim cast a spell on the audience. As Mesut reveals to the narrator, the religious schoolboys, who were

forcefully transported to the theater in military vehicles, could not resist Zaim's star power or

> speak openly about their attraction to Sunay. Perhaps it had something to do with Sunay's absolute power, the thing to which they also aspired. It may be that they were relieved by the many restrictions he'd imposed on their movements, which made it impossible to take stupid risks like inciting a riot.   (393)

Mesut's confession about the Islamic youth's admiration of Sunay, their awe of his fearlessness in exposing himself to a hostile and potentially murderous audience after the bloody coup, points to the confusion of beliefs, ideals, and lack of agency in dark times. The "flock" can be easily swayed, as Dostoevsky's Grand Inquisitor tells Christ, "Tomorrow . . . you will see this obedient flock, which at my first gesture will rush to heap hot coals around your stake" (260). Sunay Zaim, secure in the power of his convictions, also stages his suicide, possibly as a gesture of claiming agency and control over his fate, knowing that with the return of state authority to the city after the snow melts, his short-lived dictatorship will come to an end and he'll face multiple murder charges. He persuades Kadife to act in the play in return for amnesty for Blue, who is sought in connection with the murder of the institute director. He also tricks her into shooting him to death with a pistol (as part of the plot), which he convinced her was not loaded. Zaim goes out literally with a bang after a spellbinding performance that turns him into a legendary and heroic figure, a role that had eluded him in real life.

In the denouement that follows the two climactic scenes, Blue and his mistress, Hande, are killed in a police operation, Kadife serves a short term for killing Zaim accidentally, Ka is "taken to safety" by the military and forcefully put on a train, İpek decides to stay behind to tend to her own and Kadife's wounds (caused much more by their loss of Blue than by the other tragedies that transpired in the two days in Kars), and Kadife ends up marrying Fazıl and gives birth to a son. İpek, unable to have children, devotes her life to her nephew. Ka returns to Frankfurt without İpek and, without the love and inspiration that buoyed him in Kars, leads four difficult and lonely years in Frankfurt. In the end, he is killed execution-style, presumably by a group of Islamists in exile who suspect him of having betrayed Blue. Into this allegorical morality play of murder, intrigue, betrayal, despair, love, and hope, enters Pamuk as Ka's double—it turns out that he was the narrator—and friend, looking to make sense of Ka's life and death. Did

Ka die because he tried so hard to understand? Despite all the evidence he gathers and the testimonies he listens to, a clear-cut answer eludes the narrator. The murder mystery itself is set against the larger implied narrative of Turkey's recent past, as it symbolically alludes to one of Pamuk's key concerns, the unsettled accounts of an abruptly shut-down history.

Unlike *The Black Book* and *My Name Is Red, Snow* cannot find solace in the reimagined cultural-aesthetic wealth of the past. In fact, art proves to have no corrective power here and now. The poet Ka fails to offer insight and advice to those he tries to understand and help. In the hands of the charismatic theater director Zaim, art becomes complicit in literally deadly ideology. Or is it that any form of discourse, whether aesthetic, metaphysical, political, poetic, or religious, turns deadly if ideologized? Ideology spells the demise of dialectical thinking, reflection, critique, and self-understanding as well as an understanding of the other. The author-narrator maintains a position of moral integrity that refuses to blame the opposing parties for their convictions. Some Western critics have wondered how Pamuk escaped the wrath of Islamists, given the explosive nature of the book. I doubt very much that they would have or could have read the book. Most people I know—colleagues, friends, avid readers—have a hard time finishing Pamuk's novels. Pamuk's writing is often extremely strained and heavy-handed and, conversely, loose and rambling. There is little occasion for dialogue, as monologues drag on forever after they've made their point. This unedited profuseness detracts from the literary value of Pamuk's novels. But *Snow*, a novel that could have been titled *Tragedy in Kars*, like the second play within the novel, is one of his most challenging books and also his most carefully crafted work along thematic and formal lines.

Maybe Pamuk felt sorry for the critics and readers who would be struggling with *Snow* or be snow-blinded by it, so he entered the story to console them by revealing its "heart":

> Here, perhaps we have arrived at the heart of our story. How much can we ever know about the love and pain of another's heart? How much can we hope to understand those who have suffered deeper anguish, greater deprivation, and more crushing disappointments than we ourselves have known? Even if the world's rich and powerful were to put themselves in the shoes of the rest, how much would they really understand the wretched millions suffering around them? So it is when Orhan the novelist peers into the dark corners of his poet friend's difficult and painful life: How much can he really see? (259)

So is there no way to inhabit the mind and the shell of sorrow of the other? Should we try to understand, even if that understanding will never be complete but is, nevertheless, the way toward dialogue? Is there no way of bridging what appear to be incommensurable plots of different lives or of fictional and actual lives? At any rate, there is no way of letting a novel like *Snow* rest within its covers. As Paul Ricoeur states in *Oneself as Another,* "in our experience the life history of each of us is caught up in the histories of others" (161). But is this entanglement of life stories "with one another hostile to the narrative understanding nourished by literature?" Ricoeur then asks, "Or does it not find in the framing of one narrative within another, examples of which abound in literature, a model of intelligibility?" One may or may not agree with Pamuk's sympathies in *Snow* and argue that whatever message he endeavors to convey merely circles in fictions within fictions in a game of metafictions. However, as Ricoeur argues, authors can only be the coauthors of a life they narrate, play a role in a play they have not written and thus step outside the role and let the reader assume "authorship" and agency (162). The reader owes the possibility of becoming an agent of story and history to "narratives that teach us how to articulate narratively retrospection and prospection" (163).

Lost in the Labyrinth: Adalet Ağaoğlu's *Curfew*

> There is a new language to describe our nights. Being caught.
> Being late. Not making it. Over-nighting. Missing the
> deadline. Begging for pardon. My clock stopped. The car broke
> down. The bus was late . . . A new language which oscillates
> between . . . staying put and dashing for it. A horror film.
> —Adalet Ağaoğlu, *Curfew*

> What are we, and how can we fulfill our obligations to ourselves
> as we are? The answers we give to those questions are often
> belied by history, perhaps because what is called "the genius
> of a people" is only a set of reactions to a given stimulus. The
> answers differ in different situations, and the national character,
> which was thought to be immutable, changes with them.
> —Octavio Paz, *The Labyrinth of Solitude*

Adalet Ağaoğlu's ambitious experimental novel *Curfew* interlinks the quest for identity in a specific history and geography with a narrative that shifts between temporal and experiential frames—past, present, future, dream, hallucination, waking life—to represent the fortunes of modern Turkish society, buffeted by the blows of three military interventions from 1960 to 1981 and rocked by right- and left-wing terrorism, police brutality, and assassinations of prominent intellectuals, journalists, and other public figures. The first military coup, which brought down the ruling Democrat Party on 27 May 1960, was on the whole welcomed by the intellectuals and citizens of major cities, as the corruption of party leaders, their espousal of political Islam, rigging of elections, and bloody suppression of student demonstrations had begun to seriously threaten the foundations of Turkey's young democracy. The military ultimatum of 12 March 1971 and the military takeover of 12 September 1980 were prompted by political violence and growing economic crises. The unstable coalition governments could not curb the tide of social unrest and financial calamity.

Although the 12 March coup was initially welcomed by the intellectuals, it soon turned out that the high command was mostly interested in combating the specter of communism. In the aftermath of this coup, leftist intellectuals, teachers, journalists, and students were systematically persecuted. Although political violence came mostly from right-wing extremists, it was those with leftist sympathies who were relentlessly harassed by the system and its police. The extreme right operated freely, as the authorities closed their eyes to its violent acts. The years following the 1971 coup marked the emergence of the *12 Mart Romanı* ("the 12 March novel") which chronicled the harrowing experiences of a persecuted generation of progressive thinkers, workers, and left-leaning intellectuals. Ağaoğlu's *Bir Düğün Gecesi* (1979; "A Wedding Night") is considered one of the most accomplished representatives of the 12 March novel. In both *The Wedding Night* and *Curfew*, she portrays periods of historical tribulation through the personal trials of individuals caught in the crossfire of events but moves away from realism by engaging in a modernist experimentation with form and language.

The 1980 military takeover was triggered by a multiplicity of problems, including a deadlocked political system and its inability to deal with political unrest and ethnic conflict—specifically, the Kurdish separatist movement; an economy in shambles; and last but not the least, the growing violence of Islamic extremists. The events of *Curfew* reflect the government's highly oppressive and equally ineffective ways of dealing with political violence by arresting party leaders, declaring martial law, and persecuting intellectuals.

Curfew is the story of four people at the crossroads in the oppressive atmosphere of the days shortly before the 1980 military coup. Although the original title of the book is *Üç Beş Kişi* ("A Handful of People") and not *Curfew*, curfew operates as the central metaphor of the story, for it evokes the fear of being late, missing the last boat, being caught, and not making it. This anxiety of belatedness, in turn, functions as an allegory of recent Turkish history marked by a vacillation and contestation between staying put and dashing for it. The anxiety was fueled by Turkey's hastened modernization efforts, which inevitably fractured social bonds and cultural heritages and lacked the resources to catch up with the advanced nations of the West. Furthermore, *Curfew*, both symbolically and thematically, represents through its seven main characters the people of a nation in different states of repose and movement on the path of history. Some are paralyzed, staying put; others are dashing for it; and still others are taking slower steps or hesitating at the crossroads. The thematic concerns of the novel are not only mirrored at the level of form, in the use of a multivoiced narrative; nonlinear sequences; and a fluid merger of dream, memory, and lived experience. They are also reflected in its intertextual frame, in the literary allusions to works that depict parallel situations. A conspicuous reference to *The Labyrinth of Solitude*, by the Mexican writer and Nobel laureate Octavio Paz, describes Mexicans as "[p]eople who have lost their identity in the depths of their history and are trying to find it again" (*Curfew* 74). The allusion underlines the contiguity of Turkey's struggle for national identity with that of many lands thrust into the seismic upheaval of modernization movements.

Adalet Ağaoğlu was born in 1929 in Nallıhan near Ankara and studied French literature at Ankara University. In the early stages of her writing career, she published several successful plays, which explains the rigor of dialogue in her novels. One of the most prolific, innovative, and philosophical figures of modern Turkish letters, she has received many awards and honors for her work, both in Turkey and abroad. She is celebrated for her trademark portrayals of individuals whose lives and fortunes are implicated in the web of historical destiny. Because of its philosophically reflective and stylistically appealing nature, her work bears the gift of translatability in more than a linguistic sense. Since Ağaoğlu works in different genres and is a critic and translator also, she has a nuanced as well as universal perception of the literary craft. Like Georg Lukács, who saw the novel as the modern epos that restores the shattered unity of the human being with the world—albeit only in memory and imagination—she maintains that the novel resists the threat to the integrity of human consciousness, dignity, and creativity. Thus, her works are woven with threads of sociohistorical evidence and poetic and dreamlike imagery. Her poetic strategy is never a mere exercise in style. It modulates the voices of the narrative, affirming, questioning, or debating these against a background of assumptions about culture, human freedom, agency, fate, and temporality.

In *Curfew*, the ordering and depiction of events and thoughts are not stylistically innocent moves; they define the literary and aesthetic investigation of critical social issues and enter a dialectical relation with them. In *The Political Unconscious: Narrative as a Socially Symbolic Act*, Fredric Jameson systematically illustrates how forms of human consciousness and psychological mechanisms are not manifestations that emerge outside time and space but are historically contingent (152). Ağaoğlu's depiction of the fateful moments of recent Turkish history through a narrative governed by stream of consciousness and poetic fragmentation points to the larger historical narrative of a society embroiled in the complications of socioeconomic challenges it can scarcely cope with. For Jameson,

> the experience of the subject in consumer or late monopoly capitalism [is] an experience which is evidently able to accommodate a far greater sense of psychic dispersal, fragmentation, drops in "niveau," fantasy and projective dimensions, hallucinogenic sensations, and temporal discontinuities than the Victorians, say, were willing to acknowledge.   (124–25)

His inquiry focuses on how a Marxist aesthetics can bridge historical perspective and narrative analysis to gain a critical sense of the characters' actions in the structure of the work. In *Curfew*, Ağaoğlu interweaves factual context with poetic imagery and dialogic (spoken and inner monologues and dialogues) reflections to underscore the historical determinants of human character and motivation. History alternately secures and unravels constructions of identity.

Jameson's *Political Unconscious* bears strong traces of Lukács's pre-Marxist historicization of aesthetic categories in *The Theory of the Novel* in a Hegelian vein. Although the spirit of Lukács's astute study is strongly informed by Hegel's ideal of the understanding of permanence in change and of change in the permanence of essence, by his own account, Lukács did not merely embrace an orthodox Hegelianism; he drew on the aesthetic theories of German classicism and Romanticism, especially the concept of Romantic irony "as a modern method of form giving" to offer a fuller intellectual grasp of the novelistic genre. Lukács contends that since the elements of the physical world defy any form of direct and sensuous (or material) representation, "they acquire life only when they can be related either to the life-experiencing interiority of the individual lost in their labyrinth, or to the observing and creative eye of the artist's subjectivity." This is the reason why Romantics demanded

> that the novel, combining all genres within itself, should include pure poetry and pure thought in its structure. The discrete nature of the outside world demands, for the sake of epic significance and sensuous valency, the inclusion of elements some of which are essentially alien to epic literature while others are alien to imaginative literature in general. (79)

The inclusion of the poetic and the philosophical situates otherwise seemingly isolated or ordinary events in a system of regulative ideas that allows for the fullness of their understanding. In *Curfew*, Ağaoğlu positions characters lost in the "labyrinth" of history in a framework that makes it necessary, in her own words, "to allow as much weight to the technical as to the artistic aspects of the novel" ("Author's Foreword" vii).

Curfew is the darkly prescient story of seven characters whose lives are entangled in bonds of family loyalty, heritage, desire, and despair. At the narrative level, their moods, vacillations, confusions, and actions are confined to a time frame of a few hours before the start of curfew at 2:00 a.m. The way these characters, in search of an exit out of the precarious darkness that has settled on individual and collective destiny in early June, experience the precurfew hours becomes a compressed meditation on times wedged between military coups. The oppressive mood, reiterated in refrains—in the screaming headlines that tally the numbers of those who died in clashes or in the elliptical phrase, "Night-time. June. But still some time to the longest day and the shortest night," repeated at the beginning of several chapters—foreshadows the September 1980 military takeover. The book consists of seven chapters, each portraying the fears, hopes, and memories of *Curfew*'s seven characters in flashbacks, actual and remembered dialogues, and premonitions, all juxtaposed in a stream-of-consciousness mode.

Murat and his older sister, Kısmet, are from a wealthy and politically well-connected family of Eskişehir, a provincial but up-and-coming Anatolian town near Ankara that symbolizes in the author's words, "yesterday, today, and tomorrow. Its population belongs to a time and context in which people have not yet been clearly defined" (viii). Having willingly or unwittingly strayed from their place in community and history, all the inhabitants of the novel's space are living testimonies to the extremities of stress that results from a failure to settle accounts with the past. Murat, an aspiring songwriter, has turned his back on family and fortune and left Eskişehir to pursue Selmin, a pop singer he is besotted with. Selmin has sung some of Murat's revolutionary songs onstage. Their ill-starred relationship comes to an end when Selmin has a brief affair with Murat's uncle, Ferit. Ferit is a one-time bohemian intellectual who has abandoned his unrealistic hopes of saving Turkey in word and turned into a man of action. Now a successful businessman, he is a believer in rapid planned industrialization. He is also concerned with the welfare of his niece, Kısmet, who is trying to get out of a loveless, arranged marriage and go to Istanbul to be with her brother, Murat. Kısmet's close friend Kardelen, a bright and optimistic young woman from the squatter settlement, is a worker in one of Ferit's factories. She is preparing for her upcoming wedding, while trying to put behind her the trauma of being raped while in police custody.

The two characters wedded to the past and hopelessly sunk in the mire of the present are Türkân and Neval, mothers of Murat and Kısmet and Selmin and her sister, Belgin, respectively. Neval had been married to an Ottoman aristocrat and rubbed shoulders with the most powerful political figures of the republic and their cohorts. Now impoverished, she cannot give up her phony aristocratic airs and totally alienates Türkân, when Türkân finally meets the family of her son's lover. She witnesses how Neval and her daughters treat her beloved Murat like a gofer, ordering him around, expecting him to cater to their every whim and pay for their lifestyle. Türkân, cast in the role of the traditional good daughter, wife, and mother, was widowed as a young woman and stoically carries on, taking care of her senile father and dealing with her son's abandonment and her daughter's suffering. Türkân's memory of her father's dislike of her husband, a conservative landowner with a pious mask, reveals the personal factor in religious and political persuasions. Her father, Emin Bey, a secular Republican, so hated what he considered his son-in-law's religious pretensions that he became a virtual atheist out of spite. Now, infirm, bedridden, and totally dependent on his daughter and hired help, he has turned to God with a vengeance that gets on Türkân's already shattered nerves.

Through the staging of this family drama and the medium of her characters' inner lives, Ağaoğlu endeavors, by her own account, to sketch a social map of Turkey in one of its most critical moments and to define the lines where collective and individual lives intersect. In the author's foreword to the English translation of her novel, she sums up the political aesthetic of *Curfew*:

> In the confusion of these hectic hours of martial law, we get to know the predicament of a group of aristocratic relics from the Ottoman period and how they respond to the "new values," the conflict between the old lifestyle and the new which is trying to lift itself out of the villages into the cities; the feudal elements that are struggling on the threshold of the "new values." (viii)

Ağaoğlu adds that for her the most exciting aspect of writing this novel was to see which of the characters from this cast, "struggling to 'save' or 'be saved' would actually escape beyond the impassable wall—the curfew" (ix).

It turns out that Kısmet, the artistic and sheltered daughter of the "rich semi-feudal family," summons the courage to leave her family and catches the last train before the curfew out of Eskişehir station to begin a new and as yet uncharted life. Unlike her mother, Türkân, who in her inability to break away from the paralyzing bonds of family and tradition attributes her numbness to the curfew in impotent anger ("If it wasn't for this curfew, I know exactly what I'd like to do!" [121]), Kısmet scales the wall of curfew to land on the other side. At the end of the book, Kısmet turns and looks back, in her mind's eye, "with an apologetic smile at the handful of people she's leaving behind, far behind her" (247).

Although the plot revolves around inner monologues, self-reflective moments, and conversations between characters rather than actions, the narrative succeeds in creating layers of tension and suspense and maintains reader interest by a judicious use of the curfew at both the literal and the symbolic level and through adept transitions between different registers of time in memory, lived presence, and anticipation. By envisioning alternative scenarios of the past and future through the eyes of the characters, the author also underlines the possibility of peoples and nations to imagine a liberating future by reinterpreting the potential of their history. Kardelen, Ferit, and Kısmet are poised to embrace the future in their differing but equally determined ways, whereas Neval and Türkân are smothered by the rubble of the past. Selmin, Selmin's sister, and Murat, having misspent their youth, are on a crash course destined for a place beyond redemption. Kardelen is the hardworking, optimistic proletarian who represents the potential of the working class and its aspiration to join the ranks of the bourgeoisie

(in an ironic reversal of Marx's vision). Ferit is a man of both action and reflection who never travels without the German poet Heinrich Heine's *Book
of Songs* (151). He sees salvation in unbounded industrialization, while rec-
ognizing the damage it inflicts on nature and humans. He says to his friend
Asaf, one of the ineffectual intellectuals in his old crowd:

> Try as we will, we can't reconcile civilization and development with a purely
> emotional attitude to nature. How can we interfere with nature without rap-
> ing it? How can we bring machinery and nature together without making
> them enemies? But you ought to come and see some of the factories we've put
> up outside the city. They all have lovely parks and flower beds. Despite the
> concrete and timber factories stretching down the valley to Bozüyük, I some-
> times feel as happy as if I was in an unspoilt snowy landscape. Is that enough?
> Of course not.   (152)

Here the narrator steps in to stress the necessity of a new ethos, which is
articulated in various symbolic registers of the novel. Ferit knew, of course,
that nature had its own history and that the idea of some original purity could
only be a dream. History would always assert itself, and "mankind's destiny
was to assert itself in turn against the forces of history. But this dialectic had to
be creative and constructive. And memory has to be sensitive and on the alert
against destructive tendencies" (152). Such moments in the novel both point
to the necessity of modernization in Turkey and warn of its inherent dangers
for a new nation that has not passed through the prerequisite historical, political, and economic stages that constitute the foundation of the Western modern. In a more general sense, this passage also implies a critique of modernity's
faith in progress, science, and industrialization, ideals that embody the legacy
of the Enlightenment. To prevent the Enlightenment ideals of universal humanism, freedom, and primacy of reason from turning into instruments of
dominion over nature and humankind, as Max Horkheimer and Theodor
Adorno argued, it is necessary to cultivate an awareness of their dialectic unfolding in history and the ability to constructively correct their misuse.

In the end, it is Kısmet who takes the most radical step, by breaking
out of her own overdetermined history to forge a new and free identity. In
one of the most telling passages of the novel, Ferit recalls his niece's telling
him of a nightmare she had. She is in shabby old clothes but has to dress up
to go to Murat's circumcision celebration. She feels paralyzed and simply
cannot get dressed. She is surrounded by doors and mirrors, keeps dressing

and undressing, and is in total panic, since her mother tells her that Murat could end up uncircumcised because of her. She begins crying and remembers finally saying, "Mother! There are so many mirrors here that I simply can't find my own body . . ." (180). In her quest for an emancipated identity, Kısmet was supported by her enduring love for Ufuk, the activist she could not marry. Ufuk, who had been in and out of jail, trained her for a more enlightened life by having her read his favorite books. He sent her a heavily marked copy of Paz's *Labyrinth of Solitude*. The reference to Paz's book in *Curfew* is revealing, since Paz himself quotes a metaphor, "páramo de espejos" ("a wilderness of mirrors"), by the Mexican poet José Gorostiza, to describe a state of disconnectedness that strongly echoes Kısmet's cry (*Labyrinth* 21). "To become aware of our history is to become aware of our singularity," writes Paz. "It is a moment of reflective repose before we devote ourselves to action again" (10).

Curfew awakens a profound awareness of Turkey's recent past, marked by authoritarian rule, uncertainty, and fear, through the experiences of people who make up history but whose stories history fails to record. Ağaoğlu writes:

> The novel depends not on ideology, but on excavating—above all through language—the depths of human spirit. To achieve this, both aspects—human and linguistic—need to be viewed through the optic of social and economic relations and their own historical and topographical context.
>
> ("Author's Foreword" viii)

Writing through Censor and Censorship: Bilge Karasu's *Night*

> Certainly, there is a divergence between subjective aim and objective achievement. But it is not something abrupt and irrational, a distinction between two metaphysical entities. Rather it is part of the dialectical process by which a creative subjectivity develops, and is expressive of that subjectivity's encounter with the world of its time (or, possibly, of its failure to come to terms with that world).
>
> —Georg Lukács, *Realism in Our Time*

The symbolism of political angst and sense of paralysis that permeates the air in *Curfew* reaches its extreme expression in language, mood, and shock effect in Bilge Karasu's haunting novel *Night*, recipient of the Pegasus Prize in Literature. One of the most innovative writers of contemporary Turkish literature, Karasu was born in Istanbul in 1930 and studied philosophy. In 1963, he went to the United States on a Rockefeller Fellowship, and after his return to Turkey he began publishing translations along with fiction. He has published highly acclaimed novels and short stories, where prose and philosophy, image and musical motif blend with ease and test the limits of narrative conventions. He was a research associate at Hacettepe University at the time of his death in 1995. Karasu is a writer with a strong philosophical bent and stylistic flare who takes the play with style, symbolism, and metaphor to its postmodern limits.

Karasu's talent for underwriting abstract concepts by allegory has led critics to compare his work with that of George Orwell, Milan Kundera, José Saramago, and most frequently with Franz Kafka's parables of a world of transcendent desolation. *Night* also reveals a strong Nietzschean presence and has unmistakable parallels to Italo Calvino's *On a Winter's Night a Traveler* and Dostoevsky's *Notes from the Underground*. Why does this novel, for all its seeming singularity, conjure up memories of other books and call for comparisons to them? Perhaps because it is so resistant to any coherent interpretation, self-consciously interrupts itself, and undermines or disclaims every point of reference it establishes, it compels the reader to seek a vantage point through other texts with similar narrative strategies. In terms of reader-response theories, *Night* subverts the reader's "horizon of expectations" (Jauss 44)[4] to raise an awareness of other dimensions of reality and experience—in this instance, a reality censored by the state and the subconscious.

Since *Night*'s plot, if one can talk of a plot here at all, is discontinuous and disorienting, the narrative moves through metanarrative—in this instance, an ongoing commentary on the narrative by a second narrator—metaphor, and mood shifts. The historical and biographical context of the novel would confirm that what appears to be a solipsistic narrative voice is in fact a clear echo of reality. In *Night*, as in Kafka, the unity of the world is irrevocably fractured. Lukács notes that in Kafka's work "an essentially subjective vision is identified with reality itself" (*Realism* 52). One of the epigrams at the beginning of *Night*—"The movement of self-building individuality is . . . the becoming of the real world," a quotation from Hegel's *The Phenomenology of the Spirit*—is a novelistic gesture of self-reference and bears out Lukács's concept of the dialectic unfolding of subjective experience as constitutive of reality. This quotation, as well as other, less transparent allusions to the work of modern philosophers in the text, directs the reader to the novel's self-consciously intertextual character. The complex relation between the idea and its representation of a world that resists any direct representation (especially a world caught in a web of trauma) can be mediated only through a form that reflects the fragmented consciousness of the subject. Such a form is characterized by ellipses, interrupted thoughts and visions, and seemingly nonlinear episodic units.

Night starts with what appears to be an entry in a writer's diary. The entry foreshadows the subjugation of the writer's world to darkness, where "no weight or reality" will remain and only the tongue will survive, since "[t]he one reality the darkness will seem to offer is in lending itself to being spoken" (3). At the very onset, we are confronted with the problem of representation. How can language represent the trauma that is about to unfold? It can do so only indirectly, in fragments of dreams and hallucinations, in the ellipses of the narrative, or in allegories that veil horror but suggest and intimate it in images. The writer-narrator (or one of the narrators), a man of liberal sensibility, lives in a land of terror, where night workers invade streets as darkness falls and systematically engage in acts of violence, killing arbitrarily selected victims and leaving announcements about the coming of an ominous big night. Into this world of fear, persecution, and murder enters the writer's nemesis, N, a former schoolmate who has suffered a major hearing loss as the result of a childhood illness. N is an administrator in both a sinister governmental agency and a subagency and supervises two agents, a man called Sevinç ("joy") and a woman called Sevim ("love"). Sevinç and the writer become lovers and are separated and reunited during the course of the story. The narrator is blackmailed into attending a foreign conference as a mouthpiece of the regime. Sevim, also a former schoolmate of the narrator, who was once married to the administrator, struggles between her conscience and the tasks she is assigned to carry out, and her dilemma leads to her murder. All these characters lend their voices to the composition of the novel, while a running commentary by the narrator, who is or may also be the author, corrector, and creator, accompanies the text.

The threadbare plot expands and unfolds in the alternating narratives and comments of the four characters; the original writer-narrator; the blond, hard-of-hearing N; Sevinç; and Sevim. Are there four narrators here or only one? Accompanying the first-order narrative are footnotes and commentaries that recount—as in Calvino's *On a Winter's Night a Traveler*, which tells of the elusive search for the real author and where meaning is contracted between writer and reader—the creation of the story itself. The footnotes written by one or more of the narrators converge with and diverge from the initial narrative, until all the narratives flow into one another in contiguous mirrors. "How far can this go?" the exasperated reader may ask. The initial narrator answers:

> Until you see only yourself in the mirror. Until other people's eyes become your mirrors. Or rather until all the mirrors reflect you, even though you are not standing in front of them. . . . Is not everything in this world ultimately what is seen, imagined, or thought by whoever tells of it?   (136)

These words are uttered after the presumably sole narrator discloses that he made up Sevinç and Sevim and possibly even the administrator of the agency (136). He is at the moment in a hospital, where he's been held for months, and the terror outside (inside?) continues unabated. But just as we think that this was all a nightmare the narrator in the hospital had, he is shoved into a pitch-black place by "He," who says, "Now you get what you want" (141). As the place is suddenly flooded by a powerful light, the narrator sees Sevinç, who for a moment appears to be Sevim. But it is, in fact, Sevinç, who seems to be mocking him. Irritated by Sevinç's attitude, the narrator lunges at him and hits the ground. Then he sees Sevinç, Sevim, "He," and the blond deaf kid (an image of N in his school days) all laughing at him, as if they were all one bloodied face, looking back at him, "perhaps in the mirrors" or in his mind. As the strong light slowly dims, the narrator at last becomes himself; "reflected in every fragment" is the self "he did not recognize in the mirror." "Thousands of fragments. Hundreds of thousands of fragments that are no longer me at all," are the last words before B**** K***** (the author, Bilge Karasu?) signs and inscribes the dates of the production of this novel (April 1975–September 1976) (141). But wait. This BK has one last burning question, which slips away from under the signature: "Can writing all this keep one from going mad?" (142).

If readers are not totally baffled by now, what are they to make of this novel that defies the possibility of any form of truth or reason and reveals all existence at worst as a world of unspeakable evil perpetrated by murderous agencies and at best as an aesthetic product of a grotesque vision? Wherein lies the redeeming value of this narrative? We might read the text through Lukács's eyes, which saw in Kafka's evocation of the nightmarish existence of humanity "an allegory of transcendent Nothingness" (*Realism* 53). That allegory can be seen in Karasu's novel as the dark menace of fascism cloaked in a night whose limits are invisible and intangible. Or we can read *Night* with Walter Benjamin's "Theses on the Philosophy of History," which urges its historical reader, caught in the nightmare of the Nazi era, to blast the idea of the ruling powers' version of a history of progress. Benjamin writes in thesis 8:

> The tradition of the oppressed teaches us that the "state of emergency" in which we live is not the exception but the rule. We must attain to a conception of history that is in keeping with this insight. Then we shall clearly realize that it is our task to bring about a real state of emergency, and this will improve our position in the struggle against fascism.   (257)

Benjamin sees the ammunition against the rulers' conception of history in the fragmented instances of an oppressed people's memory that can evoke the emancipatory power of the past. "For every image of the past that is not recognized by the present as one of its concerns threatens to disappear irretrievably" (255). In a similarly symbolic vein, Karasu interrupts and dislodges the narrative of the present history and evokes the memory of the fighting spirit and liberatory potential of past struggles. "Here is the point, and the only point, where our thoughts are superior to theirs—and it is a clear superiority," comments the original narrator, referring to the "oppressors," "we can prove that each element of what we assert, even if it is a construct, has been realized in the past by taking the appropriate steps" (45).

Thus Karasu dismantles discourses of the rulers, of the scribes of official history and of propaganda, by the time-honored technique of making them strange and grotesque in the figures of the night workers prowling the streets; in their threats of the coming big night; in their conversion of city streets into dead-end alleys, where they would trap their unsuspecting victims. *Night*'s initial narrator combats the murdering agents of the system by exposing their truths as metaphors and opposing these with his own.

In "Über Wahrheit und Lüge im außermoralischen Sinn" ("Truth and Lie in an Extramoral Sense"), Friedrich Nietzsche reminds us that so-called truths are metaphors (coined by the powerful) that we have forgotten are metaphors. He asks:

> What is truth? A mobile army of metaphors, metonyms, anthropomorphisms—in short, a sum of human relations that were poetically and rhetorically heightened, transposed, and embellished, and after extended use appear solid, canonical, and binding to a nation.   (5: 314)

Nietzsche blurs the distinction between fact and fiction, as he argues that what is in language, in the subjective voice, is translated through repetition or habitual usage into accepted fact.

Karasu goes even further, to claim that a mental or corporeal representation may be a mere image of the world, but it can bend reality to its will:

> Lately, workers don't seem to spread out into the streets only as darkness grows and night begins to fall. On the contrary, it seems that squads of them are coming out while it is still light . . . and darkness is then falling before it should. We say that it must be a sensory aberration; wishing to believe what we say: the days must be getting shorter. . . . Are we to think that the sun is adjusting itself to them? Absurd. (33)

Not as absurd as it seems, since the reality of Karasu's world adjusts itself to the subjective vision—that is, to the articulation in language of the subject's perception. At the same time, language remains the only means to overcome the terror of the night and its own subjectivity: "For the moment the only entity that appears to have been able to survive in the dark, as we have said, is language" (6). But at the end of the first section (the end of the first notebook), a footnote claims, "This notebook is done. What is it that I hold in my hands? At most one view of the world. So?" (40). The interaction of these asserting and negating terms—reality as fully structured by language and, conversely, language as only one limited view of reality—is the area of irony, which is "the normative mentality of the novel," in Lukács's words (*Theory* 84).

Philosophical, lyrical, and eerily grotesque by turns, this profound metafictional work both refers to a national political reality and allegorizes the terrors of fascistic regimes in universal terms. In the process, Karasu incorporates and pays homage to the work and ideas of many major thinkers of modernity, while forging and preserving a writerly voice and identity distinctly his own. In the introduction to the original Turkish edition of the novel, the philosopher-critic Akşit Göktürk maintains that *Night* wreaks havoc with our need for a straightforward story line and our set expectations of narrative coherence at the risk of being rejected by the reader. "Perhaps *Night* will be called a tough text," he concludes. "Why shouldn't it be?" (8). The book is certainly not recommended reading for the faint of heart. Although the challenge of reading *Night* arises to a great extent from its philosophical and structural complexity, this complexity is at the same time the source of the novel's timeless draw. Despite its strong political undercurrent, *Night* is not burdened by tendentious and tedious rhetoric. Its affinity with allegory averts condemnation of any individual or group by name, and its tendency to irony precludes final judgments. Thus, the form of the novel that challenges the understanding of the reader also constitutes its ethical force.

Aziz Nesin's *Surnâmé*: Humor Springs Eternal

Whereas the philosophical builds opacity, humor brings clarity to complexity by exposing the structures of fallacy that imperil our understanding of the world. The prize for most effectively raising awareness of social injustice through satire, irony, political allegory, and other literary subversions goes to Aziz Nesin, arguably Turkey's best political and philosophical satirist. One of his most acclaimed novels, *Hayri the Barber Surnâmé*, focuses on problems of law and lawlessness, crime and punishment, and the simultaneous fear and awe of hardened criminals. Even though humor is often the most difficult genre to translate, his prose has lent itself to translation almost ideally and earned him an international reputation. His works have been translated into more than thirty languages, and he has won numerous awards in Turkey, Italy, Bulgaria, and the former Soviet Union. In 1956, Nesin won first place in the International Humor Writers competition in Italy and took home the Golden Palm award. The translatability of Nesin's work resides in the reflexivity of his idiom, his political savvy, and his command of irony and parody.

Furthermore, Nesin is both a practitioner and theorist of political humor. In *Cumhuriyet Döneminde Türk Mizahı* ("Turkish Humor in the Republican Era"), an anthology he published in 1973, Nesin offers an account of his career in the development of humor writing in modern Turkish literature. He sketches with considerable theoretical acumen the sociopolitical factors that have engendered the growth of political humor at different times and in different places. He observes that Turkish society lived through a period of hope, idealism, and productivity with the founding of the republic, followed by an era of decline and depression. During times of decline, people were deceived and exploited by the ruling classes. Intellectuals and dissenters were so relentlessly persecuted that they were unable to fight back. Since resistance to repression was impossible under the conditions of the day, humor became a weapon to combat the grip of tyranny. An exciting and important brand of modern Turkish humor was actually born from the inability to fight against oppression in a physical way (45). In Nesin's view, times of distress and oppression have historically generated the conditions for the growth of humor.

Aziz Nesin was born Mehmet Nusret on 20 December 1915 in Istanbul. After serving as a career officer for a few years, he became a full-time journalist and editor. He began his first job in 1944 as a humor writer for the newspaper *Karagöz*. Later he began writing anecdotes for another newspaper, *Tan*. By his own account, these anecdotes had a strong humorist slant. In 1944, after the publication of his political satire *Azizname*, a warrant was issued for his arrest. Since he had two young children at the time, he decided to hide in order to find some means for their support before turning himself in. He could hide successfully for six months in public libraries, as he continued to write, since it never occurred to the police to look for him in a library. He was subsequently jailed for four months. During his long career, Nesin assumed the editorship of many satirical periodicals and wrote numerous short-story collections, essays, a memoir, and novels. He was a political activist who dedicated himself to fighting ignorance, political oppression, and religious fundamentalism. In 1972, he set up the Nesin Foundation, for the education of children from destitute families. The foundation provides free room and board and takes on the cost of each admitted child's education until graduation from secondary or trade school.

Although Nesin was arrested many times for his political views, the attempt on his life came from religious fundamentalists, who set fire to the hotel he was staying in during a culture festival in the city of Sinop. On 2 July 1993, the mob surrounded the hotel, shouting, "Death to infidels," and started a fire that burned the lower floors of the building. Firefighters managed to control the fire, and Nesin and some guests were able to escape, but others were not so lucky. Thirty-seven people staying in the hotel were killed in the fire, and Nesin never recovered from the tragedy. The incident that made him the target of the assassination attempt was the forthcoming translation of Salman Rushdie's *Satanic Verses*, which Nesin's publishing house had bought the rights for. During the last years of his career, he believed that radical Islam posed the greatest danger to democracy and free speech in Turkey.

His troubles, however, began with the one-party Republican regime's distaste for and fear of political satire. In *Turkish Humor in the Republican Era*, Nesin tells how Cemil Sait Barlas, a representative of the National Assembly who later became minister, attempted to extend martial law after the end of the Second World War, citing the danger posed by *Markopaşa*, a humor magazine edited by Nesin and Sabahattin Ali, one of Turkey's most renowned writers. Nesin relates how Barlas claimed that the evil perpetuated by *Markopaşa* had its "roots outside" and notes that this term first entered Turkish political vocabulary with the attack on a humor magazine (58–59).

Afterward, when the Democrat Party came to power with the promise of delivering a true democracy, the first thing Prime Minister Adnan Menderes did, in his inaugural speech in the National Assembly, was attack humor magazines. Nesin writes:

> Imagine: For the first time another political party comes to power after a twenty-seven-year one-party rule. The assembly is in session. The representatives take the oath. And the prime minister of the newly formed government pounces on humor magazines in his inaugural speech, as if the country had no other worry, as if all the problems had been solved, and if they were not, the solution would depend on the silencing of humor magazines. (13)

From his personal experience as a humor writer and his study of the history of satire, Nesin theorizes that humor in general and modern Turkish humor in particular have enjoyed their highest achievement during times of political oppression. He is known to have said that being a humorist in Turkey did not require much talent, since the material for the comic was available in high doses on a daily basis. Nesin himself never missed an opportunity to capture the humor in a society where everyday life was an ongoing comedy of errors. *Hayri the Barber Surnâmé* is a matchless presentation of (gallows) humor as national pastime.

Surnâmé is the story of Hayri, a young barber sentenced to death for the rape and murder of a six-year-old boy. By his own account he is neither a pederast nor a murderer but was driven out of desperation to a desperate act that went very wrong. From the very onset, the author highlights the paradoxes that characterize both the social system, with its penal code imported from Mussolini's Fascist Italy, and the behavior of hardened incarcerated criminals. Hayri is put in the barracks of the worst sex offenders, including a necrophile and a youth who strangled his mother, with whom he was having an incestuous relationship and who was carrying his child. The heinous crimes of these sex offenders are told in a droll tone and shadowed by a parallel subtext, provided by the ironic narrator, that reflects on the social and psychological determinants of unspeakable depravity. The worst sex offenders were men who were themselves brutally and repeatedly raped before and after coming to prison. In some cases, the offender was socially and economically driven out of society and graduated from outcast to outlaw. A loyal son, Hayri worked hard to support himself and his old mother on a meager income. He was befriended by a petty criminal who first acted like a big brother to gain Hayri's trust but then one day drugged and raped him. The rapist continued the abuse and terrorized Hayri, who could not escape the clutches of this thug without leaving his mother. To get back at the monster, Hayri tried to molest his son, but when the boy started screaming, Hayri panicked and strangled the child.

In prison, Hayri appears resigned to his fate but worries about his mother, who is left all alone and with no means of support. The old woman dies on hearing the news of her son's impending hanging. Hayri undergoes a profound transformation during his four years on death row. His loss of innocence as he is abused by another ruthless thug in prison turns him paradoxically into a murderous fighter and a poet. He befriends three men in the political barracks, and for the first time in his life he feels in the company of kindred souls. The prison guards are at first reluctant to let him call on these subversives but then decide to let him visit them freely. Hayri listens to their talk with endless fascination, trying to understand and process what he hears. Gradually he gains a poignant understanding of the social determinants of crime, the prison system, and the redemptive power of knowledge. When the time comes for his execution and the imam asks him for his last words, Hayri sums up with unexpected eloquence what is fundamentally wrong with the justice system, which is supposed to reform the criminals and return them to society but does nothing of the sort:

> I believe in endless change; everything, but everything, changes continually. . . . Four years ago I committed a very grievous crime; I was guilty. But in four years, I have changed to such a degree that I am another Hayri. . . . [Y]ou are hanging an entirely different person. (193)

On these words, the hanging committee members fall silent. The narrator immediately breaks the silence and the brief solemnity of the moment by revealing the thoughts of the prosecuting attorney, who has encountered so many difficulties in organizing the details of this "carnival" that he decided to write a book, *Problems Faced in the Execution of Capital Punishment from the Angle of Our Regulations* (151):

The Prosecuting Attorney made a mental note to add this point of view to the book he planned to write. Yes, even though he believed in the necessity of the death penalty for individual peace of mind and tranquility of society, he was on the side of freedom of debate about every type of ideal; this too was an ideal, it could be debated. (193)

In the last chapters of the book, the preparations for the public hanging of Barber Hayri are portrayed in all their grotesqueness and reveal the realities of a system of justice that defies any sense of justice. Nesin's novella of black humor "could easily have turned into a lugubrious melodrama," notes Talat Halman in the foreword to the English edition, but Nesin, "a wizard of humor, a magician with words and scenes . . . can transform even the most lurid episodes into smiles of recognition, of self-discovery, of stoic acceptance of man's universal defects" (2).

More than that, I think that Nesin effortlessly incorporates into this grim tale enlightening moments of philosophical, historical, and cultural insight. His choice of genre, style, and idiom flexes the critical muscle of political satire. This work is a testament to satire as critique with political intent. At the level of content and transparent allegory, the prison functions as a microcosm of the larger society. Death by hanging is supposed to be carried out in such a way that it causes minimal suffering to the condemned man. To that end, a skilled executioner must be hired and the right type of rope must be secured and soaked in high-quality olive oil to alleviate the pressure on the neck. None of these conditions can be met in Hayri's case. The only executioner in town is a drug addict who has not had a job for a long time; a rope of required length and thickness cannot be found; and the olive oil procured with great difficulty, since it was very expensive and hard to find even on the black market, is stolen. Thus Hayri ends up being hanged in a most inhumane fashion, with a heavy clothesline soaked in water.

Hayri's story is also a debate on the use and abuse of the death penalty. However, in typical Nesin fashion, the debate is informed by laughter. The Bespectacled Gentleman, the most learned inmate among the sex offenders, who commands their respect by his vast knowledge of homosexuality and famous homosexuals of history, also proves to be an expert on the subject of executions. After giving his enraptured listeners a short history of the subject, he informs them that in most states of the United States, the condemned man dies "in a flash," in the electric chair. "That method wouldn't work with us," his listeners respond, "Could you kill a man in a flash with the current that wouldn't even light a fifty-candle-power globe?" (82)

In *Discipline and Punish*, the French philosopher Michel Foucault relates the story of a man who was executed on 2 March 1757 for attempting to assassinate the king of France. The man was drawn and quartered by six horses, his flesh torn from his bones with red-hot pincers, and his body burned to ashes in a gruesome spectacle. The horror of the execution revealed a contest between the violence of the criminal and the violence of the state. The growing public sentiment that the horror of the punishment exceeded that of the crime, incidences where civil disorder ensued when the anger of the onlookers turned from the criminal to the executioner, and the shame that attached to those charged with carrying out justice—all called for reform in the penal system. Public executions were eventually abolished, and attention shifted from execution to trial and sentencing. The courts became more concerned with correction and cure. The sector that carried out the punishment became an invisible entity working in secret.

In Foucault's terms, when the correctional focus moved from the body to the soul, the punishment that was once performed on the body was replaced by a punishment that would penetrate the heart and the soul. This change signified not so much a desire for a kinder cut but a change of objective. The judgment of crimes in the penal reforms became more and more based on the knowledge of the offender, allowing psychiatrists, sociologists, psychologists, criminologists, and armies of social scientists not only to determine the degree of the criminal's culpability but also to participate in the implementation of the sentence. Foucault offers a cultural history of punishment to show that the new power to punish derives its rules and justifications from the human sciences that analyze the criminal mind. Thus, Foucault sees punishment not only as a part of the legal system but also as a political tool for the acquisition and exercise of power. Like the madman, the criminal is the other, who can be studied, objectified, and controlled. Ultimately, the moral of Foucault's history is that knowledge can be used to define the other as incorrigible, mad, or even evil and to consolidate and exercise power against the already judged. Furthermore, the effort invested in rehabilitation cultivates and encourages criminality.

In Foucault's history, the power of institutions such as the prison and the asylum is not controlled by a dominating class but inheres in a complex configuration of micropowers or power relationships that mark all aspects of social life. Therefore power cannot be overthrown by abolishing state authority or a particular institution. It is not a centralized or totalized target. The struggle against power thus has to be localized. In Nesin, political satire becomes a form of political struggle, as its barbs leave holes in the mask of state authority and expose its hopelessly antiquated practices. Although the narrator makes clear that Hayri's hanging is the last public execution in Turkey, the decision to ban the gruesome spectacle comes almost two centuries after its abolition in Europe. In Nesin's account, the punishment, instead of providing a moral lesson for the public, totally blinds them to their own hypocrisy and exonerates them by setting up a scapegoat. Hayri is rehabilitated not by the system but by the political prisoners whose crime was to speak out against the system, a system that in turn has judged them on the same scale as the most violent rapists and murderers. Nesin's dark allegory suggests that the only hope to short-circuit systems of domination lies with activist teachers, writers, and workers.

Despite the transparency of the narrator's political stance, neither the characters nor the action assume the form of a sermon or morality play. Rather, the corrective thrust of the story unfolds in laughter and humor. When effectively used, humor can be both subversive and redemptive, as it reveals the contingency and arbitrariness of social rites. Like other tropes, such as allegory and irony, humor explains the world through both indirect and inverse forms of reference. By strategies of defamiliarization, it urges reflection on things, acts, and concepts that have gone unquestioned for too long. Because humor is "a universal human activity that invites us to become philosophical spectators," writes the British philosopher Simon Critchley, "[i]t is practically enacted theory" (18).

In *Surnâmé*, Nesin enacts philosophy, not through theory but through parody. In Nesin's use of parody, style, form, and content are interactive components that deliver a critical punch in each punch line. In literary terms, parody is usually an imitation of or an ironic commentary on another text. Linda Hutcheon defines parody more specifically as "imitation with a critical difference, not always at the expense of the parodied text" (6). Nesin writes *Surnâmé* ("festival book") as a parody of the genre by that name and frames the narrative with a satirical prologue in verse about a Sultan Palamute ("Sultan Bonito," slang for an incompetent and dictatorial head of state) who signs all kinds of human rights treaties but makes a joke of them. In his tongue-in-cheek introduction, Nesin explains:

[In the] Ottoman Era, books which described all the gaiety, extraordinary spectacles, great entertainments, colorful ceremonies, rich feasts which lasted for many days and in which the public participated . . . were called sûrnamé, which means "festival book." It's easily understood these were not festivals for people thrown in jail . . . they were festivals in honor of sultans and princes.   (8)

He then declares:

> While taking up the pen for this sûrnamé, a valuable document for our cultural history, I haven't varied a hair from the truth, so that future generations may take admonition from us. . . . One of the aims of legal punishment is that, through seeing the guilty punished, the public's conscience can be eased with a happy, "Mercy, I've been saved!"   (9)

Thousands of eager spectators spend the night before the morning of Hayri's execution in the public square to get the best viewing spots. In the morning, all kinds of hawkers, pickpockets, Koran sellers, black marketers, Gypsies with dancing bears, peddlers with atomizers spraying people with oily perfumes one can never get out, lotto and dice players, boy punks, food vendors with trays on their heads fill the square. The rich and the poor, the sacred and the profane, the high and low culture rub shoulders, united in the spirit of the carnival:

> People, rich and poor, finding themselves together among the spectators, abolished class differences and made social justice a reality. . . . The people of Istanbul, especially in recent years, due to increasing complexities of life, rising prices, growing expenses, shortage of transportation . . . lack of harmony at home, and all kinds of other troubles, not being able to go to the movie theaters, casinos, picnics, on trips and to other places of entertainment, didn't want to miss the opportunity to be entertained at this hanging festival in the heart of the city.   (179–80)

The "carnival" goers revel in the errors of the system instead of seeing the whole spectacle for what it is—scapegoating, a distraction from very real socioeconomic ills, a disregard of human rights conventions. The narrative voice does not condemn the crowd but distracts from the spectacle to reveal, by paradox, the melan-cholia (black bile) symbolically oozing from the gallows to the society at large, gathered in the square.

In a short essay titled "Der Humor" (1927; "Humor"), Freud relates the story of a condemned man who is being escorted to the gallows one Monday morning. Looking up at the sky, he quips, "Well, the week's beginning nicely" ("Humour" 161; "Na, die Woche fängt gut an" [383]). For Freud, this kind of humor, which affords the criminal a certain pleasure and sense of satisfaction, "has something liberating (*befreiend*) about it" (162). Nesin gives Hayri's last words the same liberating ring: "The Imam Efendi said to Hayri, 'May God forgive your sins!' Barber Hayri with the meaning of thank you, said 'Yours too'" (193). What makes this funny is that the imam does not get the intended meaning, and the reader has a good laugh at his expense. Freud argues that this type of humor "also has something of grandeur and elevation" (162), because it is generated by the superego observing the ego and lending it a sense of dignity and superiority that seems to say, "Look! here is the world, which seems so dangerous! It is nothing but a game for children—just worth making a jest about" (166). The grandeur of humor lies in the superego's refusal to let the ego be "distressed by the provocations of reality" and "affected by the traumas of the external world"; it enables "the victorious assertion of the ego's invulnerability" (162).

"Humour is not resigned; it is rebellious" Freud contends (163). Indeed, Nesin's pen wields the humor of the rebel. His humor shares in a sense of emancipation, even as he continues to show that—unlike in Foucault's history, where the powerful contain the otherness of the others by confining them—in our system, the prison or what it represents imprisons both us and them, everyone on both sides of the divide. Ultimately, however, in Nesin's world, humor springs eternal, poised to confront injustice and oppression and to drown in laughter the distress they provoke.

Notes

1. "[T]he Village Institutes, as originally conceived, had a very short life. After the war, they came under attack on the ground that the kind of education the institute teachers were providing to the peasants made them an easy target for 'undesirable ideologies' (codewords for socialism and communism) and incited class conflict" (Ahmad 83). In 1954, the institutes were closed and merged with existing institutes of pedagogy. In the novel *Bozkırdaki Çekirdek* ("The Seed in the Steppe," first serialized in the daily *Cumhuriyet* in 1962 and published in 1967), Kemal Tahir offers a bleak account of the failure of village institutes. He furthers the thesis that the institutes trained the students to be unquestioning followers of the regime and points to the discrepancy between the idealistic efforts of the village teachers and the questionable objectives of the ruling Republican Party.

2. Currently, the idea of reinstituting the village institutes is receiving much press. *Vatan Dersleri* (2006; "National Lessons"), the first novel of the projected trilogy *Hal ve*

Zaman Mektupları ("Letters on Situation and Time"), by İbrahim Yıldırım, a poetically gifted and politically savvy author, offers a fictionalized and insightful story of the village institutes experiment, in which he highlights the extraordinary role the institutes performed in their mission to bring education to the rural masses.

3. Since the English version is a compilation of two books by Makal, I cite page numbers in both *Bizim Köy* and *A Village in Anatolia*. The book discussed here is *Bizim Köy*. All quotations are from the original Turkish version.

4. "[A] literary work with an unfamiliar aesthetic form can break through the expectations of its readers and at the same time confront them with a question, the solution to which remains lacking for them in the religiously or officially sanctioned morals" (Jauss 44).

CHAPTER 5

Istanbul: City as Trope and Topos of Crossed Destinies

There are places where history is inescapable, like a highway accident—places whose geography provokes history. Such is Istanbul, alias Constantinople, alias Byzantium.
> —Joseph Brodsky, "Flight from Byzantium"

Die Literaturgeschichte ist eine große Morgue wo jeder seine Toten aufsucht, die er liebt oder womit er verwandt ist.
("Literary history is the grand morgue where everyone looks for his favorite dead, one whom he loves or is related to.")
> —Heinrich Heine,
> *Die romantische Schule* ("The Romantic School")

stanbul, Constantinople, Byzantium—this enduring object of poetic desire and curiosity is a sprawling memory archive of myriad civilizations, whose traces linger in the multiple idioms of the city. For its modern scribes, Istanbul has become the definitive trope of loss and melancholy, a monument of time that survives only in the faded splendor of its seraglios, in archives and libraries, and in the ruins of fortresses and walls that once protected the city. Pierre Loti, the nineteenth-century French writer of exotic fictions and travelogues, experienced the sorrow of a vanishing civilization even in an Istanbul relatively unmarred by the relentless march of the modern. During a visit to Istanbul in May 1890, he dares to express to the sultan, who invited him to see the illuminations for the Kadir Gecesi,[1] all his "melancholy regret in seeing the old things disappear, in seeing great Stamboul opening up and being transformed" (41). Nevertheless, Loti still concedes that this city, the only one astride two continents, not only embraces two divergent geographies but also guards diverse histories in its "imposing silhouette," which gives "one the thrill of old memories, the great mystical world of Islam" (6).

Istanbul's intriguing geography and history, which span divergent, interrupted, occulted, and emergent cultures, have captivated the imagination of countless writers, be they its citizens, visitors, or dreamers. In his collection of essays on Istanbul titled *Estambul otomano*, Juan Goytisolo describes Ottoman Istanbul as a riddle for Western writers. Although these writers have written extensively on Istanbul,

> the facts, anecdotes, hypothetical observations, descriptions of the interior of Topkapı Palace are transmitted from text to text without much variation, as if its [Istanbul's] authors, confronted with the enigma of the great city and unable to overcome the pull of its exoticism, gave up the uncertainty of their personal impressions to take refuge in the certainty of print that books provide.   (9)

Among modern Turkish writers, the poet Yahya Kemal (Beyatlı), his protégé Ahmet Hamdi Tanpınar, and Tanpınar's literary heir Orhan Pamuk are considered the most prominent readers of Istanbul's enigmatic character. Currently, Pamuk holds the unofficial title of Istanbul's most acclaimed literary son. Nevertheless, Pamuk would agree that Tanpınar, whose work has strongly influenced his, is the most commanding modern figure in the pantheon of Istanbul poets. Tanpınar's vast knowledge of Istanbul's cultural history informs all his writing and is integral to the solid foundation of his social and aesthetic criticism. In his poetic and critical work, Istanbul embodies both the trauma of separation from a long-standing heritage and the recuperative potential of the residue of that heritage.

Ahmet Hamdi Tanpınar: The Dialects of Art's Memory

In "Istanbul," a poetic essay in his *Beş Şehir* ("Five Cities"), Tanpınar offers a comprehensive analysis of historical transition, cultural loss, and crisis of value through an in-depth portrayal of Istanbul. However, in no way does the essay lay claim to academic exactness or historical certitude. It is neither an apology for nostalgic sentiment nor a desire to reclaim what is lost to time. Rather it reflects on the fragility of memory and how memory is shaped by the desire and the needs of the present:

> For our generation, Istanbul is something very different from what it was for our grandfathers or even our fathers. It does not enter our imagination in the

gold-embroidered caftans of the sultan, nor do we see it in a religious frame-work. The light that bursts out from this word [Istanbul] is for us the light of memories and yearnings shaped by our state of mind.

This longing for the past is not a feeling that necessarily conflicts with the present, but "we can say that the image of Istanbul that lives in us today is projected by this nostalgia" (15).

Istanbul offers Tanpınar a vast archive of cultural memory and artifacts in disarray. From the material and metaphysical inheritance left to the city by its diverse populations, Tanpınar seeks to forge a new aesthetic pedagogy for an age of change, disorientation, and confusion, a pedagogy akin in spirit to that of Friedrich Schiller's famous essay "Über die ästhetische Erziehung des Menschen" ("On the Aesthetic Education of Humanity"). While Schiller saw the modern age riven by the conflicting drives of reason and sensibility (or theory contra history, spirit contra matter), Tanpınar sees modern Turkish culture suffering from a clash of two civilizations, where an Ottoman Islamic past ended up being banned from a narrowly conceived project of moder-nity. Schiller believed that philosophy had identified the malaise of an age— modernity—at the threshold of tumultuous change, but it could not restore the breach that the opposing intellectual and cultural drives had brought about in the unity of human knowledge. He proposed to reconcile reason with sensibility through aesthetic education, which would render moral and social recuperation possible. The advent of civilization had fueled the com-peting conflicts between reason and nature and self and state. Schiller's pre-scription was play—specifically, the play drive as arbiter between the form drive (reason) and the material drive (sensibility). Schiller identifies the play drive with art and the experience of the beautiful, which can transcend the culturally overdetermined claims of rationality and materiality and reconcile the fullness of existence with the highest autonomy (5: 583–615).

In the introduction to her conceptually judicious study of Tanpınar's short stories, Sarah Moment Atiş emphasizes Tanpınar's place in modern Turkish literature as an analyst of the cultural malaise caused by "a forced leap from one civilization, theocratic and medieval, to another, modern and secu-lar" (17). By his own account, the civilization crisis was the overarching theme of Tanpınar's work. It was also the formative force behind his social and aes-thetic philosophy, which in turn shaped his poetics. Quoting Alfred North Whitehead's definition of nineteenth-century literature as "a witness to the discord between the aesthetic intuitions of mankind" and the "materialistic concepts of orthodox scientific theory," Atiş suggests that Tanpınar's enduring interest in nineteenth-century world literature, Romanticism, and symbolism corresponded to his preoccupation with the crisis of cultural conversion (185). Although Atiş states that a discussion of Tanpınar's ties to the literary and critical legacy of the nineteenth century remains outside the scope of her book, she does mention that Tanpınar acknowledged the significance of Nietzsche and Nerval in his literary development. In some ways the "characteristically Romantic strategy in dealing with the dilemma of selfhood," which transformed an essentially metaphysical problem into one of cultural division and associated "the non-rational faculties of mind—Imagination, Emotion, Spirituality, Dream, Eros—with an 'Orient,' " reflected Tanpınar's view of Turkish self-identity as a space of cultural confrontation. "Tanpınar clearly was one of those who did not take offense at the Romantic attribution of the positive aspects of non-rationality to the realm of his own cultural heritage," Atiş maintains. In fact, "Tanpınar's use of precisely this Romantic world view" points to his turn to aesthetics in search of an answer "to his own metaphysical dilemma of selfhood" (185–86).

Tanpınar's search in the archives of Ottoman Turkish cultural memory was not undertaken with the hope of restoring a morally superior or utopian past; it was an attempt to reclaim an aesthetic unity that would lend a sense of renewed selfhood and autonomy to Turkish culture. In the last section of "Istanbul," after remembering, seeing, smelling, hearing, and singing Istanbul's enchanting faces and facets, Tanpınar breaks his contemplation to refute any sense of nostalgia we may have read into the text:

> So many memories and so many people. . . . Why have I talked of things impossible to resurrect . . . ? Why does the past draw us like a well? I believe that what I am looking for are not these people, nor do I long for the age they lived in. . . . I don't think I can survive more than ten minutes even in the Istanbul of Kanunî [Suleiman the Magnificent] and Sokollu [grand vizier under Suleiman and his son Selim II]. For that I would have to give up so much that was gained and discard so many important parts of my identity. To see Süleymaniye as it was first built would be to deprive ourselves of the full splendor of our [present] familiar and beloved Süleymaniye, a splendor that turns the play of light in the waters of Bosporus to images of golden palaces and that has come down to us in the eternity of time. We taste [Süleymaniye's] beauty differently in its enriched sense because of the experience of four centuries and of our identity, whose contours are sharpened each day by its position between two different worlds of value. (101–02)

He adds that all the monuments and great figures of Istanbul's past would appear "much more naked than we can imagine," if they had not been magnified by history and memorialized by Ottoman Turkish and French artists—Proust, Debussy, Mallarmé" (102).

"Istanbul" not only articulates Tanpınar's major questions of cultural legacy and identity and civilizational conflict; it also presents a poetic concept of the city as a locus of memory, desire, signs, visions, concealment, decay, and death, reminiscent of Italo Calvino's *Invisible Cities*, which similarly writes a theory of the city not as an abstraction but as poetry. In Calvino's *Cities*, Kublai Khan, the Mogul emperor (1215–94), who senses that the demise of his empire is not far off, and Marco Polo, the famed Venetian traveler (1254–1324), sit in a garden, where Polo entertains the aging monarch with tales of cities he has seen. "Kublai Khan does not necessarily believe everything Marco Polo says when he describes the cities visited on his expeditions," are the first lines in Calvino's novel (5). From that moment on, the authority of the leading narrator of the story is undermined in terms of veracity, and the novel abstracts from the metaphysical attributes of the imaginary personified cities—with mythical names like Chloe, Despina, and Anastasia—a conceptual metaphor of the city. As the Khan and Polo discuss, between Polo's accounts of his travels, the mysteries of existence and questions of life, death, remembrance, and forgetting, the cities illuminate the inscrutability of the invisible links that bind us to the past and to the future, to nature and to others. Memory for the *Invisible Cities*, as for "Istanbul," is a concept explored through various symbolic denominators. Marco Polo says of the city of Zaira that it

> consists of relationships between the measurements of its space and the events of its past: the height of the lamppost and the distance from the ground of a hanged usurper's swaying feet; the line sprung from the lamppost to the railing opposite and the festoons that decorate the course of the queen's nuptial procession. . . . As this wave from memories flows in, the city soaks it up like a sponge and expands. (10)

The city does not speak of its memories but contains them; the memories are inscribed in every step, pole, and window and at every corner, where the signs are re-marked by scratches, lines, or nicks.

Tanpınar's Istanbul also carries its past in the intricate details of its old houses, the lyrics of its composers, the verses of its poets, and the recipes of its delicacies. Polo's account of Maurilia is a fabulated version of Tanpınar's

observation that Istanbul's face has been touched up by history and therefore appears more romantic and poetic to us now than it would have been
in the past. In Calvino's Maurilia, the traveler is invited to visit the city and at
the same time look at some old postcards that showed it as it used to be. If the
traveler did not wish to disappoint the inhabitants, he would praise the
postcard city but take care to register his regret within certain limits:

> [A]dmitting that the magnificence and prosperity of the metropolis Maurilia,
> when compared to the old, provincial Maurilia, cannot compensate for a cer-
> tain lost grace, which, however, can be appreciated only now in the old post
> cards, whereas before, when that provincial Maurilia was before one's eyes,
> one saw absolutely nothing graceful and would see it even less today, if Mau-
> rilia had remained unchanged.   (30)

Of course, Tanpınar's subject is a real city, whereas Calvino refers to several
fabulated cities. However, we find out that each of Polo's fantastic, exoti-
cally named places are in essence the same place, the city of Venice. Polo's
myriad allegories of the city—as desire, design, sign, death, dissimulation—
unite at home in Venice. Tanpınar's search for a meeting ground with the
past begins and ends in Istanbul, a city overwritten with the same allegorical
attributes.

At the end of the Istanbul essay, Tanpınar poses the question that
drives his art: "This is our greatest problem: where and how are we to connect with the past? We are all children of a crisis of consciousness and identity, we are all caught in a more intense version of Hamlet's 'to be or not to
be' question." Crises create the need for self-reflection, and "[a]s we own up
to this question, we can also claim a more solid ownership of our lives and
works of art" (103). His celebrated novel *Huzur* (*A Mind at Peace*) hands
out this question to four characters, İhsan, Nuran, Suat, and Mümtaz, who
take turns, in the four chapters named after them, debating their author's
assignment. *A Mind at Peace* is a novel of ideas, wrapped in a love story
that runs its tragic course against the background of a time of acute anxiety, as Turkey stands on the brink of the Second World War, which it desperately tries to stay out of. While the story is told in a straightforward
manner, without the intrusion of postmodern riddles, its questions only
raise more questions, and the polyphonic structure of the novel creates a
complex web that suspends issues and postpones answers. The dialectic of

ideas and ideals that move the narrative resists closure and signals that the search will go on.

What makes this novel so compelling despite the long debates carried out by its characters is its *terkip* ("composition"), a term Tanpınar often uses to describe Istanbul. For him, Istanbul's uniqueness resides not only in its history, art, architecture, and stunning natural beauty but also in the masterful blend of all these elements, which also comprises its sounds, smells, southerly (*lodos*) and northerly (*poyraz*) winds, Ramadan nights, tombstones, poor neighborhoods, colors at sunset, broken marble fountains, and much more. *A Mind at Peace* presents Istanbul as a "composition" of these myriad elements and mimics this characteristic of the city in the novel's own symphony of themes, forms, and moods. It reveals a political and social conscience, yet it is neither a political novel nor a work of realism. It is engaged in ideas but not a thesis novel. It is about Istanbul, using the city not merely as a setting or a character but also as a compact encyclopedia of cultural references. It is a seemingly realistic account of a time, place, and people, but its realism is compromised by unmistakably Romantic literary conventions: a ghost who enters the world of the living in a seamless flow of narrative, as in magic realism; dreamlike reveries; the doppelgänger motif; and a prose narrative interrupted by poetry, song, and flashback (the two middle chapters represent the protagonist's memory of the past year's events).

It is widely known that *A Mind at Peace* is an autobiographical novel (Moran 1: 270); its romantic-idealist protagonist, Mümtaz, is the author's double, and his older cousin İhsan, who became a surrogate father to the orphaned Mümtaz, is modeled after the poet Yahya Kemal. The weltanschauung that informs the narrative coincides with Tanpınar's essayistic expressions of his cultural theory and is embodied in Mümtaz, İhsan, and Mümtaz's lover, Nuran. These three characters speak their ideas and convictions in one voice. The protagonist's intense love affair with Nuran is portrayed as a union of minds and glosses over the physical aspect of the attraction. Mümtaz appears to be in love with his double, the mirror image of his soul. The antagonist in the story, if we can call him that, is Suat, a fascinating but seemingly callous and morally bankrupt character who poses the antithesis to the thesis shared by Mümtaz and his two doubles. Suat is in competition with Mümtaz for Nuran's love. In a way, he is also Mümtaz's double (they are relatives), the evil twin, or, in Freud's definition, the uncanny.

The uncanny figure appears in the Romantic novella in the form of a ghost or stranger who is both strangely familiar and threatening. On the basis of E. T. A. Hoffmann's novella *Der Sandmann* (*The Sandman*), Freud developed a theory of *das Unheimliche* ("the uncanny"). In a nutshell, the experience of the uncanny arises from the repression of any aspect of the individual's affective life and in time takes the form of anxiety and fear. But this fear (which is personified in fiction) is nothing new or strange, because it was once part of the individual's psychic life that became alienated through the mechanism of repression (Freud, "Uncanny").[2] In *A Mind at Peace*, Suat consistently destroys Mümtaz's peace of mind and arouses his anxiety. Yet Mümtaz can never quite grasp the reason for his fear of Suat, since at some level he feels strangely drawn to him—possibly because he shares some of Suat's ideas but cannot admit that to himself.

My reading of Tanpınar through the lenses of other major thinkers should not imply that he was directly or unquestioningly influenced by them or that his work is philosophy light in fictional garb. Cultural theory is a vast field of cross-disciplinary and intertextual subfields and connections. As a scholar and artist of immense learning and many talents, Tanpınar was a cultural theorist *avant la lettre*. His synthesis of the Western humanistic tradition with a refined sense of the Ottoman Islamic aesthetic avoids both imitative gesture and false nostalgia. His subjects are poeticized and theorized, understood in the symbolism of their own times as well as in the context of our modern allegories. Like the Romantics, whose critical legacy continues to influence modernist and postmodernist sensibilities and who were keen on recovering past cultural traditions in the mold of the modern, Tanpınar does not shy away from looking back. That he maintained his aesthetic and moral convictions in the 1950s, when his mode of Romanticism was shunned and some version of social realism was all the rage, secured his work an enduring status far from the madding trends. If originality lies in a synthesis (his notion of *terkip*) that offers alternative and imaginative ways of looking at life's big questions—the meaning of existence, identity, memory, death; the role of faith, art, science in human life—then his work is unpretentiously original. Such a synthesis, however, calls for a corresponding configuration of literary forms and narrative conventions. *A Mind at Peace* offers a carefully wrought (and at times slightly overwrought) texture that negotiates form and content.

The novel begins one August morning almost twenty-four hours before the declaration of the Second World War and ends twenty-four hours later, as the war is declared. İhsan, Mümtaz's cousin, is gravely ill with pneumonia, and the household is infused with sorrow and anxiety. A third-person narrator gives a background sketch of Mümtaz's life: the death of his parents at an early age and his bringing up and education by the much older İhsan, a historian who was a prisoner of war in Egypt during the First World War and worked in an underground organization during the War of Independence. There is little action and much reflection in this first chapter, but the narrator offers detailed sketches of Istanbul's old neighborhoods, whose destitution and distress reflect the mood of the city and its inhabitants. Mümtaz, who is running errands for the family and looking for a nurse, witnesses signs of impending war in the city—troops that stop traffic; people rushing to banks to withdraw their money; a businessman who rents a store owned by İhsan's family, planning to stockpile tin and leather for the black market. İhsan's physical illness and Mümtaz's spiritual illness (we find out that his great love, Nuran, has left him to go back to her ex-husband) allegorize the ailments of a nation suffering from the economic cost of two recent wars and the melancholy state of Istanbul's denizens. Disease is everywhere; even the streets are ill; one street looks "as if afflicted by leprosy" (64). However, during his long day's journey through the city, Mümtaz not only is busy taking in the sights and wallowing in his melancholy but also gets lost in thoughts of books, music, and poetry (of the Occident and the Orient), reciting verses, remembering passionate intellectual and emotional moments with Nuran. The foray into thoughts of books and art tempers the sorrow and anxiety caused by İhsan's illness, the impending war, and the loss of Nuran:

> The truth was Mümtaz led a double life like the cobbler in *The Thousand and One Nights*. On the one hand, the memory of his happy days did not leave him; but as soon as the sun rose, the night of separation took hold of him with all its pain. (62)

Characteristically, Tanpınar here introduces the idea of a double life, a leitmotif in his work and philosophy, through another story. *A Mind at Peace* unfolds as a web of intertexts. At the level of form, the steady flow of ideas and citations that course through Mümtaz's mind are told in an almost stream-of-consciousness mode that is usually reserved for a first-person narrator. However, here we have a third-person narrator who appropriates, so to speak, what belongs to a first-person narrator. As Berna

Moran observes in his fine analysis of the novel, an obvious identification of the author-narrator with Mümtaz becomes an integral part of the narrative technique. What is narrated in the novel by the third-person narrator, who keeps a certain distance from the story sometimes turns out to be identical with Mümtaz's stream of thought. Moran cites a passage from the book, where the author-narrator talks about the beauty of the night, which can be matched only by the sublimity of music, and describes the night as "the *peşrev* of the moon."[3] When the narrator pauses, Mümtaz echoes him: "this is the Ferahfeza Peşrev of the moon" (1: 271), a poetic way of saying that "the beauty of the night foretells the appearance of the moon or is an overture to the moon." Moran speculates that since the novel was known to be autobiographical, Tanpınar wanted to distance himself from it by using a third-person narrator; however, because such narration took away from the immediacy of Mümtaz's ideas, Tanpınar opted at places for an internal monologue and the narrator-author-protagonist identification (270–71).

The second chapter is an ode to love, nature, and art, all harmonized against the breathtaking vistas and dreamlike settings of Istanbul. In contrast to the sorry sights of the city portrayed in the first chapter, the second chapter is bathed in golden light. Mümtaz and Nuran, whose husband left her and their daughter for another woman, meet and fall in love. The two lovers are thoroughly schooled in classical Turkish literature, music, and the arts, and Istanbul becomes the witness to their *grande amour* as well as the common object of their affections (and obsessions). The city is almost like the child they never had a chance to have (Nuran's daughter never accepts Mümtaz). In this chapter, narrated as memory, poetry and song as well as reflections on art predominate and define Tanpınar's characteristic stylistic gestures. The narrator inscribes Istanbul's sites with poems, citations, songs, and memories in such a way that the cityscape and each text cited continuously refer to, reflect on, and explain one another.

The dominant reference is to music. The analysis of Tanpınar's references to classical Turkish music, his constant evocation of a multitude of *makam*s to describe both natural sights and metaphysical states, would be the topic of another reading. Tanpınar is an equal-opportunity employer of aesthetic forms and references, so his fascination is not limited to classical Turkish music. In a letter to a fellow writer, he acknowledges, "My real working life began when I started getting a taste of Western music" (qtd. in Moran 1: 275). The narrative composition of his novel resembles the movements of a symphony, where the combination of themes in one chapter is repeated on modified scales in other chapters.

Another formal device Tanpınar is fond of employing is synesthesia, which was a common poetic play of Romantic literature. It serves him particularly well in his evocations of Istanbul's sights. The lights that Bosporus's waters reflect, offer "eyes a great taste" (111); the shores of Bosporus remind the narrator of the girls of yore "swimming in the mother-of-pearl dreams of mirrors." In fact, in Bosporus each sensation reflects another; everything is a reflection; even people could be "from time to time reflections of many things they did not know" (115). The intriguing sounds of this chapter, however, can overwhelm. With each outpouring of Mümtaz's emotions, the romance gets more over-the-top, the "mixtures" (*terkips*) more complicated. The passionate blood Nuran inherited from her forebears was "a strange mixture. It was prepared by pounding it with the strange hammer called Turkish music" (137). The balance that effective poetic expression requires wanes, and the prose yields to cadences of high melodrama. Moran argues that it is possible to divorce the melodramatic excess of the story in this chapter from the person of the author-narrator and attribute it instead to Mümtaz's character, who experiences the beauties of nature, woman, city, and art simultaneously and thus with aching intensity. Nevertheless, Moran also admits that Tanpınar uncharacteristically oversteps the limits of poetic moderation and "falls victim to his emotions" (1: 283). However, as in tragedy, the heights of happiness are harbingers of sorrows to come. At the end of the second chapter, clouds descend on the dreamlike world of the lovers, as Nuran's ex-husband wants Nuran back and her child wants her father back. Then Suat, a cheating husband and Nuran's longtime admirer, whom for some mysterious reason everyone around Mümtaz is eager to welcome back, appears on the scene to strike the deadly blow to Mümtaz's short-lived bliss.

The third chapter—also a flashback, to the last act of Mümtaz's drama—switches from the emotionally overwrought atmosphere of the second chapter to a scene of philosophical and aesthetic debate, where Suat is the antithetical voice whose apparent nihilism flies in the face of the optimism İhsan and Mümtaz try to maintain in a difficult time. Here İhsan, the historian, is given long and barely interrupted monologues on the overwhelming challenges facing the nation. The scene is a dinner party that turns into a seminar, as the friends gathered at İhsan's place begin responding to his comments, raising questions, and suggesting complementary arguments or counterarguments.

Even though the lecture-like monologues get repetitive and cramp the flow and flair of the story, this section, which reads like an essay, provides a mini-cultural history of Turkish fortunes. It is impossible to do justice to the fullness of the reflections articulated here, but they contribute richly to contemporary debates on the legacies and burdens of the past, memory and forgetfulness, memory and identity, and tradition and modernity.

In the second chapter, Mümtaz and Nuran had debated similar questions. In Mümtaz's words, the Orient may have been a world frozen in mummifying tradition, but it was in possession of a great secret, its oneness with the universe. "Perhaps it found this antidote, because it felt the agonies to come," Mümtaz muses. "But let us not forget that the world can only be saved from this point" (170). Later he mentions the need for an identity each nation finds in its past (171). İhsan believes in the compatibility of tradition with modernity, in their codependence, and in equal support for both, for

> they are the two sides of the same coin. On the one hand, we are in a cultural and civilizational crisis, on the other hand we need economic reforms. . . . We were born of the liquidation of an empire. This was an old agricultural empire. We are still struggling within its economic conditions.   (246–47)

He contends that the Westernization movement, seen as a measure to stop the decline of the Ottoman Empire during the Tanzimat period, ended in a crisis of civilization due to lack of planning, inadequate knowledge, and economic deterioration. The Republican era reforms were not grassroots movements, and the people, instead of leading the revolution, trailed behind it and had to catch up with the state instead of the other way around. The dinner company experiences temporary relief from the pain of "cultural split," when the *ney* virtuoso Emin Bey performs for the guests. The music of the mystical ritual leads the narrator into a metaphysical reverie:

> Why does longing constitute the major part of our spiritual life? Are we seeking the eternity we were created of? . . . Or are we, as children of time that molded us but has no pity for us, crying for our transient and lost selves? Are we striving for perfection or complaining about the ruthless order of time?   (267)

The spirit of the gathering is disrupted by Suat's arrival. Armed with cynicism and emboldened by alcohol, Suat has come to deconstruct everything İhsan defends or Mümtaz holds sacred. "The Orient has never been free," he declares. "We give up our freedoms so easily, on every occasion" (283). He is a strangely Nietzschean figure, quotes Nietzsche (without mentioning him) almost verbatim when he responds to İhsan's statement, "You cannot transcend morality," with "Why not? For a person who lives beyond good and evil? You talk about authority [*velilik*]; my hero does not want authority but freedom. Only when he is free, does he become a god" (288). İhsan sees the divine internalized in us as conscience and dismisses Suat's arguments—Suat "carries within him the god he killed" and practices "a negative theology" (295)—as irrelevant. İhsan points out that Suat's torments have already been lived a hundred years ago, since Hegel, Marx, Nietzsche, and Dostoevsky, who have been there, done that (300). Mümtaz tries to defend Suat on the grounds that the man is tormented, but İhsan has no patience with one individual's "belated" problems (301). After Nuran ignores the love letter Suat sends her, and when Suat realizes that Nuran and Mümtaz are planning to tie the knot, he commits suicide in the couple's apartment. That night, when Mümtaz and Nuran come home and find his body hanging from the ceiling, their already strained relationship snaps. Nuran, totally unnerved by the incident and possibly holding Mümtaz and herself responsible for the tragedy, leaves for good.

The fourth chapter takes us back to the present, and "like a symphony, picks up the form and themes of the first chapter" (Moran 1: 291). Mümtaz's subjective trials now take on a larger social significance. The real and present danger precludes a resolution in art and ideas. The manuscript on Sheikh Galip, which Mümtaz has been unable to finish, no longer concerns him. He is oppressed by the gloom of the day, smarting from the news of Nuran's impending marriage to her ex-husband, and exhausted in his efforts to find a doctor for İhsan. The oppression of the first chapter is intensified, and Mümtaz's questions and fears take on renewed urgency, causing him to doubt his convictions. He feels he is seen as an "aesthete of decadence" (172) and wants to distance himself from that perception. He joins a group of friends at a café who are discussing the fate of the country in the wake of the war. His imagination dwells no longer on personal trials but on the faces of the small people—the porter, the vendor, the waiter—who will all be drafted and die for something they know nothing about. In the portentous atmosphere of the day, the war is announced, and Mümtaz and his author-narrator engage in a self-reflection so intense and deep that there is almost no way out of it. The questions of conscience, responsibility, and courage, expressed in an inner monologue, are echoed first by the doctor whom Mümtaz is taking to İhsan and later by Suat's ghost, who taunts and tortures Mümtaz. The doctor, a man of science, contemptuous of superstition, an aficionado of Western classical music—we are told that he was listening to a violin concerto when Mümtaz called on him, the same concerto that Suat repeatedly played all day long before killing himself—finds Mümtaz's idea of hybrid cultural identity naive: "The East and the West do not meet. We tried to unite them. We even thought we found an original idea here. But the experiment has always been attempted and only yielded Janus-faced people" (368).

The final encounter with Suat's ghost further problematizes the author-narrator-protagonist's position on the possibility of reconcilable duality. When Mümtaz tells Suat that he does not remember his ever looking so beautiful, "like Botticelli's angels," Suat interrupts him: "Drop these meaningless analogies! Can't you ever speak without likening something to something else? Haven't you all understood how you have complicated things because of this bad habit?" When Mümtaz insists on knowing why Suat appears so beautiful, Suat's response is, "Those of one mind are always beautiful" (388). If we take the ghost to be Mümtaz's double (he tells Mümtaz, "I never left you, I was always with you" [387]) or his experience of the uncanny, which comes from a repressed fear, as Freud would have it, we cannot look for a logic of finality in the novel. All the theses have met their antitheses. But maybe there is a synthesis in sight. Suat offers to take Mümtaz to Hades, telling him that he does not have it in him to "bear these burdens." As despondent as he is, Mümtaz, refuses: "No, I can rise to the challenge of my burdens, and if I can't, I am prepared to be crushed under them, but I won't come with you" (390). In the final analysis, Mümtaz does not give up the challenge, and Tanpınar does not give in to the solace of unequivocal answers to the questions the novel poses: Can tradition be reconciled with the imperatives of modernization? Can there be accord, where history is not shared? Should we persist on maintaining "an anarchistic individualism" (283) or relinquish the dreams of the Orient and get on the Occident Express?

Orhan Pamuk picks up these questions and stakes out a field of cognition for them in a bildungsroman that begins and ends in Istanbul.

Istanbul as Borgesian Encyclopedia: *The Black Book*

> I would say that what I did in *The Black Book* was to find a narrative texture to match the force, colors, and chaos of life in Istanbul. The winding sentences of the book, those vertiginous baroque sentences that spin on their axes, appear

to me as arising from the history and chaos of the city and its present riches, irresolution, and energy. *The Black Book* was written with the motivation to say everything about Istanbul at once, and the book tries to say a lot of things at once. The book also aspires to make *The Thousand and One Nights* come alive in Istanbul.

—Orhan Pamuk, *Öteki Renkler* ("Other Colors")

Writers, both Turkish and Western, who have referenced Istanbul as an archive of poetic memory are legion. Among them, Orhan Pamuk is arguably the one whose life is most intensely and inextricably bound to the historical text and texture of the city. His international fame rests to a great extent on his untiring and ongoing examination of Istanbul's fabulous stories and histories, on his ability to write and rewrite Istanbul, to map its psychic geography, to decode its complex signifying systems, and to restore its histories of the curious and the marvelous. The announcement of the Swedish Academy that awarded the 2006 Nobel Prize in Literature to Pamuk cited him as a writer who in the quest for the melancholic soul of his native city has found symbols for the clash and interweaving of cultures.

Pamuk sees himself as the Istanbul novelist par excellence. He maintains that his city has always been successfully represented in short tales, in snapshots, and in symbolic detail, but never panoramically. He claims to be the first novelist who has seen the city in its full depth, through its history and geography, seen it panoptically through its soul, its materiality, and its illimitability (*Öteki Renkler* ["Other Colors"] 294–95). He represents the city simultaneously and alternately in episodic, epic, and encyclopedic form and as part biography and part autobiography. He views *The Black Book* as "a personal encyclopedia of Istanbul" and as a "history of many personal memories" of the city:

> In *The Black Book*, I finally did something I've been wanting to do for years, a sort of collage, bits of history, bits of future, the present, stories that seem unrelated . . . To juxtapose [all these] is a good technique for signifying a meaning that should [only] be intimated, indirectly alluded to. (*Öteki Renkler* 139)

Pamuk's Istanbul, then, is not a text of a verifiable past. Rather, it is a stage of lived history, where the past comes into being as a vision of the present projected backward. This is one definition of memory, as memory is rarely about the past but instead about how the past is remembered or reconstructed in and for the present. And the reconstruction always entails a measure of lack or loss.

Metaphors of loss—the loss of people, things, landscapes, languages, identities—and of mourning fill Pamuk's multiform accounts of Istanbul. In *The Black Book*, Pamuk tropes the trials of Turkish modernity as an allegory of loss and disappearance at the level of both individual life and collective culture. The novel demonstrates how a specific city, Istanbul, evokes its past and how the confluence of historical memory and current crisis can forge new identities to break the deadlock of destiny. The specificities of Istanbul's history, its place as cradle as well as cemetery of major civilizations, and the strategic importance of its unique geography—in short, the vast horizon of its texts and contexts can be grasped only through multiple disciplinary and aesthetic approaches, through a Herculean—or, rather, Hegelian—encyclopedic effort.

In *The Black Book*, possibly his intellectually most ambitious novelistic undertaking, Pamuk defies limitations of genre, discipline, and discourse to fashion an encyclopedic and panoptic representation of Istanbul in the guise of a murder mystery. This not-so-little black book of numerous Istanbul addresses has, in turn, generated volumes of critical essays, which see it as a theory of the postmodern novel itself, a cultural history of Istanbul, a picaresque novel, a detective novel, an encyclopedic novel, a quest in the tradition of mystical Islam, and an extended meditation on identity. With a nod to all the fine critics who have interpreted the book from every angle, I read it as a quest, as a bildungsroman about rebuilding or a new *Bildung* ("education or formation"). The quest unfolds in the form of a detective story in which writer, reader, and protagonist are all *Bildungsreisende* ("travelers on the road to *Bildung*"). This is *Bildung* with a twist; it is a second *Bildung*, a re-formation. Reading the novel as an expression of the desire for a new *Bildung* suggests that the cultural pedagogy of modernity requires correction. The path to reform goes through a reeducation, designed to recall memories where erased or forgotten knowledges are restored. The path winds through various sites of Istanbul, through apartments, offices, stores, underground storehouses, which are all compact memory archives. The city turns into a miniencyclopedia of cultural history.

A Hegelian spirit haunts this attempt at *Bildung* through memory. In Hegel's *Phänomenologie des Geistes* ("Phenomenology of Spirit") the subject acquires *Bildung* by studying a blueprint of remembered forms. Phenomenological recollection culminates in absolute knowledge. In *The Black Book*, remembering an occluded history leads to a corrected knowledge of that history. Since Pamuk has stated that meaning is only implicated in this book in bits and pieces of past, present, and future, the reader-critic can work only with fragments—like the miniaturists in his *My Name Is Red* who were allowed to work only on the fragments of a picture that never came together in a whole. The fragments of my hermeneutic interest focus on the three interrelated concerns of the book: the mourning of a culture lost to a mismanaged modernity, the quest for re-presenting that culture as a corrective endeavor (*Bildung* as rebuilding a lost cultural legacy through remembrance), and turning the city into an encyclopedic site of a new pedagogy. The first point is not expressly stated in the novel but constitutes an overarching theme of Pamuk's oeuvre; the last two are thematically and structurally inherent to the multifaceted story.

In the conventional disguise of a detective novel, *The Black Book* sustains the interest and energy that are necessary in order for readers to meander with the narrator(s) through the labyrinthine alleys of Istanbul. The extensive tour of Istanbul and the narrator's quest, interrupted by fantastic visions, stories, and intertextual inserts, write the city, in the first instance, as a living critique of failed modernity. Interwoven with the phantasmagoria of the traumas inflicted on the city in the process of a hastily planned and clumsily executed modernization are Borgesian visions of an alternative, unwritten civilization that revise the poorly written, incoherent draft of Turkish modernity. From the numerous historical strata of Istanbul, Pamuk reconstructs a cultural archaeology, whereby the city emerges as a triangulated site of critique, instruction, and the recovery of aesthetic imagination.

Goytisolo detects in the wildly branching architecture of *The Black Book*, which he reads as the mirror of "a palimpsest city," an outstanding example of an aesthetic of multivoicedness and stereophony that is characteristic of the end of the millennium and its flawed worldview. In response to a ruling culture of modernity that is impoverished, anemic, and slavishly imitative of Europe, Pamuk performs Antoni Gaudi's bon mot, "originality is a return to origins."[4] Thus, Istanbul quits the scene of many so-called realistic novels, where it is depicted without the benefit of its historical contexts, and emerges as a site of archaeological finds that match the vast intellectual fund of the book ("Orhan Pamuk'un Kara Kitap'ı" 297–98). Goytisolo deeply sympathizes with the critical combat of writers and intellectuals of the Islamic world who see in radical secularization or Westernization reforms an eradication of Islam's ancient intellectual traditions. In its broader context,

Pamuk's critical engagement is with the inevitably dire consequences for his land of an imitative Westernization. His multiple-centered critique plays itself out in the fortunes of Istanbul's denizens, who mirror the destiny of the nation. In *The Black Book*, the scale of the city, in terms of its historical gravity, coincides with that of the nation. So what really happens in this novel that seems to encompass such a multiplicity of visions?

Galip, a lackluster lawyer and married to his cousin Rüya, with whom he has been in love since childhood, comes home one day to find a note from his wife saying that she is leaving him. Galip sets out to find his missing wife. He learns that Celâl, a newspaper columnist and Rüya's stepbrother, also vanished and at the same time. Galip rightly assumes that the two, who had always been very close, are in hiding together. At first he thinks this is a practical joke, a kind of a game all three of them used to play as children. He goes to the office of the newspaper publisher, where Celâl is employed, to see if he can find some clues to Celâl's whereabouts. When he fails to discover any answers to this missing-persons mystery, he starts reading Celâl's old columns for clues. The clues lead him to paths of personal and public experiences, histories, and further mysteries, all contained in the labyrinthine architectonics of Istanbul as both city and text.

Galip comes to realize that many of Celâl's observations address him. He understands Celâl's writing as an apostrophe, a criticism of society directed at his person. Galip recognizes himself as the personified abstraction that symbolizes a Turkish intelligentsia in search of an identity in a cultural vacuum. His search for Rüya and Celâl turns into a search for his own identity. He starts writing Celâl's columns for Celâl, enters his apartment, starts living there, takes phone calls as Celâl, and impersonates him for an interview with foreign journalists. Mistaken for Celâl, Galip is followed by a stranger and gets death threats. Finally, he assumes Celâl's identity fully. We are told in the beginning that Rüya and Celâl will be murdered, but we never learn why or by whom. After reading the next 356 pages of this voluminous tome, meandering through the mysteries of the city and the story, ransacking the entire texts of Celâl-Galip's columns, we come up empty-handed, with no clue about what happened. This story is not about facts, solutions, or closure; it is an allegory, at once transparent and laden with heavy cargo. As in all Pamuk's books, proper names perform an allegorical function. In Arabic, Galip's name means "victor," Rüya is "dream," and Celâl "grandeur, glory, or magnificience." Galip is in search of a lost dream. In this quest, he encounters the fiery criticism of the voice of the people, who fault the intelligentsia for having sold out to the hollow values of the West and having exchanged a cultural heritage for the false promise of progress.

Pamuk's allegorical tale references several works of Islamic mystical literature, most notably the philosophical romance of another Galip (the eighteenth-century Ottoman Turkish poet Şeyh Galip), *Hüsn ü Aşk* ("Beauty and Love"). *The Black Book*, constructed out of framed narratives and inter-texts, is not merely a bold foray into the postmodernist camp. It forges a subtle yet powerful *Ideologiekritik* from the exemplary status and the sublime chaotics of the city. During the time Pamuk was at work on *The Black Book*, Istanbul was experiencing the shock of an unprecedented population explosion. Modernity had already left its indelible imprint on the city. But the inhabitants of the city and the nation are not citizens of the West; they are an altogether different species. Transported and translated into its Turkish version, modernity appears as what the Turks have dubbed an arabesque culture, which implies less the idea of an intricate design than that of a grotesque hybridity. It is a displaced modernity, one that has dislodged the foundations of a long-standing culture and driven it underground.

One of Celâl's columns about a subterranean gallery of mannequins in Istanbul, "Master Bedii's Children," is a sublime baroque allegory of the repressed indigenous cultures. It is prefaced by a quotation from Dante, "sighs rising and trembling through the timeless air," from canto 4 of *The Inferno* (*Black Book* 52). Master Bedii, the narrator tells us, was the patron saint of mannequin making. He created the mannequins for the first Naval Museum, founded under Sultan Abdülhamid's edict. These mannequins were made from a carefully selected array of materials, including wood, plaster, wax, and human hair, and were so lifelike that visitors to the museum were awestruck by the real human form of historical figures. But when the Sheikh al-Islam of the time sees these miraculous figures, he is livid, since imitating Allah's creatures so perfectly amounts to nothing less than a competition with Allah, and so the mannequins are removed. "Prohibition, which occurs very frequently in our history of never-ending Westernization," remarks the narrator, "did not snuff out Master Bedii's spontaneously ignited fire of craftsmanship" (53). For years Master Bedii tries unsuccessfully to place his "children" in a museum. He teaches the craft to his son and continues with unabated passion to make new mannequins in his basement.

During another wave of Westernization reforms in the early years of the republic, when Western fashion has replaced Ottoman Turkish garb, Master Bedii sees his moment of opportunity and takes his mannequins to the fashionable stores that have begun to display mannequins in their windows. But the store owners refuse to use them, for "the mannequins he made didn't look like the models from the West who taught us style; instead, they resembled our own people" (54). So these mannequins, who represent us, our authentic selves, seem forever doomed to living in a bleak dungeon. They remind the narrator "of the gods who had suffered the loss of their innocence as well as the loss of their awesome shadows exaggerated in the dim light; of penitents who consume themselves for being someone else" (56–57).

This allegory of abject mannequins is one of the many embedded narratives that comment on the crisis of values and identity that characterizes modern Turkish society. Pamuk sees in an Istanbul steeped in the melancholy of this loss the intractable crisis of Turkish modernity. Although this crisis is city/nation (Istanbul/Turkey) specific, the travails of modernity, as many have commented, meet their most concrete images in the purview of urban spaces. James Donald writes:

> The republican city, the city as public sphere, and the rational planned city continue to articulate the despair and hopes of modernity. . . . Those who fantasize about turning the city into an efficient machine . . . see it as a territory to be bounded, mapped, occupied, exploited, a population to be managed and perfected. (182)

They live in the dream of Enlightenment rationality. To impose a rational order on the city, to ensure the educating of the model citizen, and to follow this dream can lead only to a replaying of the anxieties, repressions, and censorships that provoke the dream.

When Galip attempts to prepare a rational plan of action to find Rüya (the double allegory of a lost past and a false dream?), he confronts failure, danger, and nothingness. When he finds his identity and loses Rüya and the dream forever, he is liberated. It turns out that Rüya was brutally murdered in Aladdin's store. This store, unlike the underground mannequin gallery, is a real store, owned by a certain Aladdin and located right across from the police station in Nişantaş, an actual neighborhood of Istanbul. Aladdin's real name is not Aladdin, but everyone calls him that. It seems fitting, since he is like the genie in the story of Aladdin in *The Thousand and One Nights*. The customer is the master, and Aladdin carries just about anything that customers need: cigarettes, imported whiskey, pantyhose, a thousand and one brands of soap, cologne, shaving cream, detective novels, photonovels, pine-flavored bubble gum, rose-scented ink, toys, tax forms. You name it, you get it. This store, a neighborhood fixture for forty years, which resisted the fate of many small businesses that went under with the proliferation of supermarkets and department stores, reflects—despite the fascination it holds for Pamuk as a unique Istanbul landmark—the insatiable greed of a consumerist society:

> People . . . suddenly all wanted musical cigarette boxes as if they were going out of style, or they all went ape over Japanese fountain pens no larger than your little finger; then they'd lose interest the next month, and they all wanted pistol-shaped cigarette lighters. . . . Then . . . the leftist and the conservative, the God-fearing and the godless . . . all purchased at Aladdin's the rosaries that came in all colors and all shapes, and they went to town fingering the beads. (39)

What remains, of the country's Westernization process is this mere desire for consumption, stripped of all meaning and value.

It is rumored that Istanbul is home to a thousand religions, orders, and cults. Synagogues, cathedrals, Greek Orthodox and Armenian churches, mosques, shrines, Muslim and Christian cemeteries are all part of the cityscape. No cultural memory has erased the other. Here memory lives at once diachronically and synchronically. Like his author, Galip assumes the pose of the city walker, flâneur, who wanders through the streets and alleys of Istanbul, recollecting a cultural past in the currency of memory. Galip graduates from being a character in the novel to a narrative device, an epistemic form that underlines the importance of historical inheritance for critical self-reflection.

The travels and travails of the postmodern flâneur in the urban landscape have a historical link to the mission of the bildungsroman's protagonist. As a palimpsest of texts and contexts, *The Black Book* moves within and across the boundaries of metafiction, philosophical reflection mediated through fiction, and the bildungsroman as a site of learning and formation. The classical German bildungsroman was the product of the late eighteenth and early nineteenth centuries. *Bildung* as a concept of comprehensive education (academic, social, and worldly) came to be seen as the foundation of the nation. The typical hero of the bildungsroman leaves home to acquire *Bildung*, whose course takes him to other places and opens up opportunities for other encounters. After passing through a series of real and symbolic educational stations, the hero returns home as an enlightened citizen.

Galip returns home with a sense of a newfound identity after his travels through Istanbul. Of course, this is a second *Bildung* for him, one that supersedes the earlier *Bildung* that makes him a properly educated citizen in the Enlightenment mold. Each of Pamuk's novels marks the path of a particular *Bildung* or learning experience for its author. In *The Black Book*, the city itself is transformed into a site of education and a pedagogical tool. It educates both the author and the reader and joins them in a hermeneutical pact. Pamuk performs this educational mission by revealing Istanbul as an encyclopedia of an occulted history, a history whose recovery and understanding will lend the modern Turks a sense of who they are and give them a chance for reconciliation with their historical selfhood.

Borges's imaginary and idealized land Tlön is founded on the power of language to create a reality in the idealistic sense. Forged in and by language (in both senses of the term *forged*, as faking and as making with great effort), Tlön's origin is one of Borges's favorite texts, *Encyclopedia Britannica*. The encyclopedias of the Borgesian universe belong more to the genre of the Romantic encyclopedia than to that of the *Encyclopédie* (1772) of the French philosophers. The *Encyclopédie*, the product of Jean le Rond d'Alembert and Denis Diderot's prodigious efforts, had a strongly pronounced secular bias and championed the Enlightenment ideals of reason and skepticism. But if D'Alembert and Diderot were able to produce, despite many setbacks, a complete encyclopedia, Borges's encyclopedias are always incomplete, with pages missing; they must be reconstructed from fragments. Their status inevitably calls to mind the other universal encyclopedia project, that of early German Romanticism.

The German Romantics' penchant for creating a new mythology found its concrete expression in their encyclopedia project, which remained incomplete, composed of fragments on a vast range of poetic, philosophical, and scientific subjects. The German Romantics envisioned an amalgamation and reconciliation of diverse modes of knowledge that had been separated by conflicting discourses and traditions. One of the most prominent figures of early German Romantic philosophy, the poet-critic Novalis, whose *Das allgemeine Brouillon* ("The General Brouillon") was an outline of the universal encyclopedia, believed that the greatest truths of the age could be found in the connections among the long-separated parts of total knowledge. In the reunited field of knowledge, each idea would be considered a philosopheme with respect to the whole. For Novalis, everything strange or unknown could be explained by encyclopedic observation, and nature itself was an encyclopedic, systematic index that reflected the human intellect. Schooled in the tradition of German idealistic philosophy yet resistant to all systematization, the early Romantics found themselves in a dilemma with respect to the form of the encyclopedia. Ultimately, they decided to cast it in the mold of their favorite genre, the philosophical fragment. This form entailed both an economy of expression and the possibility of self-extension and revision. The early Romantic ideal of the text was open-ended and self-generative, one characterized by infinite progressivity. The Romantics also regarded the novel as an encyclopedic form that encompassed diverse genres. Thus they wrote their novels as fragments and considered all the novels of any one author as constituting a system of works that repeated and completed one another.

The Romantic concept of an encyclopedic novel that is both a fragment and an infinitely rewritable text allows for a steady deployment of theoretical imagination that is evident in Borges's "Tlön, Uqbar, Orbis Tertius" and other fictions. It also coincides with Pamuk's philosophies of identity that are drafted, revised, and rearticulated as they move from book to book. In his *The White Castle* and *The Black Book*, the question of identity is not only treated thematically but also reflected stylistically in the rewritable structure of the novels. These two books and *My Name Is Red* also have an encyclopedic range that finds its sources in Turkish and European writers' works, used-book stores, museums, villas, cemeteries, and Istanbul's numerous memory archives. Pamuk does not necessarily attempt to reinvent a past for the reader in search of identity; rather, he offers an encyclopedic landscape and opens the visible and invisible archives of Istanbul for examination and review. The reader joins the author on the *Bildung* path that winds through the city and is alerted to sites resonant with politically contested meanings and memories.

The Sea-Crossed Fisherman: Death in Troubled Waters

Whereas Pamuk's and Tanpınar's Istanbul is an overwritten history, one in which the authors attempt to configure from yesterday's memories a cultural manifesto of metaphysical import, Yaşar Kemal's Istanbul is a living and very physical presence. Kemal paints Istanbul's less traveled roads, its outskirts, shores, and islands with the same brush that gave his Çukurova novels a transcendent hue, something that a reader who is not in the least familiar with the region could take away.

In *The Sea-Crossed Fisherman*, a story of Istanbul's small coastal towns on the Marmara Sea, Kemal conjures an Istanbul memory that the cultural historian and the philosopher often overlook: the lost unity of man and nature, the harmonious work of ecosystems, and the communal solidarity that protected the fishermen and their sea against the invasion of destructive forces. Istanbul's history and legends have largely risen from its waters; its unrivaled strategic importance is inextricably linked to the Strait of Bosporus, which opens to the Black Sea in the north and the Marmara Sea in the south (and Marmara connects to the Aegean Sea via the Strait of Dardanelles). The sight of numerous fishing boats on the Bosporus and Marmara, accompanied by Istanbul's ubiquitous seagulls, has steadily been fading into oblivion because of the water pollution's toll on the fish population.

Kemal shows us the vanishing splendor of Istanbul's seaways, the disappearance of Marmara's irresistible dolphins, and the tragedies brought on by an economy that rejects ecologically sound ways of expending natural resources. *The Sea-Crossed Fisherman*'s bleak portrayal of the capitalization of greed that bleeds the fish population dry and turns the unemployed fishermen into drug and gun runners parallels a narrative of individual human tragedies. Kemal's novel shows the inconvenient truth of impending ecological disasters, the illogic of a fake capitalism that destroys its raw material for short-term profit without any plan of regenerating natural capital, and the human cost of forced migrations caused by loss of livelihood due to environmental destruction and poorly envisioned industrialization. Like Calvino's invisible and continuous cities, Kemal's Istanbul depicts the hidden gangrene of urban blight that is not contained by the city's geographic borders but becomes contiguous with the earth's terrain. "Perhaps the whole world, beyond Leonia's boundaries, is covered by craters of rubbish, each surrounding a metropolis in constant eruption," Marco Polo says, referring to the concept of the "continuous city," characterized by unchecked consumption and waste. The boundaries between modern cities (and by extension between countries) become "infected ramparts where the detritus of both support each other, overlap, mingle" (*Invisible Cities* 115). Kemal's concept of nature and his plea for its protection are not bound by regional and national concerns; the poet sees nature as a critical source of sustenance for human life and art in a universal sense.

Readers familiar with Kemal's *Memed, My Hawk* will recognize in *The Sea-Crossed Fisherman* the theme of noble banditry or the bandit romance transported from the Taurus Mountains to Istanbul's shores. In translating this theme into an urban idiom, however, Kemal consciously parodies its excessive appeal to public imagination, its mishandling by police forces, and its collateral damage. The book opens with a scene in the coffeehouse of a small coastal village, a scene out of some misplaced western, where Zeynel Çelik, an orphaned young migrant from the northeast shores of the Black Sea, kicks the café door wide open and coolly guns down the local gangster İhsan. The only person there to react is Fisher Selim, the eternal outsider. Selim wrests the gun from Zeynel, slaps him hard, but lets him go. Zeynel becomes a fugitive and a legendary bandit in the popular imagination, and the villagers, who have always treated Selim as an alien, lose no time in somehow putting all the blame on him.

We find out that Zeynel's whole family was brutally murdered in their home on the northeastern tip of the Black Sea coast, when he was a young child. The severely traumatized child was brought to Istanbul, to the home of Laz Refik, a neighbor from his old village. Zeynel remained in a catatonic state until sixteen or seventeen, when he suddenly turned into a hell-raiser. Even though after the shooting in the coffeehouse Zeynel attempts to burn down Selim's house twice, succeeding the second time, Selim's compassion for the wronged and persecuted compels Selim to protect Zeynel to the bitter end. While Zeynel has to hide from the police as an outlaw, Selim has to stay away from the community as an outcast. Rumor defines, shapes, and alters the destinies of these two men, whose lives intertwine as they travel through Istanbul's turbulent underbelly, its outskirts, and its seas. Selim, a self-sufficient romantic and veteran of the Turkish-Kurdish civil war, strives to keep his "family" of dolphins out of harm's way and lives with the hope of finding the nurse he fell in love with while recovering from war wounds in a hospital. Both men are pursued by their own ghosts and visions and exist more in the steadily growing concentric circles of rumor and myth than in reality.

Selim, a frugal loner who is trying to scrape enough money together to build a house for the flaxen-haired nurse Gülizar of his dreams, draws the suspicions of the villagers and their enmity, even though he is the first one to run to everyone's aid. What makes him suspect more than anything else is his outsider status. When the tongues start wagging, the first comment is, "Does anyone even know where he came from?" (14). Like his author Kemal, Selim came to Istanbul from the plains of the Toros (Taurus) mountain range along the Mediterranean coast of Turkey. He is, however, of Circassian origin; the designation comes from the Turkish *Çerkes* and refers to the Islamic people of Caucasia who were forced into exile after the Russian invasion of Caucasia in 1863. Selim's solitary lifestyle, eccentricities, and reserved manner also draw suspicion and isolate him further from the community. He is rumored to have murdered a fisherman and confiscated his fancy boat. Villagers suspect that he has hoarded millions and complain that he is a miser. Many consider him mad, because he adopted a dolphin and his family, looks after them, and holds them closer to his heart than his fellow villagers.

When demand for dolphin oil begins to turn Marmara into a hunting ground, Selim pleads with the fishermen, who rush to Istanbul to get their share of the spoils, to spare the dolphins:

> "Don't do this. . . . The dolphin is like a human being, it *is* human. To kill it is worse than killing a man. Why, it is even holy—it protected our Prophet Jonah and kept him in his belly for forty days and forty nights . . ." And he always ended up with the same words: "You'll anger the sea, you'll make her cross with us."
> (36)

Thus, the nickname Sea-Crossed Selim. With a couple of like-minded fishermen Selim goes to the province governor, sends telegrams to the president, the prime minister, and representatives of the National Assembly to stop the massacre, all to no avail. But when he loses his best friend, the pet dolphin, and his family, he is inconsolable and begins searching every corner of the sea. Rumors start that the dolphin was his lover, " 'The man who's lost his heart to a dolphin' . . . 'Who's fallen in love with a dolphin and made a mate of him' " (36). The narrator occasionally interrupts the story in defense of Selim, to refute rumors, to set the record straight. On one such occasion, he remarks:

> Perhaps Fisher Selim could never have put these thoughts into so many words [as the narrator arrests Selim's stream of consciousness]. . . . Why was a human being so blind to the world around him, to the sea, the clouds, the fish, the birds . . . ? Friendless, confined in ghastly darkness, hiding his face in his hands, shutting out the light?
> (62–63)

Yet human beings are also capable of sublime feelings, appreciative of the beauties of music, nature, love. Since time immemorial, humankind's song has been "a paean of thanks" to nature's joys and beauties but also to "pain and darkness and wickedness even, for things of beauty, lost and found again, for the joy of reunion" (63).

The story is told almost exclusively in the third person by a first-person narrator. He is the only one to get close to Selim and his thoughts, and in their conversations the narrator switches to the first person. He is the author's double, as he is a writer, whose books Selim has seen, " 'I've seen them,' he said, pleased. 'With a horse on the cover, orange on one, blue on the other, and with the rider holding a gun and the horse going at a spanking gallop . . .' " (29). What Selim describes is the original cover image of Kemal's *Memed, My Hawk*. Buried in the dialogue between the narrator and Selim is a definitive clue to the narrator's identity. But why does the narrator identify himself as the author? In a novel that is neither thematically nor formally metafictional, what motivates the author to introduce himself into the text? In the context of Kemal's other works and statements, his identification with the narrator endorses the views presented in the novel. This is especially true of the ideas Selim stands for, as Kemal, like Selim, has been a strong voice in environmental protection and a champion of the working poor.

Although the third-person narration has the effect of objectifying the story, the author-narrator clearly observes events through Selim's eyes:

> Nobody remembers what year it was, that accursed year when dolphin oil became a precious commodity. Foreigners were eager to buy it and one drop was worth a gram of gold. Fishermen flowed into the Marmara from everywhere . . . and soon a fierce hunt was on, more like a wholesale massacre. . . . The cries of the dolphins still echo over Marmara, the shrieking as they were caught— harpooned, dynamited or shot dead. (35)

The massacre pollutes the sea and the shore, and, as the narrator and Selim predicted, the net result of crooked capitalist growth turns out to be the depletion of Marmara's fish population. Kemal characteristically avoids tendentiousness by letting the sun shine through the smoke from the cauldrons where dolphins are boiled, by tempering pictures of ecological plunder with Istanbul's kaleidoscopic colors: "A fresh evening breeze was rippling the smooth water, and the sun, a soft roseate mauve, sat on the horizon under a welter of clouds, orange, purple, green" (31).

The multihued atmosphere of the city is reflected in the cultures of its multiethnic populations. Selim frequents the watering holes of Kumkapı, an Istanbul neighborhood on the shores of Marmara, where Turks, Kurds, Armenians, Circassians, Georgians, the Laz, and the Roma—the Roma famous in all Istanbul for their haunting music—mingle. But a perpetual wanderer and exile, Selim eventually feels alienated from the bedlam of Kumkapı's bars and settles in Menekşe, a small fishermen community on the outskirts of Istanbul and home to many migrants from Anatolia. As Selim's quiet life, planting olive trees, fishing and frolicking with the fish, is violently interrupted by the carnage in the sea and Selim feels more and more alienated from the other villagers, he seems to slowly sink into madness. The search for the pet dolphin and the flaxen-haired nurse, who wears a white cap with the red crescent, both long lost, becomes an overpowering obsession. Their apparitions haunt him in his descent into the chaotic underground of Istanbul and in his aimless wanderings. At times in his boat, he sees "first her [the nurse's] hand rise out of the water, followed by the white cap with the red crescent, the flaxen hair blowing in the breeze, the large deep-blue eyes reproachful" (101). His decline into a hallucinatory state parallels the image of Istanbul sinking into a quicksand of debris and destruction. As Selim and the city seem to be in decline, Zeynel appears buoyed by his celebrity status.

Zeynel became a hero for killing a ruthless gangster. Since he remains at large, his fame spreads at breakneck speed. A public hungry for sensation, an ineffectual police force eager to close the case, and the media feeding the frenzy catapult him into the status of legend. On the run from the police, haunted by his past, and overcome by a paranoid desire to take vengeance on Selim, Zeynel is trapped in his own living hell. The newspapers run stories and pictures of his endless exploits. He is linked to a millionaire's daughter, to two other women, to several murders, bank robberies, rapes, and each time the police arrive at the scene, he slips away. Police get hundreds of tips and leads, but he remains elusive.

But who are these Zeynels? The real Zeynel reads about the exploits of the constructed one in awe:

> Every morning Zeynel bought the newspapers and read word for word the account of Zeynel Çelik's adventures, thrilled to the core, admiring the handsome, broad-shouldered man in the photographs, . . . forgetting that this was not Zeynel Çelik at all, then suddenly freezing at the realization that the gangster they were talking about was he himself.   (155)

Even though each crime is laid at his door, the public, instead of going into panic or trying to catch him, do their share to protect him—and, of course, they end up protecting others pretending to be him. Since he is not the man in the photographs, neither the public nor the police have any idea what the real Zeynel looks like, so the police never notice him, even when he is under their noses. The double motif here appears not as the uncanny but as sheer parody. As every sensational crime is credited to Zeynel, his doubles proliferate, until he is totally stripped of his real self and becomes an urban legend. As tales of his bravery and exploits make the rounds, Zeynel sinks into abject misery, living in constant fear of being caught. When he decides to flee the country, no one but the compassionate Selim is willing to help the fugitive.

The final meeting of the two men in Selim's boat ends in the inevitable tragedy of their star-crossed relationship. While Selim risks everything to take Zeynel to the Greek island of Limnos, Zeynel, gripped by his delusions, tries to kill Selim, who involuntarily strangles him in the ensuing struggle. Eventually Selim, who has single-handedly tried to fight the forces of a crooked capitalism, ends up killing Halim Bey, a ruthless landowner and industrialist, the Istanbul version of the agha in *Memed, My Hawk*, and, like Memed, who disappeared in the mountains, he vanishes into the vastness of the sea. Kemal rewrites Memed parodistically by re-creating him both in the person of Zeynel, the tragicomedy of the noble bandit who becomes a hero through mistaken identity, and in Selim, who despite his madness very consciously shoots to kill Halim Bey, as the landowner embarks on wrecking the shantytowns of Istanbul's fishermen.

Although Kemal does not have the philosophical bent and the memory-making skills of Pamuk and Tanpınar, his Istanbul is more vibrant than theirs. The sounds, smells, and textures of the cityscape come to life in his poetically inflected language, ably translated by Thilda Kemal. The famously contrasting faces of the city are reflected in the disparate fates of its citizens. As a modern novel, *The Sea-Crossed Fisherman* dazzles not only on account of masterful storytelling and sheer poetic vision but also as a tale of genuine social concern and moral compassion. The story of the killing of dolphins, whose closeness to human beings is the stuff of myths and legends, drives home the horror of ecological destruction at the highest visual, emotional, and cerebral levels. Without the need for modernist-postmodernist props, Kemal tells the tragedy of modernization that involves the domination of nature, the exploitation of human labor, the loss of small communities, and the ontological sense of displacement that is the burden of modern human beings. But the thematics of social concern does not interfere with the story, either as commentary or as sermon. The political message is not an operative agency in *The Sea-Crossed Fisherman*; rather, it breathes in the same environment as the novel's characters and becomes the face of their passions. Kemal intervenes in social spaces not to preach but to stir moral indignation through heartbreaking drama and a sense of justice awakened by the power of poetry.

Notes

1. Kadir Gecesi is the twenty-sixth night of the holy month of Ramadan, a night of celebration.
2. In Hoffmann's story, the main character, Nathanael, when he was a little boy, was told that the Sandman would throw sand in his eyes if he didn't go to sleep. After witnessing his father's death in an alchemy experiment conducted by a shady character, Nathanael becomes traumatized for life. The phantom of this character repeatedly appears to him in different shapes and represents the fear of losing his eyes and also something both familiar and repressed from his childhood—the story of the Sandman.
3. *Peşrev* is a movement—the prelude or overture—of a complex composition in Turkish classical music.
4. Antoni Gaudi (1852–1926), a Catalan architect, is a name often cited in Goytisolo's work. Goytisolo is fascinated by Gaudi's fantastically intricate and irregular style. I translate from a Turkish translation, by Gül Işık, of Goytisolo's article ("Orhan Pamuk'un Kara Kitap'ı").

CHAPTER 6

Scheherazade's Progeny:
The Modern-Postmodern
Will to Fiction

Postmodernism was not the invention of literary critics, but
literature can certainly claim to be one of the most important
laboratories of postmodernism.
— Steven Connor, "Postmodernism and Literature"

Yıldız Ecevit notes that the Turkish novel has for the first time,
through modernism and postmodernism, met Western Romanticism. Personally, she finds the newly found freedom of the contemporary Turkish novel from a long history of unadulterated realism a cause for
"exuberant" celebration with regard to aesthetic creativity. She states that the
increasing number of Turkish novels marked by the experimental, formal,
and avant-gardist aspects of modernism and postmodernism heralds an aesthetic revolution, "and, like all revolutions, it generates excitement" (12).
Ecevit makes clear that she is referring to the formal and stylistic features of
European (and especially German) Romanticism of the late eighteenth and
early nineteenth centuries. The discourse of philosophical and literary Romanticism in Germany was a critique of the epistemological certainty that
had come to be associated with the Enlightenment. Philosophical Romanticism challenged the limitations of Kantian philosophy that confined human
understanding to the experience of the phenomenal world. It broke through
the confines of logical and ordered thought to expand the limits of understanding through art and imagination. In literary Romanticism, this break
took the form of narratives that were dreamlike, nonlinear, dialogical, and
marked by a mixture of genres (prose, poem, song, epistolary) and texts.
For the early German Romantics, the organic blending of these forms
could be realized in only one genre: the novel. Therefore, the genealogy of

the intertextual, fragmentary, and metafictional forms attributed to the postmodern novel is traceable to the roots of Romantic aesthetics.

In the trajectory of Western intellectual and cultural history, postmodernism, which emerged as a response or challenge to modernism, has formal and conceptual features that parallel those of Romanticism. On the other hand, modernism, which sees itself as a rupture from tradition, moving toward ever new horizons yet maintaining its faith in the containability of forms and the understanding of the observing subject, retains the memory of the Enlightenment ideals of reason and progress. Because the terms *modernity* and *modernist* and *postmodernity* and *postmodernist* are often used without qualifiers or interchangeably, it is important to remember that modernity refers to an epoch of Western intellectual history that begins with the Enlightenment and Immanuel Kant's critical philosophy, which was instrumental in freeing truth from the monopoly of the Church and placing the possibility of all understanding in human faculties. In historical terms, *postmodernity* refers to a postindustrial worldview that underscores the reasons for the necessity to supersede the value systems of modernity, which is associated with the Enlightenment and the Industrial Revolution. *Modernist* and *postmodernist* also refer to cultural and aesthetic movements that conjugate the formal reflections of these historical markers—although they may not always be in a synchronic continuum with them.

The definitions of *modernism* and *postmodernism* as well as those of their relation, difference, contiguity, or dissonance are legion. For purposes of my argument, I skip the history of the debate and limit the discussion—like a good modernist—to a set of three coordinates that, to some extent, negotiate the historical and cultural aspects of these movements. These coordinates can be seen as historical markers or transition points and are based on aesthetic-literary, cultural-socioeconomic (Fredric Jameson), and philosophical (Kant, Jean-François Lyotard) axes. However, in the purview of the terms *modernism* and *postmodernism*, it is not unusual to see their semantic fields overlap, come in conflict, or expand to take in a host of cultural phenomena that do not necessarily refer to coeval histories.

In architectural terms, *modernism* refers to a style that seeks to break away from tradition, rejects historicism, aims at formalized abstraction, and becomes the harbinger and embodiment of everything totally new or never before seen. Its belief in technological and scientific progress views as obsolete traditional forms of building and use of space. Postmodernism in architecture, on the other hand, is marked by a return to history, references to a diversity of styles—known as the citation style—and a meeting of forms.

In literature, modernist and postmodernist styles often coincide in their formal practices. We see the invasion of the postmodernist literary terrain by fragmented subjectivities (e.g., in the hallucinatory visions of Kafka's characters), fractured images, subversion of mimetic representation, and multiple points of view, all of which are characteristic of modernist or high modernist literature. Thus, the term *postmodernism* remains caught in an irresolvable ambiguity that suggests that modernism has either been surpassed or superseded by postmodernism or is coextensive with it. It would be fair to assume, nevertheless, that at least in formal terms, postmodernism is marked by a decidedly expansive use of narrative self-consciousness, Romantic irony, and the seamless integration of the fantastic into the real—as in magic realism.

In world-historical terms and in the context of the specific developments in Western capitalism, postmodernism represents in Jameson's words the "cultural logic of late capitalism." Jameson delineates the growth of capitalism in three stages. The first stage is market capitalism, characterized by industrial production for national markets and by the rise of the bourgeoisie. The aesthetic reflection of this era is cast in the formal manifestations of realism. This classical era of capitalism is followed by monopoly capitalism, which ushered in the rise of imperialism tied in with the creation of world markets in nation-states. The cultural reflection of monopoly capitalism manifests itself in modernism. The last stage of capitalism's development is multinational capitalism, where global markets cross national borders and mark the erasure of the bourgeois ego. Jameson calls this stage "the waning effect" (*Postmodernism* 15), and says that "faceless masters continue to inflect the economic strategies which constrain our existences" (17). Thus, if the ego or subject has lost its bearings in time (or history) and the language "to organize its past and future into coherent experience," it would be difficult to imagine "how the cultural productions of such a subject could result in anything but 'heaps of fragments' and in a practice of the randomly heterogeneous and fragmentary and the aleatory" (25).

Postmodernism emerges as the cultural derivative of multinational or late capitalism. With the disappearance of the bourgeois subject, the conception of genius also expires, and the postmodernist artist cannot claim originality or expressive inventiveness but rather recycles the cultural artifacts and memories of the past. For Jameson, an economy driven by spectacle, style, and consumption rather than by production is the propelling force of postmodern culture. The global entertainment industry, which realizes itself "within a predominantly visual or aural postmodern production" (38), fascinates us

> not so much in its own right but because it seems to offer some privileged representational shorthand for grasping a network of power and control even more difficult for our minds and imaginations to grasp: the whole new decentered global network of the third stage of capital itself. (37–38)

Jameson's logic of capitalism's destiny may be on the money, but his equation of the three phases of capitalism with realism, modernism, and postmodernism is, at best, formulaic and reductive. For him, "the postmodern sublime" can be adequately theorized only in the ungraspable power and control of global socioeconomic systems (38). Ironically, Jameson, himself a modernist by virtue of his penchant for abstraction and categorization, pens a master narrative to account for postmodernism, which is a cultural phenomenon that effectively resists the logic of master narratives.

Jean-François Lyotard's *The Postmodern Condition* proposes a more persuasive understanding of postmodern sensibility in epistemological and cultural terms (but without real historical bearings). In Lyotard's view, both modernist and postmodernist aesthetics attempt to behold what Kant and the Romantics called the sublime, that which is unmanageably complex and expansive and eludes all understanding and imagination. Modernist and postmodernist art recognize this crisis of representation and willingly aspire to imagine the unimaginable, conceive the inconceivable. "[M]odern aesthetics is an aesthetics of the sublime, though a nostalgic one," writes Lyotard. "It allows the unpresentable to be put forward only as the missing contents" (81), containing them in a recognizable form that evokes a degree of comfort and pleasure in the viewer or reader. But the postmodern is cognizant of the unmanageable enormity of its representational task, of its inability to grasp contemporary experience (and reality) in its totality. Thus the postmodern

> puts forward the unpresentable in presentation itself. . . . A postmodern artist or a writer is in the position of a philosopher: the text he writes, the work he produces are not in principle governed by preestablished rules. . . . Those rules and categories are what the work of art is itself looking for. (81)

The noncoincidence of the world and its representation is what he frequently refers to as their incommensurability. He agitates against the illusion of totality and controlling forms. That illusion, "the nostalgia of the whole and the one . . . the reconciliation of the concept and the sensible" (81–82), comes at a terrible cost. The final sentence of the book is a battle cry: "Let us wage a war on totality; let us be witnesses to the unpresentable; let us activate differences and save the honor of the name" (82).

In the final analysis, while both the modernist artist and the postmodernist one shocked sense and sensibility with their portrayals of a modern world in chaos, the modernist tamed or contained chaos in form, whereas the postmodernist caught the turbulent wave and rode it, giving in to rather than resisting its energy. As Steven Connor puts it:

> Modernist work was shock requiring later analysis. . . . Postmodernist work attempts to draw experience and meaning, shock, and analysis into synchrony. Being modernist always meant not quite realizing that you were so. Being postmodernist always involved the awareness that you were so.   (9–10)

Although the modern and the postmodern converge at many points in their representation (or resistance to representation) of the real world, the postmodern preserves with a keener awareness the sense of the fractured myths of life, of the insurmountable complexity of modern life and its traumas, and of the sublime. Therefore the metafictional, parodic, and analytic forms of narrative are more pronounced and frequent in postmodern texts than in modern ones.

Further, as opposed to the modernist subject's originality and the work's "newness," in postmodernist art the "fiction of the creating subject gives way to the frank confiscation, quotation, excerptation, and accumulation of already existing images" (Crimp 53). In literature, the postmodernist passion for citation, appropriation, revision, and annotation finds its field of play in parody. Parody, however, should not be seen as a prevailing norm of postmodern literary practice, for, as Linda Hutcheon states, it "is a complex genre, in terms of both its form and its ethos. It is one of the ways in which modern artists have managed to come to terms with the weight of the past" (29). Although Hutcheon attempts to keep the operative fields of irony and parody apart, her emphasis on the "double and divided" nature of parody and its "authorized transgression" (26) draws parody and Romantic irony into a shared mission of simultaneously subverting illusion and creating new levels of illusion (30).

The modern Turkish novel does not fully agree with any of the various representatives of the postmodernist school, because it did not go to school with them, and its relatively short history is not coeval with their histories. Judging from its interest in regional history, one can even surmise that it was homeschooled. In effect, the postmodern Turkish novel is a synthesizing embrace of high modernism, postmodernism, and emphatic local identifiers. I take issue with critics who read into the modern-postmodern Turkish novel a defensive sense of its belatedness or who emphasize its historical belatedness as an analytic category. The postmodern, as Lyotard put it, is caught in a paradox of temporality. It certainly transcends national boundaries (and creates its own forms, as do all other novels coming out of specific nations) as it emerges in a globalized economy, as Jameson would argue, but it is also marked by deep self-reflection on its historical destiny. The progression of the modern Turkish novel may not have taken the path of its Western counterparts. But its rather impressive achievements, starting with the early years of the republic, can be attributed to its timely and perceptive assessment of the possibilities the novel offers with regard to alternative narratives of self and history. The predominance of women postmodernist writers of the Turkish literary scene and their success in employing the genre may have something to do with the broad range of new languages postmodernism has offered to historically underrepresented or marginalized voices.

Treasures in the Trash: Latife Tekin's *Berji Kristin: Tales from the Garbage Hills*

The search for a language that represents what has not been represented is evident in Latife Tekin's works and words. One of seven children of a mother of Kurdish Arabic roots and a father who was a migrant worker in Istanbul, Tekin was born in 1957 in a small village of Kayseri. She grew up in a multilingual environment, and when at the age of nine she moved to Istanbul with her family, she found the language of this enormous metropolis foreign to her linguistic world, which had been nourished by memories of Kurdish and Arabic, tales of the Roma, magic spells, and stories of jinn (spirits that take the shape of human beings or animals in Islamic legends). The family struggled to make a living in the impersonal and unwelcoming environment of the metropolis but slipped more and more into poverty. With trepidation and sorrow, Tekin had to distance herself from the family and from unskilled work in order to finish school. By her own account, she began to write in opposition to the dominant language, seeking to create one that gave voice to what she felt was her voicelessness. The idiom born of her writing is both a fragmentation of language and a confrontation of different languages—the secular and the vernacular, the colloquial and the poetic, and the mundane and the magical.

Tekin's first novel was *Sevgili Arsız Ölüm* ("Dear Shameless Death"), a semiautobiographical story of a mother, suspended between the supernatural and natural world, and her daughter, who adapts herself to city life better than the rest of her family while still retaining her sense of the magical. When the novel burst onto the Turkish literary scene in 1983, it created quite a controversy, for it broke the taboos of a realism that had become tendentious and trapped in thematic and aesthetic limitations. Tekin's second novel, *Berji Kristin: Tales from the Garbage Hills* (1984; translated into English in 1993) conjugates all the forms of her unique, highly metaphoric, and wryly nonrepresentational language. The unusual title indicates the peculiar dualities that define the lives of the villagers and other marginals who have moved to the shantytowns at the edge of the metropolis. Berci (spelled with *c* [pronounced like the English *j*] in the original title) and Kristin are two feminine nicknames that are not proper nouns as such but refer to the quaint practice of naming among the village and shantytown folk. Berci, we are told, is the name given to the young girls of the village who assume the task of milking cows, and their status (or worth) is measured by how well they perform this skill. Kristin, on the other hand, is clearly not a name of Turkish origin; it is a Christian name, which Crazy Gönül, one of the inhabitants of the shantytown, is known by. Crazy Gönül, who "was given the official title of 'The First Whore of Flower Hill,'" unapologetically practices the oldest profession and responds to those who try to shame her with a simple, "I've got to live!" (145). Referring to the binary values inscribed in the title, Saliha Paker, *Berji Kristin*'s translator, comments that "the rise and decline of the community on the garbage hills is symbolized by the female attributions in the title: 'Berji' for innocence, and 'Kristin' for prostitution" (14).

The colorful, divided, and tragicomic community of these squatters reflects, however cryptically, a larger history of the division between the two nations, which was portrayed in a different idiom in Karaosmanoğlu's *The Alien*. Furthermore, the various dwellers of this makeshift housing project, the old-timers, the newcomers, the nonpermanents, and the fly-by-nighters

represent more universally the modern city, whose margins always display
the melee, blight, and distress artfully concealed at its center. In the time-
honored tradition of the allegorical, the time and place of the story are not
indicated in the novel. The reader assumes that the location of the settlement
is somewhere on the outskirts of Istanbul, where in the 1960s and 1970s
thousands of illegal makeshift huts were built overnight out of cardboard,
cast-off materials in the city's garbage dumps, paper, cloth, and manure, only
to be demolished the next morning by the sanitation workers, the police, or
the gendarmerie. These dwellings, known as *gecekondu* (literally, "landed at
night"), had neither water nor electricity and were faced with the constant
threat of being torn down without notice at any time of day or night. Despite the danger of serious illness from the waste of nearby factories, constant
police raids, threat of robbery, and every imaginable and unimaginable ad-
versity that sprouted in the poisoned earth of the shantytowns, *gecekondu*s
mushroomed around the city, as more and more peasants, who had lost their
fields to landlords or could no longer find work in the village, migrated to Istanbul in hopes of making a living. As the town of Garbage Hills (which the
settlers rename Flower Hill) grows in leaps and bounds, so do the troubles of
its inhabitants. The silver lining to this darkly humorous tale is etched in the
extraordinary world of words that Tekin conjures up. The magic of the book
lies in this language and not in a Turkish version of magic realism.

Magic realism is a loaded and often loosely used term that refers to an
unsignaled intrusion of the fabulous and fantastical into an objective or realistic account in a text. It was first used by the German art historian Franz
Roh (1890–1965) to describe altered reality in postexpressionist painting
but later came to be synonymous with a certain kind of writing by Latin
American authors such as Miguel Ángel Asturias, Alejo Carpentier, and most
notably Gabriel García Márquez. Márquez's *Cien anõs de soledad* (*Hundred
Years of Solitude*) is considered the major example of the magic realist style,
and the scene where one of the characters suddenly levitates and flies off to
heaven while hanging her laundry is often cited as the definitive moment of
magic realism. In his preface to the English translation of *Berji Kristin*, the
renowned critic and novelist John Berger remarks, "I have never read another
book like this one. And perhaps you haven't either. True originality is unusu-
ally difficult to define because it gives the impression of existing for the first
time and this—fortunately—precludes generalizations" (5). Berger's statement testifies to the novel's radical departure from all literary conventions.
By the same token, the book can turn off readers, since an excessive use of

metaphor may wear thin, especially when the figurative loses sight of its referents and the text becomes the playfield of free-floating signifiers.

Tekin relates the many stories of the inhabitants of Garbage Hills, who, by force or circumstance, are relegated to a life among the refuse. They literally and figuratively forge a recycled culture, with its own synthetic idiom, out of the fragments of their various memories and heritages. Like a landfill composed of strata of castoffs, the text carries layers of storytelling forms, and the episodic structure of the novel mimics the spatial organization of the settlement, where the individual dwellings are not arranged in a recognizable order or design but are, nevertheless, parts of an entity. Recounted by a nameless narrator and almost totally free of dialogue, *Berji Kristin*'s stories interweave the fantastical fabric of fairy tales and local legends with the all-too-real experience of physical and material dearth on earth.

One wintry night, the flimsy roofs are torn away and carried off by the wind, which also lifts the babies from their cradles and carries them off. The parents run after the wind in panic and retrieve the infants. The trauma of the event gives rise to song and legend. As in fairy tales and fables, nature is anthropomorphized and speaks. The dwellers fasten the roofs, praying they won't fly off again, but the birds of the city flock to the "Wood and Plastic Neighborhood" and poke fun at the roofs that tried to imitate their flight:

> Wee wee rooftops
> Won't you wing with me?
> Drop the babies' cradles
> And fly away free.   (18)

When feisty Tirintaz Fidan instructs the ladies of the community in the fine art of lovemaking and urges them to own up to their sexuality, the wind carries her "night lessons" to the men and seduces them in their dreams. Dreams, daydreams, and the inner realities of the shantytown folk are projected onto the outside world as songs, litanies, fables, and rumor, which shape, monitor, and redefine the settlers' experience of reality. Berger remarks:

> The story-teller of the tales is rumour. As a means of expression rumour is not much approved in places where certitude rules. Law courts. Ministries. The offices of managing directors. . . . Rumour is worse than myth for it is uncontrollable. . . . [It] is a mass reaction to trying to follow, anticipate and hold together events which are always on the brink of chaos.   (7)

Berji Kristin's universe siphons off its energy from chaos and at the same time imposes, by homegrown legend, meaning on the chaotic and the aleatory. Güllü Baba, the oldest and wisest resident of Garbage Hills, is a soothsayer and healer, a character who is another version of the much-maligned sheikh figure in *The Alien* and Makal's *A Village in Anatolia*. Whereas the village sheikh of the earlier novels ripped off the gullible peasants with his faked powers, Tekin's is an interpreter of dreams and maladies and a healer who cures the stricken with the tears of his blind eyes. He lost his sight when he took a bad fall on a dam construction job. He composed a song about his blindness, in the tradition of the Anatolian bards, and sang it better than anyone else:

> The eye is the mirror of the soul it's said
> My soul is many coloured, my eyes dead
> I broke my mirror in a fall
> No use at all!   (40)

This blind seer's gnomic prophesies foretell the future of Garbage Hills, a future that will bring in more and more jobs, in the factories and businesses moving into the area. Güllü Baba sees the fate of the squatters inscribed on their foreheads, "in deep black letters, factories, wind and garbage. These would be bringers of good luck and bad." On the bright side, "women and children would stop scavenging and fill them [factories]," but the cost of prosperity would be untreatable dis-ease, malady, and environmental death: "The factory waste would alter the colour of the earth, the howling wind would scatter, and murmurs would turn into screams" (46).

The harbinger of good luck and bad appears in the form of the wandering Jew, Mr. Izak, who belongs to "no homeland" and is "as humble as the streams that [run] between the hills"; he shows up one day and builds a makeshift refrigerator factory on the slopes of the garbage hills. In the beginning, he fraternizes with the shantytown's settlers, embracing them all as "Garbage Brothers," wearing workers' overalls and pouring "sweat like all the others" (83). However, shortly thereafter Mr. Izak turns into the stereotype of the money-grubbing Jew, begins to exploit his garbage brothers ruthlessly; hires some of them to work underground, where, according to rumors, he is manufacturing parts for firearms; and turns a blind eye to the poisonous gases from his factories. As compensation, he distributes liters of milk to the settlers daily and has a mosque built. Mr. Izak is a complex and mysterious type, a Mephistophelian figure who represents moral ambiguity, changing from good and considerate to ruthless, greedy, and exploitative, then to apologetic and back to hard and heartless. Just as he appeared one day out of nowhere, he suddenly disappears, having "signed his name clearly in chemicals on the skies above the garbage hills." Although his physical body is gone from Garbage Hills, his "legacy" is inscribed in the song, "The man who wrecked the huts is gone / The man who woke the dead has fled / To distant lands and homes with pools" (100).

Although Tekin portrays with amused awe the social awakening of the squatters, who graduate from exploited working class in toxic factories to union strikers and from fly-by-nighters to townspeople whom the powers that be must reckon with, her stereotypical depiction of the greedy Jew and portrayal of Garbage Hills residents' glaring prejudices against other others and outsiders raises questions about representational bias. While the Romanies, whose history is narrated by the very knowledgeable resident amateur historian Honking Alhas, are portrayed as unjustly persecuted yet talented and colorful people, the Alevis, a minority sect of Islam that does not abide by the pillars of Sunni Islam, do not fare so well. In one of the most affecting scenes, the men of the Garbage Owner set the cardboard houses of the Romanies on fire and burn to ashes the seagulls they had healed and the clever bears they had trained to perform many tasks, along with several Romanies. But there is no trace of pathos in the portrayal of the Alevis. The residents view their move to their settlement with suspicion, call them by the derogatory name Kızılbaş ("crimson head"), and perpetuate in song and story the still widely held prejudice that links them to incestuous practices.

Kurd Cemal is portrayed as a fearless, independent, and enterprising figure who commands the respect of the settlers and stands up to the Garbage Chief. He trains the young drifters to say, "Here in garbage land we are the one to lay down rules and regulations," and his name turns up in "thousands of different stories" of daring and bravura (76). Rumors start that he will become a town councilman and build a movie theater in the middle of the garbage hills. While the settlers approve velvet curtains and leather seats for the cinema, Cemal has other plans. He is about to develop a new squatters' quarter not in the garbage hills but where they end. To carry out his scheme, he bribes the Garbage Chief to sell building plots to unsuspecting factory workers in his name, in the forest area beyond the hills that is being turned into heath. One day the workers go to the heath after their factory shifts, dig the ground, and set up random huts, only to be faced with demolishing trucks a few days later. Lo and behold, they laugh at their own stupidity instead of blaming Cemal—they would have hunted any other capitalist with sticks and stones and demanded their money. Instead of generating resentment, Cemal's scam becomes a source of mirth: "The people laughed for days at their own innocence and henceforth all such swindles were known as 'Kurd Cemal's Cinema,' a name which spread to other neighborhoods and factories" (78).

A discerning reader may be perplexed by the not-so-subtle stereotyping of the Jew and the Alevi (and, to some extent, even the Romanies) against the glorification of Kurd Cemal. Granted, the narrative avoids high-handed moralizing and ideological posturing and uses humor and language play as equalizing forces; but it is hard, in this instance, not to detect the narrator's own cultural bias. Paker's observation that "Latife Tekin stood as a challenge to the mainstream fiction of the 1980s by rejecting 'realism' in favour of a highly metaphorical perception of reality" (12) explains the author's stylistic choices, but the choice to stereotype does not fall under the rubric of metaphoric ambiguity. Tekin has repeatedly maintained that she writes against mainstream Turkish and Western literatures and has defined her writerly objective as the creation of a language of the poor and disenfranchised, since these have been excluded from the dominant discourse. This claim underscores the concept that ownership of language grants the speaking subject legitimacy and power. The command of metaphor, which can appear in the form of a shared secret language and inside joke or refer to specific cultural notions, confers the speaker power over those who cannot understand the code. For Tekin's characters metaphor opens a space of solidarity and comfort in a hostile world. Metaphor also constitutes an alternative way of seeing reality. But if it perpetuates bias instead of liberating us from the fetters of cliché and intolerance, it becomes self-defeating. A reading of *Berji Kristin* attuned to the tone and style of the narrative cannot fail to notice the absence of humor—otherwise in abundance in this book—that could have tempered the clichéd portrayal of the greedy and enterprising Jew. The stereotypical portrayal of certain ethnic types, which cannot be excused as poetic license or explained away as a criticism of society, since these types do not represent the larger society, is a puzzling and problematic aspect of this otherwise spirited (spirited in many senses of the word) novel.

Humor can undermine the stability of reading and meaning and lighten the burden of lived experience. In one of the most irreverent stories in the book, a mosque made of tin plate immediately blows away with the wind, echoing Aziz Nesin's legendary laughter and confirming Milan Kundera's practice of provoking laughter to hold terror at bay. Tekin makes rumor an indispensable part of humor: "The rumour spread that if anyone found the minaret [of the destroyed mosque] and brought it back, everything they touched would turn to gold." But the collective effort to find the minaret is in vain, and the lengthy discussions about the lost minaret end in the decision to build a new mosque. The squatters also make it imperative to add one more commandment to the Five Pillars of Islam: "Thou shalt hold down the minaret at night." "It was decreed that children, the handicapped, nursing mothers and pregnant women would be excused from holding the minaret, and it would be counted as a sin, if they did" (26–27). The Five Pillars of Islam are belief in the oneness of God and in Muhammad as his final prophet, daily prayers (*namaz*), giving alms, fasting, and visiting Mecca for those who are able. The parody here refers to fasting and daily prayers, since the only ones excused from following these commandments are children, the sick and handicapped, pregnant and nursing women, and travelers.

In the final analysis, this overlay of irreverence over Garbage Hills parts the dark clouds of factory fumes and mediates among different kinds of laughter: laughing at the comedy called life, laughing at ourselves, laughing with others. Although the residents of Garbage Hills and we implicitly know that the woes and wails of the squatters will not end, this unhappiness can be transformed into self-understanding, solace, and even power. The residents of Garbage Hills, who altered reality by renaming their community Flower Hills, have shown that they can change their fate by taking the law into their own hands. That law is the law of language, administered and enforced (and reinforced) in song, protest, petition, rumor, and demonstration.

Aslı Erdoğan's Sublime Sorrows: From Istanbul to Rio de Janeiro: Postmodern Itineraries

> In some remote corner of the universe, cast into countless
> flickering solar systems, there once was a star where clever
> animals invented knowledge. That was the most arrogant and
> the most untruthful moment of "world history"—yet indeed

only a moment. After nature had taken a few breaths, the star
froze over, and the clever animals had to die.

—Friedrich Nietzsche,
"On Truth and Lying in an Extra-moral Sense"

In the real world, there is nothing deep enough to hold what
is in you; yet you, with your life, your death, and all your
dreams are naught but a speck in the monstrous infinity
of truth.

—Aslı Erdoğan, *Kırmızı Pelerinli Kent*

Aslı Erdoğan's *Kırmızı Pelerinli Kent* ("The City with the Red Cape") is a
semiautobiographical novel of a very different hue from that of the books so
far discussed.[1] Written by a multilingual, highly educated, and philosophically minded physicist, the book is predicated on two separate levels of reality: the reality of an objective account and that of a fiction embedded in the
real world of the novel. These two levels are recounted by two different
author-narrators, who appear to be the same person, although only one of
them can close the narrative. As in Karasu's *Night*, a novel that *The City
with the Red Cape* closely resembles in its metafictional status and mood, it
is difficult to tell the two narrators apart, since the author inhabits the language of both. Erdoğan's life, mind, emotions, and studies are very much in
her work, a work that repeatedly poses questions of certainty and uncertainty in both an affective and a reflective mode. At the same time, the
author constantly blurs the distinction between perception and reality, ob-
server and observed, and strives to close the gap between subjective experience
and the external world in memory, in imagination, and most emphatically
in writing. However, the author Özgür of the novel *The City with the Red
Cape* within the novel of the same title by Aslı Erdoğan warns of the risk involved in any attempt to capture reality or truth in writing: "Everyone who
picks up the pen has to struggle greatly with this question: How much truth
can I bear"? (80).

One of the youngest literary talents to appear on the modern Turkish literary scene, Erdoğan was born in 1967 in Istanbul. She graduated from
Bosporus University (formerly Robert College) in Istanbul with a degree in
computer science. She went on to complete an MS in physics. In 1991, while
in graduate school, she went to Geneva to carry out research in the field of

high-energy particles at CERN (European Center for Nuclear Research). But her heart was in writing, and for a long time she led a double life, doing her scientific work during the day and writing feverishly at night. Her first novel, *Kabuk Adam* ("Crust Man"), was published in 1994, when she was in Brazil working toward her doctorate. She ended up staying two years in Brazil but quit her scientific work to devote herself full-time to writing. Her short story "Tahta Kuşlar" ("Wooden Birds") won the Deutsche Welle award in Germany and was translated into eight languages. Her second novel, *The City with the Red Cape*, published in 1998, garnered critical acclaim both in Turkey and abroad and was translated into French and Norwegian. Erdoğan has tried her hand in many genres: novel; short story; essay; and exhibition catalogs, in which she fuses the essayistic and the aesthetic in texts that resist classification. She is reportedly working with a film director friend on a script. It is clear that we have not heard the last of this passionately driven writer.

Erdoğan did not begin writing *City* until after she returned to Istanbul. Her fictionalized memoir of the Rio years is completely reconstructed from memory, and the distance in time lends the writing its simultaneously dreamlike and nightmarish tone. Like Orhan Pamuk's Istanbul, James Joyce's Dublin, and Kate Braverman's Los Angeles, among others, Erdoğan's Rio emerges as a major character of the novel, a character both fascinating and murderous, liberating and imprisoning, exhilarating and stifling. Like Erdoğan's native Istanbul, Rio is a city of hybrid colors and cultures, of beauty on a grand scale, of sharp contrasts, of high points (steep hills, magnificent villas, beautiful people, intense pleasures) and the lowest of the low (ruthless criminals of every sort, horrible slums, abject poverty, ubiquitous street crime). Beginning with the title of the book, the city is personified as a seductive, sensuous, and sinister character draped in a red cape. At the surface, the tone of the first narrator's voice registers an acute sense of alienation, fear, disgust, and rage toward the city, conjuring up the image of a bullfight, where a powerful but unsuspecting creature (like the narrator) is goaded on and enraged by a matador with a red cape. The bull is alone, the other of the human being (and, like any other, is feared and has no rights), and the enemy. The nation of spectators cheers the matador and jeers at the bull. It is a game of kill or be killed. But even if the bull escapes death and manages to kill or wound the matador, he is killed at the end of the game by other matadors standing by. That is precisely what happens to Özgür in Erdoğan's novel. Özgür, who hates her name, which means "free" or "independent," manages to dodge danger and death several times before Rio's bloody arena, its red streets, claim her, when unseen killers shoot her in the back in the Blue Hill favela.

The structure of the novel is unusual: it moves the story in and out of two shifting frames, and each narrative level intersects with and reflects the other in a game of doubling and mirroring. The first third-person narrator (unnamed, the thinly disguised author) relates the story of Özgür, who is in Rio to work on her doctoral dissertation at an unnamed university. For a number of reasons, emotional and financial, Özgür cannot go on with her academic work and starts writing a novel in a green notebook, while giving English lessons to survive financially. The novel is titled *The City with the Red Cape*, and Özgür composes its chapters under several titles and subtitles that simultaneously reflect the faces of the city and the moods of the narrator. The protagonist of her novel is her double, Ö. The novel within the novel appears in italics. However, the different typeface does not necessarily demarcate where the embedded novel parts begin or end, since the two narratives are intertwined in such a way that the first narrator apparent, presumably the author; the second author-narrator, Özgür; and Özgür's narratee, Ö., seem to speak in the same voice.

The novel within the novel is initially told in the first person, but as the story progresses, it switches back and forth between first- and third-person narration and ends in the voice of the third-person narrator, who is also the survivor of the tale and of Rio's inferno. The chaos of the novelistic structure represents a microcosm of the chaos not only of Rio (and the jungle) but also of the world. Noticing how everything cut down in the jungle grows back overnight, how each felled tree is immediately replaced by gigantic bushes and poison ivy, the first narrator remarks, "Chaos replaces order; fragments the whole; the wild the tamed. . . . An unmistakable proof of thermodynamics in a universe said to be ruled by the laws of physics" (81). Only writing offers the possibility of order over chaos. Özgür keeps saying she needs to write to impose order on the chaos within and without, to manage the turbulence in her soul and Rio's dizzying and volatile life: "Writing means, in the first instance, putting in order, and if Rio could be described in one word, it was CHAOS" (29). To be sure, in this case writing contains the chaos, since the story is bound by the borders of the text, but it does not or will not impose order on it; the writing swerves in and out of three levels of reality.

The immediate reality is that of the material book with the signature of its author, Aslı Erdoğan. Erdoğan writes an autobiographical fiction in which the protagonist Özgür is her alter ego. Özgür, like her author, is also writing a novel about her life in Rio. Her alter ego, in turn, is Ö., who, even though she is Özgür's representation, emerges as a character more real, having more flesh and blood, than her author:

> This willful woman [Ö.], who grew more independent by the day, was constantly stealing the role of the author and upstaging her in grand dramas. It is as if Özgür's colorless soul had been refracted through a prism and acquired all the colors of the color wheel. (94)

What happens at the structural level of the story articulates a multitude of issues about life and writing: the problem of truth in autobiographical writing; the limits of life and fiction and the line between the two; the recursive symmetries of chaos and order, modern existence as hell on earth, the modern city as jungle, and death as the end of writing. Özgür's green notebook, filled with notes, comments, and parts of her novel, addresses all these questions of fictional creation and philosophical reflection. Against Rio's red light (the red of its heat, its blood-stained streets, its rage), which stops Özgür in her tracks and paralyzes her emotionally, the notebook gives her the green light to move into an oasis of peace, solace, and creativity. She takes the novel fragment hidden in the notebook with her everywhere, "like a good luck charm, and whenever she wanted to take refuge in her inner world, she would write no matter where she was" (42).

The red city and the green notebook reflect the opposite faces of a split self that imposes its own contradictory reality on both. Rio is a character larger than life, but it is all surface. "Wherever I went in this vast world, I saw superficiality, but here it has become an art form" and "Superficiality is a worldwide epidemic, but here it is a religion" (30) are frequently heard comments by Rio's exiled citizens, who were "washed away to tropical waters by Northern currents and caught in Rio's nets" (29). There is no safe harbor in Rio for the exiled, the wanderer, the adventurer. The city robs them of their last possessions, material and moral, from the old world. Özgür/Ö.'s values were now like the "heavy, impractical suitcase she had carried here from Turkey. The old rules of the old world were not valid here" (11). Rio empties not only the baggage of the exile but also the exile's self, leaving an "empty shell subject to destruction, decay, and the mercy of time that spares nobody" (83). South America, "a package of fantasies, promises, fairytales . . . an empty canvas upon which all dreams can be sketched," draws to its paradoxically welcoming and repelling bosom

> old Nazis, fugitives from the law, international terrorists, fallen dictators . . . those looking for the lost Atlantis or for their lost "selves," those who think music, dance, and addiction are the cure for the pain of existence . . . those who have left their conscience behind along with their coats and boots and are after dirt-cheap children's asses . . . and incorrigible romantics who have lined their walls with Che posters and run to this quicksand to rescue something, since there were no ideals left to fight for in their own countries.   (77)

Yet there is nothing to save and everything to lose in this bottomless, insatiable furnace of desire and violence. Rio devours its own exiles along with its others who have come from afar.

Özgür remembers that the first film she saw about Rio was *Black Orpheus*.[2] Black Orpheus hails from the favelas of Rio, a musician who travels through the death-and-chaos-smelling streets of Rio during Carnival to find his Eurydice, who was kidnapped by a figure wearing a death mask. He reaches the depths of Hades with his magical guitar, which opens locked doors, and finds his beloved in the midst of a Candomblé ritual (Candomblé is a religion of African roots). Just as it seems that he has triumphed over death, Orpheus opens his eyes, which had to remain shut during the ritual, "like all the Orpheuses of history, before it was time. . . . The only thing that remained of Black Orpheus, destined to die in a *favela*, was his guitar" (41). Like Black Orpheus, all indigenous and excentric exiles of Rio are doomed to a premature banishment from the land of the living. They are the only characters drawn with the brush of compassion in the intertwined branches of the two novels.

Senhor de Oliveira wanders in a crazed state the streets of the favela. One night, drenched from the rain, clad in rags, and with stinking, disheveled hair, he enters a bar where Ö. is spending her birthday alone. He accosts the disconcerted woman, who tries to avoid him, but then astonishes and enchants her by quoting Keats in impeccable Oxford English. Ö. is mesmerized by this enigmatic figure and learns from the bar patrons that he was a leading Brazilian painter in the 1980s, spent years abroad in England, and introduced Brazilian painting to Europe (68–72). Senhor de Oliveira then reemerges in Özgür's narrative, where he seems to have no memory of having met Ö. The narrator's friend Eduardo tries to explain to her that Oliveira is mad and cannot understand her and in passing mentions that his name is Eli. On hearing his name, Oliveira shows no response, but Özgür recites Christ's last words in Aramaic on the cross, "Eli, Eli, lama sabachthani?" (75; "My God, my God, why hast thou forsaken me?").

Erdoğan dedicates *The City with the Red Cape* to the memory of Eduardo, another forsaken soul "killed in Santa Teresa with a stray bullet." An impoverished street vendor, Eduardo had given the house he inherited from his father to the homeless and lived in a bamboo hut. He was a sweetly mad, kindhearted cocaine addict, who reportedly was a talented painter in his past life. An "unadulterated bum," Eduardo "indefinitely postponed settling accounts with the world" (42). He gave the narrator, whom he called "the very name of loneliness," gifts on every occasion. Even though many of these gifts were things the narrator would never use, she kept them as mementos, since "no one besides the soft-hearted, crazy Eduardo had given her anything in Brazil where she spent two birthdays" (64). Ultimately, the real gift of Rio's lost souls to the narrator or narrators is the gift of their stories, which like Scheherazade's tales keep death at bay. At the head of the chapter "The New World" stands a telling quote by Robert Pinget: "The only thing that remains outside writing is death" (109).

This nightmarish portrait of Rio becomes paradoxically a kind of homage to a magnificently alive city—"Rio de Janeiro was perhaps the only city that did not succumb to the melancholy of Sunday evenings" (150)—which by its vastness and diversity of images, metaphors, spaces, and characters; its sensuousness as well as callousness; and its nakedness and masks dazzles the narrator(s) and becomes the source of the aesthetic and philosophical inspiration of the narrative.

In one of the most conspicuous metafictional instances of the novel, we are told, "For a long time Özgür looked for a writer who could exchange the real but inconceivable world in which she lived with a fictional but more real one" (83). At several places, the reader is informed of the conditions of the novel's inception, its status, and its transgression and alteration of the real:

> Once she [Özgür] aspired to write a fully autobiographical novel, "a record of traumatic events," as she called it in one of her humorous moods. . . . But a completely different story came into being; a story that belonged to another woman, to Ö., a story Özgür "had not lived," even if it "had happened to her." . . . She seemed to be more concrete, more real, more human than Özgür. More alive than her even after she was killed with a single bullet near the Blue

Hill *favela*. In the end, when she was strong enough, she was going to cut loose, push Özgür aside, and move on. (94)

The philosophical problems of truth and illusion, fact and fiction, concept and representation loom large in the jungles of the city. Chaos lends itself to form only to break out of it in a dialectic of creation and dissolution. A quotation that prefaces the chapter "Downhill," which is attributed to Jacques Derrida but is actually Derrida's citation (217) from Nietzsche's "On Truth and Lie in an Extra-moral Sense," is a maxim that courses through the text: "Truths are illusions about which it has been forgotten that they are illusions" (87).[3] To the philosopher's provocative perception, the author or first narrator adds the physicist's symbolism: "The equation of chaos is actually very simple. Life = life. Death = death. But we are all trying to formulate our own equation and make the world equivalent to it. Such unawareness!" (149).

In the final analysis, in whatever category a reader sees *The City with the Red Cape*—as an autobiographical novel, a narrative of exile, an urban novel, an essay on existential angst, a philosophical reflection—the book's power lies more in the poetry of its language and in the lyrically modulated voices of its narrators than in any one of its allegories and metafictional strategies, although these are presented in a virtuoso performance. The novel is the product of an author who inhabits a specific history and identity (Turkish, female, urban, poet, physicist, multilingual, oversensitive), yet it is not monopolized or dictated by these specificities. It resounds at an existential level, in a place marked by stages of resistance, struggle, pain, loss, and finally recovery, a place many know intimately.

Orhan Pamuk's *My Name Is Red*: Deadly Representations

> The struggle of man against power is the struggle of memory against forgetting.
> —Milan Kundera, *The Book of Laughter and Forgetting*

> If you ask me, this book [*My Name Is Red*] narrates, at the deepest level, the fear of being forgotten and the tragedy of art doomed to oblivion.
> —Orhan Pamuk, *Öteki Renkler* ("Other Colors")

The divine, because it is unsayable, can only be represented
allegorically.
　　　　　　　　—Friedrich Schlegel, "Dialogue on Poetry"

My Name Is Red is arguably the novel that made Pamuk a household
name among literature professors and literary critics in the United States.
Shortly after its release in English translation, it received rave reviews. In
addition, it began appearing on the syllabi of college courses and among
the recommended-books lists of prominent writers. The novel has been reviewed in numerous English-language publications, and search engines will
lead the interested reader to archives of interviews and book reviews. Many
of these reviews offer similar snapshots of the novel. In one of the first reviews, in the *New Yorker*, John Updike draws parallels, by now familiar, to
the philosophical games of Jorge Luis Borges, Italo Calvino, and Umberto
Eco. For Updike, Pamuk's "ingenuity is yoked to a profound sense of dou-
bleness and enigma" (93) that alludes to the deeply entrenched dualities
characteristic of Turkish society. The view of Turkish society riven by cultural duality has so frequently been read into Pamuk's novel that it has become a trope. I do not wish to imply that Updike's review is clichéd.
Updike offers an incisive rationale for the universal appeal of the novel and
gives a reasonably clear summary of a book that is hard to summarize, as enamored as it is with fragmentation and digression. Furthermore, he provides a succinct cultural context for the story and apposite references to its
endless inventories à la Borges.

　　While many reviewers dutifully point to Borgesian forking paths and
recursive symmetries of plot and form and to Calvino's play with perspec-
tives and allegories of memory, there is silence with regard to the role of
modern Turkish writers in Pamuk's literary formation. In his essayistic
memoir *Istanbul: Memories and the City*, Pamuk pays homage to Istanbul's
four melancholic poet-chroniclers whose work has had a strong impact on
his life and writing: Ahmet Hamdi Tanpınar; Yahya Kemal, a poet; Reşat
Ekrem Koçu, a historian encyclopedist; and Abdülhak Şinasi Hisar, a novelist-
memoirist. Pamuk writes, "[T]hese four heroes . . . opened my eyes to the
soul of the city in which I live. For these four melancholic writers drew their
strength from the tensions between the past and the present, or between
what Westerners like to call East and West" (111). All four taught him how
to unite his love of Western literature and modern art with the culture of

Istanbul, but Tanpınar is the writer with whom he feels "the closest bond" (110). By Pamuk's own account, *My Name Is Red* is the book that most visibly incorporates Tanpınar's critical notion of the aesthetics of cultural memory (*Öteki Renkler* 168).

In the lectures for his university course "Roman ve Meseleleri" ("The Novel and Its Issues"), Tanpınar maintains that in the East, literature has not been complemented by other arts, most notably painting, which Islam forbade (158). Therefore,

> Our experience of the human is in our language, the range of vocabulary constructs the human being. A novelist is first and foremost an encyclopedist. Flaubert is an encyclopedia; Balzac was an encyclopedia. A novelist surveys and delimits his field. Seeing becomes discipline. (170)

As a professor of Turkish literature and art history, as well as a poet, novelist, and critic, Tanpınar was a Renaissance man of Turkish culture and clearly set a high standard of authorship for himself and other novelists. Certainly Pamuk's major novels—*The White Castle, The Black Book, My Name Is Red,* and *Snow*—hold themselves to this standard by their encyclopedic range as well as by their literary craftsmanship. The greater popularity of *My Name Is Red* derives from all of Pamuk's literary strategies: metanarrative gestures, framed stories, the foolproof appeal of the detective format, and the encyclopedic taxonomies of Borges's invented encyclopedias. The encyclopedic display of cultural mysteries is more beguiling in *My Name Is Red* than in his other books. It is in the manner of Borgesian imaginary or encyclopedic taxonomies that, in Michel Foucault's words, all the known landmarks of our thoughts, designed to order the wild chaos of things, break down. "In the wonderment" of such inventories, which abound in *My Name Is Red,* what we suddenly comprehend is "the exotic charm of another system of thought," the limitation of our own ways of thinking, and the threat to "our age-old distinction between the Same and the Other" (*Order* xv).

Since *My Name Is Red* has been widely reviewed and eloquently analyzed by leading Turkish critics, including Berna Moran, Jale Parla, and Yıldız Ecevit, I start with what I am *not* going to do: give a comprehensive plot summary, which would be impossible anyway; comment on the metafictional structure of the novel, which has been overtreated and is obvious to anyone who has read Pamuk's other novels; assess its art-historical veracity; assess its historical accuracy (the English translation has a chronology appended to it, which I recommend that the reader consult); or discuss the ubiquitous concern with the East-West debate. Pamuk says:

> I don't think the main issue in this book is East-West. It is the miniaturist's torment, the artist's anguish. Art, life, marriage, happiness are the themes of this book. The East-West wanders somewhere in the background.
>
> (*Öteki Renkler* 155)

Pamuk's own comments on *My Name Is Red* provide clues to a more fruitful line of investigation. He considers the invisible *meddah*, whom we know only by his voice and who is murdered by a fanatic sect, "the real hero" of the book and says that he feels the same pressures as the storyteller of his story:

> To write novels in a half-closed society like ours with its half-baked democracy and profusion of prohibitions, is to assume, to some extent, the role of the *meddah*. Not only political sanctions, but also taboos, family relations, religious bans, the state, and many others exert pressure on the writer. In this sense, the historical novel expresses the need for a costume change.   (154)

While heeding Pamuk's thoughts about his novel, I would like to comment on some aspects of it that transcend its frame and connect to concepts of enduring interest. These aspects are what I call the interaesthetic character of the novel, which finds expression in a style rich in synesthesia (we see strong echoes of Tanpınar in this respect); in the Romantic fable of a talking world, as performed by the *meddah*; in the dialectic of image and script; in reflections on art and memory; and in the question that looms behind all image and script: the problem of representation that, as philosophies of aesthetics have shown us, is suspended in allegory or resolved in the sublime. These issues reflect my own hermeneutic bias, but they also coincide with many of the questions other critics have raised. What happens in this whodunit that generates such a complexity of viewpoints, in this detective story that aspires to relate the threat of a cultural sea change in one of the most powerful and long-lasting of Eastern empires?

In a nutshell, *My Name Is Red* tells the story of mysterious murders among the court artists of Murat III (1574–95), who has secretly commissioned a certain Enishte uncle-in-law or brother-in-law to gather the four finest miniaturists of the day to prepare an illustrated book in the Venetian style in honor of the thousandth anniversary (in the lunar calendar) of the Prophet's emigration to Medina with his followers. The miniaturists are in the dark about the form and function of the final product, and each works on a fragmentary part of the whole. (This fragmentation is reflected in the structure of the story.) The artists do, however, have a vague notion of the danger involved in their assignment. Since Islam forbade pictorial representation—thus the concentration of imagery in Islamic calligraphy—they are afraid that they may be engaged in a blasphemous enterprise. Of the four artists, Zarif ("Elegant"), Kelebek ("Butterfly"), Zeytin ("Olive"), and Leylek ("Stork"), only Elegant is vehemently opposed to this sacrilege. Elegant is killed by an unnamed murderer—who tells his side of the story in the chapters "I Will Be Called a Murderer." Later Enishte is also slain, by the same assassin, who believes that Enishte's illicit project serves to feed this master artist's ego. The surviving artists are caught in a bind of ambiguous feelings about their project, resisting the sin of portraiture yet being powerfully intrigued by it. As the artists continue their work in uneasy secrecy, the cleric Nusret of Erzurum is fomenting discontent and agitating against the blasphemy of images. Believing that all the misfortunes that have rained on Istanbul were brought about by those who strayed from the path of the Prophet, Nusret's followers murder the storyteller in a coffeehouse.

Although Pamuk identifies most with the storyteller of his tale, the character of Kara ("Black") comes closest to being a traditional protagonist, as he is thrust in the role of detective in order to win the heart of the "princess" in the embedded fairy tale of the novel. Black is Enishte's nephew and back from Persia after twelve years of working as a secretary in the service of pashas. Enishte, who became enamored with the work of Venetian masters during his travels and aspires to their style, nevertheless hesitates to reject tradition altogether. Thus he enlists Black to invent stories for the pictures. The miniatures of the Persian masters circumvented the ban on images by considering them as ornaments to enhance the beauty of writing.

In his youth, Black apprenticed as a miniaturist but felt he was not up to the task and exiled himself after Enishte refused his request for his daughter Shekure's hand (Shekure is the name of Pamuk's mother). When her father is murdered, Shekure, whose husband has not returned from the war and is assumed dead, marries Black (she is pursued by another suitor, her missing husband's brother, Hasan). However, she refuses to consummate the marriage until Black finds and brings her father's murderer to justice. So Black runs around Istanbul—the fairy-tale suitor who must slay the dragon—to win Shekure's love and eventually finds out that Olive was the murderer. In the confrontation between Olive and Black, Olive critically wounds Black but is himself killed by Hasan. The love story has a bitter-sweet ending. Black wins Shekure, but it is not clear if she gives herself to him out of pity or love. A crippled and broken man, he lives a quiet life by her side. Her sons, Orhan and Shevket (Shevket is the name of Pamuk's brother and the name behind some real-life sibling rivalry), never forget that it was their uncle Hasan who killed their grandfather's murderer. Hasan flees Istanbul, never to be heard from again. Enishte's book is never finished; its pages end up in the treasury, bound together with unrelated illustrations from Enishte's workshop. An era comes to an end:

> Thus withered the red rose of the joy of painting and illuminations that had bloomed for a century in Istanbul, nurtured by inspiration from the lands of Persia. The conflict between the methods of the old masters of Herat and the Frankish masters that paved the way for quarrels among artists and endless quandaries was never resolved. For painting itself was abandoned.   (411)

The melancholy that accompanies Black for the rest of his life reflects the demise of an era that represented a cultural quest on a social scale and a personal quest for Black. The end of the novel is vintage Pamuk: the author inserts himself in the narrative. The finale is spoken by Shekure, who says that she has told the whole story, "which is beyond depiction," to her son Orhan, in the hope that he might one day write it down. She says:

> [D]on't be taken in by Orhan if he's drawn Black more absentminded than he is, made our lives harder than they are, Shevket worse and me prettier and harsher than I am. For the sake of a delightful and convincing story, there isn't a lie Orhan wouldn't deign to tell.   (413)

This plot threads through many others, which are mostly digressions on art, style, history, and memory. Like the serial novels of the nineteenth century, the novel consists of many chapters, most of them short, told from the viewpoint of twelve characters, living and dead, human and nonhuman, and the color Red. The first of the fifty-nine chapters is spoken by the slain artist

Elegant; nonhuman characters or concepts are given voice by the storyteller. Pamuk does not wear his learning lightly, and the intellectual weight has to be distributed among the characters. Because many of the narrators (and suspects) sound like they take turns reading from the same academic book, at some point they become barely distinguishable from one another. But the storyteller has a distinct voice and, like the chorus of Greek tragedy or of epic theater, provides a running commentary on life, love, and art.

After performing the roles of two dervishes, animals (a dog, a horse), inanimate objects (a tree, a gold coin), and concepts or allegories (Death, Satan, Red), the *meddah* delivers his ultimate virtuoso performance of woman. Celibate all his life, the *meddah* confesses that as a youth he was tempted to cross-dress and experienced, in feminine attire, a physically powerful sense of womanhood. His song of wanting to belong to both genders and to the East as well as to the West not only underscores the double-doubling motif that runs through Pamuk's work but also suggests that dualities (including gender duality) are social and cultural constructs. And constructs are forms of representing. None of the entities presented by the storyteller has an inherent meaning but is given what can only be interpretive or culturally contingent meanings, as the Devil makes clear:

> Even though I can assume every imaginable form, and though it's been recorded in numerous books tens of thousands of times that I've successfully tempted the pious, especially in the lust-kindling guise of a beautiful woman, can the miniaturist brethren before me tonight please explain why they persist in picturing me as a misshapen, horned, long-tailed and gruesome creature with a face covered with protruding moles? (289)

In *My Name Is Red*, the question of identity, which figures prominently in Pamuk's other novels, is implicated in the problem of representation. Since representation can never fully coincide with what it represents or capture an entity in its entirety (since it can never be the same thing that it represents), it can only signal its reference in some form of doubling—like a mirror image, which is both identical and nonidentical with what it reflects. Or, veiled as a trope, it can refer to an object or concept indirectly or symbolically. Since both language and picture (or poetic language and painting) attempt to represent, refer, and bestow meaning, they are often paired in discussions of aesthetics. Music, as arguably the least representational— or the most immediately and directly experienced—art form is usually not triangulated with word and image in these debates. However, W. J. T. Mitchell redefines the pairing of verbal and pictorial signs as one of dialectic opposition:

> [P]oetry, or verbal expression in general, sees its signs as arbitrary and conventional—that is "unnatural" in contrast to the natural signs of imagery. Painting sees itself as uniquely fitted for the representation of the visible world, whereas poetry is primarily concerned with the invisible realm of ideas and feelings. Poetry is an art of time, motion, and action; painting an art of space, stasis, and arrested action. (47–48)

Walter Benjamin suggests a certain resolution to this opposition, in allegory. Allegory not only embodies the dialectic of word and image but also acts as tool and trope of memory. Allegory is the picture of arrested unrest ("erstarrte Unruhe") ("Zentralpark" 666); it is the snapshot of the historical moment in the relentless march of time. Like memory, allegory fragments the face of real history and reconfigures shards of time in images. The images are open to revision by the interpreting artist (*Ursprung* 354).[4] In *My Name Is Red*, the miniaturists work with fragments, narrators reconfigure stories, and Pamuk does both.

By uniting the two opposing realms of poetic expression and picture, Pamuk remains true to Tanpınar's notion of looking for cultural inheritance not by criteria of historical, generic, or aesthetic division or compartmentalization but in the wholeness of art itself. Tanpınar incorporated musical motifs into his poetry and prose and lent spirit to the word with tempo and imagery. Pamuk states that while writing *My Name Is Red*, he was drawn to Tanpınar's observations about the novel that focused on the signs and traces cultures leave in novels rather than on the character or characteristics of their authors. He observes:

> When Tanpınar talks about the very close relation of nineteenth-century French novelists to pictorial arts, what he cleverly suggests is not that novelists who are interested in pictures see better but that a culture intimately related to pictures imparts to its language certain descriptive powers. I don't know if taking note of these points in Tanpınar's essays on the novel has something to do with a novel I'm now working on about Ottoman miniaturists and questions of seeing-narrating. In any case, we should remember that Tanpınar was very fond of quoting Yahya Kemal's words, "If we had painting and prose, we would have been an altogether different nation." (*Öteki Renkler* 168)

Tanpınar's interaesthetic approach to his art resonates in *My Name Is Red*. Pamuk has undoubtedly expanded, in a postmodern idiom, on Tanpınar's ideas about aesthetic unity and cultural heritage. He has also been inspired by some of Tanpınar's stylistic mannerisms, such as a liberal use of synesthesia.

Color figures prominently in Pamuk's universe, as evidenced from the titles of his books and the names of his characters. However, in *My Name Is Red*, Pamuk not only metamorphoses colors into conceptual metaphors that explain the world but also creates an expanded world of human perception through his emphasis on synesthesia. As life goes out of him through his murderer's blows, Enishte, shouting at the top of his lungs in pain, refers to the greenness of his scream: "The color of this howl would be verdigris, and in the blackness of evening on the empty streets, no one would be able to hear its hue; I knew I was all alone" (173). In chapter 31, "My Name Is Red," Red marshals all the senses to intimate "the sense" of red, which, when touched with the tip of the finger, would feel like a mix between iron and copper; burn the palm, if handled; taste like salted meat; fill the mouth; and smell like a daisy, not like a red rose (188). The color and waft of these ideas and images sweep across the pages of the book and lend sustenance to its thematic concern that miniature art, as developed by Persian masters, is a unifying medium of representation, where text and image join not to represent a thing or concept as real (in a human sense or through human eyes) but as an allegory of an all-encompassing or divine vision.

However, the image or allegory of divine vision is given to the miniaturist only in memory. And memory untainted by earthly vision comes only in blindness. This allegory of memory and blindness is narrated in Olive's retelling of Head Illuminator Master Osman's illustration of how master Persian miniaturists achieved "Allah's vision of His World." Blindness was not a curse but rather the ultimate reward Allah bestowed on the miniaturist who had spent a lifetime searching for Allah's image of earthly life, who tried to see the world not as human beings saw it but through His ubiquitous vision. The miniaturist who expends himself in the search for divine vision can attain this reward only "through recollection after blindness descended. . . . Allah's vision of His World only becomes manifest through the memory of blind miniaturists" (80). The divine perspective does not resemble that of human beings who, like Venetian painters, see things through limiting perspective. It neither magnifies nor shrinks its object; it sees everything as it really is, as in the moment the world emerged from Allah's memory, freshly created. I refrain from discussing the art-historical accuracy of this claim.

What is of interest to me is Pamuk's implicit thesis about memory and representation, a thesis that undergirds much of his fictional and critical work.

Memory is human, not divine, thus fallible. It is selective and subject to revision. The miniaturist who aspires to the truth of divine memory can achieve this vision only like Oedipus in blindness, where the possibility of perspective (seeing things from different angles) or perspectival truth no longer exists. The struggle for truth, earthly ambition, and conflict ends when vision and, with it, the possibility of (re)vision perish. Representation can be implicit in a worldview or ideology and can consolidate and perpetuate them. It can shape and control the way we see ourselves and the ways others see us. This philosophical intuition takes concrete form in *My Name Is Red*, where a treatise on the lost art of Ottoman miniature painting becomes a portrait of how different forms of representing—divine versus human, truthful or real versus stylized, actual-scale versus in-depth perspective—signify the struggle for cultural hegemony.

Olive, the consummate artist, is caught between these antinomies and two masters: Enishte, who is intrigued by Venetian masters, and Master Osman, the guardian of an Islamic cultural inheritance, of the work of Persian artists. Olive fails to mediate between tradition and novelty, is trapped in conflicts he cannot negotiate. His inability to escape from absolutes makes him at once victimizer and victim, murderer and martyr. By drawing the pictures for the *meddah*'s tales and like a true allegoricist completing the word with the image, he becomes the allegory of cultural casualty himself. Ecevit correctly notes that this orchestration of storytelling with drawing of images is not an Ottoman tradition but represents a fiction that Pamuk invented in his desire to join picture with narrative (148).[5] Like Tanpınar and Pamuk, Enishte sees all creation as a synthesis of antitheses and a union of different traditions and styles. "Nothing is pure," he responds to Olive just before the miniaturist stabs him to death:

> In the realm of book arts, whenever a masterpiece is made . . . I can be certain of the following: Two styles heretofore never brought together have come together to create something new and wondrous. . . . To God belongs the East and the West. May He protect us from the will of the pure and unadulterated. (160–61)

Pamuk's postmodern signature under this novel bears the fusions and revisions of the binaries present-past, word-image, and life-fiction. In this signature lie both the literary-historical and pedagogical values of the novel. Besides the thriller factor, color fest, love fest, and relative accessibility of content, which all appeal to the nonspecialist reader, Pamuk's novel makes for interesting reading in the classroom. I say this with some trepidation, because, like many readers, I feel that the book could have benefited from a few cuts on the editing board and some moderation in historicophilosophical excursion. Nevertheless, because of its shifting borders among different art forms, cosmologies, and story lines, the novel is open to a multitude of teaching approaches and interpretive categories. Its focus on the problem of representation puts it in touch with many domains of human inquiry. As a novel that registers a broad range of speech forms (the sacred and the profane, vulgar and rarefied, carnivalesque and philosophical), it conforms to Bakhtin's notion of heteroglossia. For Kundera, this novel would be an embodiment of robust Rabelaisian joy and excess of contraries and of the "nostalgia" the modern novelists feel "for the superbly heterogeneous universe" of a novel like *Gargantua and Pantagruel* and "for the delightful liberty with which they [the early novelists] dwelt in it" (*Testaments* 4). Just as Rabelais starts his novel by letting Gargantua drop onto life out of his mother's ear, so does Pamuk start his story by letting a dead man speak from the bottom of the well his murderer threw him in. In both cases," the contract between the novelist and the reader must be established from the outset" (4). It has to be made clear to the reader that the story that follows cannot be taken at face value, that the road ahead goes through a universe where the Ottoman Islamic artists' adoration of Allah's glory is juxtaposed with the explicit homoerotic desire of master miniaturists for their apprentices, and where the expression of sexually charged infatuation walks around unveiled alongside words of divinely inspired love. In this world, the blind can see the world as God created it, heterodoxy confronts orthodoxy, and color becomes the form of excess.

In *Testaments Betrayed*, a book that Pamuk reviews in *Öteki Renkler* Kundera mourns the loss of the Rabelaisian joy and abandonment that characterizes the last stages of modernism in the European novel, where the ordinary is pursued to its bitter end and a "sophisticated analysis of gray on gray" holds sway (31). Kundera sees the first notable rejuvenation of the novel at the end of the twentieth century in the literary works appearing outside Europe. What he calls "the *novel from below the thirty-fifth parallel, the novel of the South*" testifies to the revolution in the novelistic realm (30). This form is exemplified in the work of writers such as Salman

Rushdie and the French-speaking Antillean novelist Patrick Chamoiseau. Kundera states that he is "delighted by that imagination without understanding where it comes from." He speculates that Kafka, his fellow Czech writer, may have been the catalyst for this change, since Kafka "gave legitimacy to the implausible in the art of the novel" in the twentieth century. "The novel of the South" represents "a great new novelistic culture characterized by an extraordinary sense of the real coupled with an untrammeled imagination that breaks every rule of plausibility" (30). The non-European novel is infused with "extraordinary coincidences; colors on colors."

Of course, Kundera, given his conviction in the superiority of European culture, cannot quite bring himself to fully acknowledge the vitality of "the novel of the South." He embraces the phrase "culture of excess" that Rushdie uses in *The Satanic Verses* to bear on the excessiveness of color and coincidence in the novels of non-Europeans authors. Now the danger is that "in Europe, [the] tedium of gray; outside Europe, [the] monotony of picturesque" will prevail. Nevertheless,

> The novels created below the thirty-fifth parallel, though a bit foreign to European taste, are the extension of the history of the European novel . . . and are even astonishingly close to its earliest beginnings; nowhere else today does the old Rabelaisian sap run so joyfully as in the work of these non-European writers. (31)

Although Pamuk is justifiably critical of Kundera's Eurocentric bias in *Testaments Betrayed* (*Öteki Renkler* 234), he would probably agree that *My Name Is Red* corresponds almost ideally to Kundera's notion of defying the constraints of the plausible, not to escape in a world of fantasy but to understand the world better.

Kundera recalls a conversation he had with Gabriel García Márquez. The Colombian novelist told him that it was Kafka who had taught him how to "write *another way*" (*Testaments* 52)—that is, to engage the fantastic to deepen understanding. Kundera asks and answers:

> How to both apprehend . . . [the world] and at the same time engage in an enchanting game of fantasy? Kafka managed to solve this enormous puzzle. He cut a breach in the wall of plausibility; the breach through which many others followed him, each in his own way: Fellini, Márquez, Fuentes, Rushdie. And others, others. (53)

Among these many others are Turkish novel's modernist-postmodernist authors, such as Tanpınar, Yaşar Kemal, Pamuk, Ağaoğlu, Karasu, Tekin, Erdoğan, and others, others. What ultimately separates their work from many a modernist-postmodernist novel that addresses questions of identity, representation, and memory is a merger of two very different reserves of cultural capital.

Notes

1. All translations from *Kırmızı Pelerinli Kent* are mine, since the English translation, by Amy Spangler, was not available to me at the time of this writing.
2. *Orfeu Negro*, a classic 1959 film, by the director Marcel Camus, retells the Orpheus and Eurydice myth during the Rio Carnival. It was a box-office hit in Turkey.
3. "[D]ie Wahrheiten sind Illusionen, von denen man vergessen hat daß sie welche sind" (Nietzsche 5: 314 ["Über Wahrheit und Lüge im außermoralischen Sinn"]).
4. For a comprehensive account of Benjamin's theory of allegory, see his *Ursprung* 340–58.
5. "That the *meddah* tells his stories accompanied by drawings is the fictional solution that Pamuk, who wants to join narrative and picture, comes up with. This is not an Ottoman tradition but a technique used by *Bänkelsänger*, who were medieval German storytellers, similar to the *meddah*" (Ecevit 148).

The composition of the novel is the paradoxical fusion of
heterogeneous and discrete components into an organic
whole which is then abolished over and over again.
    —Georg Lukács, *Theory of the Novel*

It is characteristic of philosophical writing that at every turn it
must confront the problem of representation anew.
    —Walter Benjamin, *Ursprung des deutschen Trauerspiels*

It is characteristic of modernity that it must forever lament the loss of gods and the assurance of divine truths. For Friedrich Hölderlin, the departure of Greek deities signified the end of humanity's harmonious unity with the world and the disorienting arrival of the modern age. Thus, modernity was born of an absence, of a lack of grounding reference. The certainty of divine truth was supplanted by the thinking ego and its reality as this ego was constituted in language. In "Die Zeit des Weltbildes" ("Time of the World Picture"), Martin Heidegger argues that the transition to modernity involved the replacement of a medieval world picture not merely by a modern one but also by the transformation of the world itself into a picture. The fundamental event of the modern age was the conquest of the world as picture (94). This picture is no longer a copy or imitation of the world; the word *picture* in German (*Bild*) now means "constructed image" (*Gebilde*), a product of representing "des vorstellenden Herstellens" (94). The modern subject, Heidegger maintains, creates reality in representation; the world itself becomes a picture by the representing subject. However, the loss of the truth of Being and the attempt of the thinking, imagining subject to fill the void with its structures of signification—language, image, representation—forever point to the incompleteness and belatedness of reinstating that which is lost. "All that is solid melts into air, all that is holy is profaned," writes Karl Marx in the *Communist Manifesto* (58).

The anxiety of belatedness that marks modernity stems from the apprehension that we—like Adalet Ağaoğlu's characters in *Curfew*—are perpetually late, miss the deadline, fail to seize the moment to solidify our ground or to find it. Modernity cannot catch up with itself. The Mexican modernist poet and critic Octavio Paz, in whose concept of Mexican identity Ağaoğlu sees parallels to the Turkish situation, laments modernity's failure to find its bearings, for "nothing has replaced the old principles, faith, or reason. . . . Industrial society has lost its center. . . . [I]t cannot return to its beginnings and thus recover its powers of renewal" (*Corriente* 170). Almost all societies and cultures, even those removed from one another by thousands of miles or centuries, have lived through the traumas and contradictions of the modern age and continue to do so.

Thus, the idea of the belatedness of Turkish modernity and culture, though endowed with a good degree of specificity, is not an isolated experience. In a special issue of the *South Atlantic Quarterly, Relocating the Fault Lines: Turkey beyond the East-West Divide*, contributors analyze the fortunes of Turkish modernity and its anxieties of imitativeness and belatedness as these are reflected in art, literature, and popular culture (Güzeldere and Irzık). I would argue that the conditions for the development of the modern Turkish novel have enabled it to take into its purview a great diversity of themes, idioms, and ideologies and to negotiate these in reimagined forms and styles. The symbolic possibilities of the novel and its ability to unapologetically subsume different genres and temporalities do not lend credence to charges of imitation and belatedness, since the novel does not have a determinate form but one that evolves in its passage through time. A novel can treat belatedness as a theme and analyze its attendant anxieties and traumas and can also comment, in a metafictional or ironic mode, on its own belatedness or debt to other texts. However, none of these acts make a novel a copy, a secondhand story, or outmoded, since the novel is, by its very nature, a synthetic and intertextual construct. The temporal boundaries of the novel are not absolute, and seniority is not a measure of novelistic value.

Nurdan Gürbilek argues that social, cultural, and literary criticism in Turkey "is mostly the criticism of a lack, a critique devoted to demonstrating what Turkish society, culture, or literature lacks" (599). This situation is not a discursive fallacy but the outcome of a society trapped in the contradictions of its belated entry into the modern age. Thus, literary criticism faults literary works either with not being original and masquerading as the other in poorly imitated Western costume and custom or with looking pathetic in some kitschy local costume. Gürbilek assigns the critic the role of guiding Turkish literature to its true potential by stopping the cant about lack and deficiency and working with concepts that create an understanding of the vicissitudes that constitute selfhood in our troubled modernity. She also correctly observes that all modern literature "is always belated to a genuine experience" (625). In a more fundamental sense, belatedness is inherent in the philosophical (and aesthetic) problem of representation itself, which is always a re-presentation—making present what is no longer present. The problem has been with us since time immemorial; however, it has come into critical consciousness only with the arrival of modernity.

I agree with the reader-response theories that the text is a virtual entity and comes into being only in the practice of reading, in a kind of dialogue between writer and reader. The prerequisite for a dialogue is a common language between text and addressee, in which the text reveals its secrets. The dialogue between text and reader is most apparent in the structure of metafictions that dominate Pamuk's novels, where an ongoing commentary by different narrators or by *the* narrator, who frequently admits himself into the spectacle of the plot and plots, runs parallel to the stories. These metanarrative ploys reveal the act of constructing the work. It is not only Pamuk's work that presents its mode of realization in its form. The novels of Adalet Ağaoğlu, Bilge Karasu, Latife Tekin, Aslı Erdoğan, and to a certain extent Tanpınar often make the mechanics of their composition transparent to the reader. Modern novelists and theorists of the novel, including Benjamin, Bakhtin, Kundera, Ortega y Gasset, and Tanpınar, emphasize the role of form in shaping content and ideas in the novel. Benjamin further argues that the novelistic form creates from within the space of self-reflexivity:

> Among all representational forms [*Darstellungsformen*], there is one in which the Romantics have most decidedly developed [a dialectic of] limitation and expansion of self-reflexivity. . . . This absolute symbolic form is the novel. What is most striking in this form is its seeming lack of boundaries and rules.
> (*Begriff* 98)

Thus the freedom and diversity of the poetic form allow it to be both a critical forum and a space of generative symbolism.

Tanpınar rightly observed that criticism requires acculturation into philosophical thought. "We don't have philosophers and writers who look at social life solely from the angle of ideas," he lamented. "Therefore, literature cannot find in its environment the material it needs" (*Mücevherlerin Sırrı* 183). What Tanpınar is looking for is not just literary criticism. At the time, he does not have at his disposal the vocabulary that differentiates among literary criticism, literary history, and literary theory. The formation of a cadre of literary scholars—a wish Tanpınar often expressed—would preclude the proliferation of reductive and ultimately detrimental enunciations of aesthetic judgment and the conflation of differentiating forms of critical evaluation. Nevertheless, any criticism that adds to a better understanding of a work of art or literature requires the critic to draw, in varying degrees, on all three forms of evaluation.

Literary criticism is a judge of taste; it evaluates, appreciates, depreciates a work of literature, speculates about its effects on the reader. As Antoine Compagnon notes, "it proceeds by sympathy (or antipathy), by identification and projection. Its ideal site is the salon, and the press is one avatar, not the university; its first form is conversation" (9). Its addressee is an informed reader, but not necessarily a professional or specialized one. It often assumes the form of book reviews in the Sunday supplements of daily newspapers, short columns in cultural journals, or even reader reviews on bookstore Web pages. Literary history, on the other hand, chronicles the context of texts. It does a genealogy of texts by undertaking a research of factors apparently extrinsic to the aesthetic core of a work, such as reception, literary sociology, or canon formation. Gürbilek sees these two types of criticism or some combination of both lacking in vision and capacity in terms of an adequate assessment of Turkish literature.

Literary theory is the most reflective and philosophical mode of studying literary texts and also their most unrelenting interlocutor. It leaves no stone of assumption unturned. Nevertheless, the questions it poses seem fairly fundamental: What is literature? By what criteria should it be judged? Are these criteria ideologically implicated or historically contingent, or are the values upheld by the work universal or specific? However, Immanuel Kant, whose *Critique of Judgment* became the reference point for various schools of formalist criticism, maintained that aesthetic judgment eludes these external criteria and that the work of art is characterized by the apparent contraries (at least in translation) of "Zweckmässigkeit ohne Zweck" ("purposiveness without purpose"), which is understood as coherence and harmony of form without an ultimate goal or hidden agenda (128).[1]

Form remains a formidable determinant in the representational task of the novel. The novelistic form, as Benjamin observed, expands and contracts to accommodate the representational and contemplative requirements of a given novel. The novel as such is already a constellation of forms. Virginia Woolf characterizes the novel as a cannibalizing form that devoured all types of art. She speculates that it will continue to devour more forms so that in the process of its own generation and reinvention, the novel written in prose will "have something of the exaltation of poetry. . . . It will be dramatic, and yet not a play. It will be read, not acted" (224). Mikhail Bakhtin maintained that in those ages when the novel was a predominant form—most distinctly beginning in the second half of the eighteenth century—all genres were more or less "novelized," subsumed within the supple borders of the novel. The consumption of "parodic stylizations of canonical genres and styles" is endemic to the novel, although the novel never allows these stylizations to stabilize and consistently parodies fashionable novels of the time (5–6). Writing in the 1920s, Ortega y Gasset believed that the novel as a genre had pretty much exhausted its thematic possibilities, but he exalted its form as the source of its highest aesthetic achievements. The artwork's content or material is not a guarantee of its worth: "el oro de que está hecha no consagra a la estatua. La obra de arte vive más de su forma que de su material" (101; "the gold it is made of does not sanctify a statue, a work of art lives more on its form than on its material"). Like Bakhtin, Ortega maintains that the power of Dostoevsky's novels rests on the extraordinary form and technique that underwrite the complexity of his characters (102). For Tanpınar, formal composition enables the writer to control the totality of the work; "its importance lies in the influence of form on content" ("Roman" 156). The form, then, molds, sustains, guides content, and functions as content's (aesthetic) engine.

I find it interesting that both Bakhtin and Kundera anoint Rabelais's *Gargantua and Pantagruel* as the novel par excellence of the formal manipulation of convention through ambiguity, humor, and allegorization. Bakhtin's analysis is too detailed to summarize here; however, what he emphatically underlines in Rabelais's story is its ability to purge history of the transcendent values that cling to it and its reaffirmation of the authentic world. Rabelais does this by the destruction of all "habitual matrices" and the creation of new matrices through unexpected links ("allogisms") and linguistic refigurations through syntax, etymology, and morphology within the form of a "fantastic realism" (169). Kundera, looking similarly at the form of the novel, sees in its fantastical spaces, where the polemical and the corrective blend in aesthetic form and where a heterogeneity of idiom presides, the essence of the novel, "*the realm where moral judgment is suspended*" (*Testaments*

6, 7), the space of the Nietzschean "beyond good and evil." One can argue that they overstate the case, that we are not even talking about a novel here—*Gargantua* became a novel in time, as Kundera remarks, when later novelists, including Rushdie, were inspired by it—and that compared with the great novels of the modern pantheon, it looks bawdy, dated, out of place, a naughty romp in the Renaissance camp. Furthermore, it remains largely unread, even in college courses.

The point is, comparing novels in terms of ours and theirs (historically and geographically) or judging them by such elusive and unstable yardsticks as authenticity versus imitation, sacred versus profane, or polish versus crudity adds nary a notch to the understanding of the novel and burdens it with ideological baggage. The novel's force lies in the potential of its symbolic forms, in the vastness of its diachronic and synchronic horizons, and in the possibility of a reconstellation of its social insights, allusions, memories, and languages for other times and readers. Just as a book "becomes fully and radically a *novel*" (Kundera, *Testaments* 7) when it suspends moral judgment, so does commentary become genuine criticism when it forgoes unreflected judgment. Whether referentially or allegorically, visibly in language or hidden in the folds and crevices of language, the modern Turkish novels discussed in this book offer radical insights into the conditions of historical trauma, of political revolutions and revolutions in knowledge and culture, and of civilizational clashes. That is why the Indian students celebrated Halide Edib's *Shirt of Fire* as a symbolic endorsement of their will for independence; why Aziz Nesin's *Surnâmé* is the most compelling indictment of the death penalty pronounced with Rabelaisian laughter; why the Tanpınar renaissance in contemporary Turkish letters or the international fame of Orhan Pamuk is intimately related to questions of national, ethnic, and cultural identity in the wake of worldwide migrations and displacements; why Latife Tekin's *Berji Kristin* evokes for John Berger the sensation of an original language that embraces memories of myth; or why Bilge Karasu's *Night* can conjure up images of fascism in such an emotively and cerebrally powerful way as to leave no reader unaffected.

To establish criticism and critical practice as a legitimate enterprise and a participant in cultural history, the critic has to enter a genuine dialogue with the writer-author-novelist. Tanpınar saw the realization of a culture of *Kritik* (in its double meaning as "criticism" and "critique") only in an academic context. I think that many modern novelists, such as Tanpınar, Ağaoğlu, and Pamuk, are astute readers of their own and others' work, but the legitimization of literary and cultural criticism as an academic discipline would certainly renew the relevance of the writer's work with each age and generation and ensure what Benjamin called its "afterlife" (*Fortleben*) ("Aufgabe" 53). He considered both translation and criticism as the second life or the "survival" (*Überleben*) of an original work (51). Despite the dim view some writers take of critics, without criticism there can be no afterlife for a book. Considering that the modern publishing industry grants many a good book only a brief shelf life, the survival of books depends increasingly more on the interest of critics and teachers to review and teach them and to disseminate and make accessible their insights for a larger audience.

It is also important to read novels comparatively, through other texts and contexts. As Borges, Calvino, Pamuk, and others have shown us, each text reflects another or others in a series of mirrors, through which we see ourselves. The truth of literature's inevitably intertextual heritage comes to word in an insightful remark by Umberto Eco's narrator in *The Name of the Rose*: "I had thought, each book spoke of the things, human and divine, that lie outside of books. Now I realized that not infrequently books speak of books: it is as if they spoke among themselves" (342). Comparative critical practice leads to self-reflexivity, which is an integral part of philosophical thought. This practice is a far cry from comparing the Turkish novel with Western models and coming up with the verdict "deficient," the kind of criticism Gürbilek justifiably and eloquently takes issue with. The aim of comparative literary study is not to rank works on a numerical scale but to put them in a dialogue with one another, through which each will be enriched and gain deeper clarification. Comparative study also enhances pedagogical practice. I have found that reading Pamuk's *The White Castle* against Calvino's *If on a Winter's Night a Traveler* in a course on metafictions gives students a concrete historical and cross-cultural sense of this literary technique. Karasu's *Night* proved a worthy companion to Kafka's "The Metamorphosis," and Nesin's *Surnâmé* provided a parodic clarification for Foucault's intellectual history of institutions and power in *Discipline and Punish*.

Because of its simultaneously expandable and delimiting borders, the novel proves to be an ideal genre for study in comparative literature courses. The structural capacity of the novel to devour other genres; its formal ability to employ different narrators and thus narrative voices and other aesthetic forms, such as musical motifs and variations; and its intertextual and dialogic character all work to negate absolutes or dualities that hamper the possibility of critical pedagogy and make it a genuinely transcultural form. By virtue of the generosity of their poetic imagination, novels can incorporate diverse views and values that would be contradictory and inimical in other forms of discourse. Pierre Bourdieu correctly contends that taking oppositional positions in art and literature, "often inherited from past polemics, and conceived as insurmountable antinomies, absolute alternatives, in terms of all or nothing," may structure thought, but it "also [imprisons thought] in a series of false dilemmas" (193).

The task that faces the modern Turkish novel is not resisting imitation—after all, even Pamuk's universally recognized achievements are not spared comparison with the incomparable Calvino, Kafka, or Borges—or striving to achieve some arbitrary notion of Turkishnesss or opposing to the dilemmas and traumas of modernity, which millions of earth's inhabitants also face, a lovingly restored past. Rather, the task at hand is to defuse the power of entrenched antinomies and imagine a history of dialogic possibilities. In his classic work on the experience of modernity, *All That Is Solid Melts into Air*, Marshall Berman notes that the early visionaries of modernity, such as Marx, Nietzsche, Carlyle, Mill, and Kierkegaard understood the ways modern social structures and technology controlled human lives. But they also

> believed that modern individuals had the capacity both to understand this fate and, once they understood it, to fight it. Hence, even in the midst of a wretched present, they could imagine an open future. Twentieth-century critics of modernity almost entirely lack this empathy with, and faith in, their fellow modern men and women. (27)

Even though Berman considers Foucault just about the only contemporary writer who has had a good sense of modernity, he sees in Foucault's notions of a world imprisoned in institutional fetters no possibility of either freedom or criticism. Berman counters Foucault's "iron bars" with Paz's dynamic and dialectical sense of modernity. For Paz, *dialectical* can be understood in its original sense as dialogue, a dialogue born of a contradiction or conflict. In the concluding essay of his *Corriente alterna*, Paz contends that a new form of movement that continuously makes and remakes itself will transform the paralyzing disorientation of modernity. This dialectical movement will deploy the revolutionary power of contradiction and enable the "third world" to "finally walk" ("y el 'tercer mundo' al fin empezará a caminar" [223]). Berman sees in Paz's re-vision of modernity the understanding of forces that connect us across time and space to others and help us understand the contradictions that rule our lives: our need to be rooted in stable pasts and our desire for insatiable growth, which erases those pasts; our quest for identity, which we seek in allegiance to national, ethnic, and religious groups, and our fear of being left out of cosmopolitan and international spaces; our desire to cling to our values and our obligation to suspend moral judgment with respect to other worlds into which modernity throws us.

Contemporary Turkish society is experiencing these contradictions in a very concrete and intense way. Political Islam vies with the desire join the European Union, which openly resists the admittance of an Islamic nation. Ethnic conflict flies in the face of national identity. Women make great strides in all aspects of political, economic, and social life, but deeply rooted, traditional societal norms exact their toll on their hard-earned rights. Turkish novelists of the early republic, in the early 1920s, intimated these challenges. Their writing embodied the tension between the climactic expectations of the nation and reality's anticlimactic pull.

Tanpınar did not live to see the renaissance of his works but heard the rhythm of these contradictions clearly and used his art as a scene of alternative ways of understanding the deep differences in his culture. His work imagined the reconciliation of Islam with secularism in the practice of daily life and in the continuity of cultural traditions that divest both religion and the laicist state from their respective absolutes and ideological fetters. He often moderates dialogue in the novel to negotiate oppositional positions. In his *Mahur Beste*,[2] Molla Efendi, a devout and tolerant Muslim man, states, "What we call Orient, Islam are the forms we have created in our lives in this land" that are in Islamic calligraphy, poetry, and architecture. The pure Muslim he is addressing admonishes him, "You don't think like a true Muslim." Molla Efendi responds:

> [O]n the contrary, I think exactly like a true Muslim, but [do not think of Islam] in the abstract. . . . The Islam [I practice] is the legacy of my forefathers, who have been intimately connected to the life of this land for the past two hundred years. . . . This Islam has rules that I believe in like everybody else, but behind these rules there are people and a whole life that illuminate them and lend them meaning.

Letting Molla Efendi speak on his behalf, Tanpınar contends that the magic of religion resides in the spirit of the people and does not take its orders from the clergy or any institution of religious authority. That spirit can even accommodate "Frenk [Frankish] invention, but its shape will remain ours" (124–25).

In his fictional works, Tanpınar demystifies Islam and recasts its divine mystique in cultural and aesthetic terms. In his critical work, he attributes the lack of a humanistic tradition in the East to Islam's obstruction of philosophical thought:

> We do not have a humanistic work to emulate. The Islamic religion had blocked the path to philosophy. Furthermore, the [Islamic] mystics rejected the world. Under the circumstances it was impossible for us to grasp the world. In all of Eastern literature there is not a single work that mediates between duty [*vazife*] and emotional proclivity [*his*].   ("Roman" 158)

It is interesting that he uses the translation of the binary terms *Pflicht* ("duty conditioned by reason") and *Neigung* ("inclination and desire conditioned by sensual life"), whose unity formed the humanistic ideal of Goethe and Schiller's classicism. The balance of *Pflicht* and *Neigung* underwrote good morals, and the concept became the signifier of the ethical ideal in an age burdened by the turmoil and trauma of the French Revolution, Napoleonic Wars, and early stages of industrialization. Tanpınar's generous worldview embraces the belief in the recuperative force of an aesthetic and popular Islamic culture along with the ethical ideals of Western humanism, and his work expresses the desire to refigure a beneficent tradition in novel form: "All things considered, today's problem is to create values anew. And these would have to be adapted to the present, as they are re-created" ("Edebiyatımızda" 146).

We have seen that Tanpınar put considerable emphasis on the idea of reconfiguration to ensure the preservation of cherished traditions and their adaptation to the demands of the day. However, his sense of reconstellation does not entail a genuine dialectic. In other words, what he seems to suggest is that once the reconciliation of old and new values is realized, the situation will be stabilized. There is nothing to indicate that the resolution may be "pregnant with its contrary," as Marx's felicitous phrase goes ("Speech" 577). He could not have foreseen the degree of intensification of contraries that took place less than two decades after his death.

The challenges facing modern Turkish society and its novelists and critics demand an ongoing attunement to the ever-changing nature of patterns of identity formation, solidarity, religious and ethnic affiliation, and contingencies of history and economy. Neither literature nor criticism allow for a direct, immediate, or effective intervention in social or political reality, but they can build and consolidate intellectual community. Any literature worthy of its name awakens in us feelings of awe and respect for the diversity of human imagination and instills a sense of the ethical by its resistance to commit to absolutes. Ultimately, however, it is *Kritik* (both as criticism and critique) that teaches us what to look for in literature and how to practice its model of thinking dialogically.

Dialogue among oppositional groups cannot be expected to overcome irreducible differences; however, it can defuse built-up aggression. When Tanpınar, who was a staunch supporter of Atatürk's Republican Party and of his successor, İsmet İnönü, also advocated respect for Islamic Ottoman culture and way of life, he set an example, a pedagogical wake-up call, a preemptive response to charges of cultural extermination by the neo-Islamist intellectuals. Although, unlike Halide Edib, Güntekin, and Karaosmanoğlu, Tanpınar cannot be seen as one of the architects of a literature of nation building (not only was he younger than these three writers but also, as a student, he was sequestered at the university at the time they witnessed the War of Independence, were involved in it, and wrote its stories) and although he is a writer of metaphysical rather than political interests, he has never questioned the historical necessity of abolishing the sultanate-caliphate and instituting a secular republic. Orhan Pamuk incorporated the spirit of Tanpınar's weltanschauung in his own work. However, as the product of an age of intensified political, religious, and ethnic consciousness and conflict, he has been vocal about Turkey's historical errors and the failure of the state to deal with ethnic conflict. Despite his admiration for Tanpınar, he questions Tanpınar's exclusion of non-Islamic and other ethnic groups from Istanbul's historicocultural map. Indeed, Tanpınar's writing may appear naive and negligent about questions of ethnicity. However, these questions come from a political consciousness that postdate him. In his day and context, Tanpınar strove to diagnose the roots of social and cultural traumas while preserving the integrity and autonomy of his craft.

In a highly politicized culture, the writer has to negotiate between artistic integrity and the pull of social conscience, between poetic sensibility and critical reason, between the need for representation and the awareness of how representation can be co-opted by ideology. At the same time, these constraints open up the possibility of dialectical and dynamic escapes. Poised at Europe's last frontier, in the interstices of two and more cultures, the modern Turkish novelists of this study reflect on their often precarious historical and geographic position between worlds. The impasses of Turkish modernity have urged them to articulate questions that have joined them in an implicit dialogue with writers of faraway times and lands. The demands of critical reflection, dialogue, and pedagogy cross geographic, historical, and disciplinary boundaries and urge us to seek paths not yet taken and, like Scheherazade, tell stories not yet told to keep (cultural) battle and death at bay.

Notes

1. In his discussion of the "analytic of the beautiful," Kant defines taste as the faculty of judgment that refers to imagination's free conformity to law. The judgment of the beautiful arises from a subjective agreement between imagination and understanding, whereby imagination shows a conformity to law without a law (*Gesetzmäßigkeit ohne Gesetz*). In this schema, an aesthetic idea is a representation to which no concept is adequate. Imagination and art enjoy flexibility within limits, regularity without rules, and design without design (in the sense of intention, aim, or purpose). Kant's notion of aesthetic autonomy has been a major influence on modernist and postmodernist literary theory.
2. This title is untranslatable, only paraphrasable. *Mahur* is a *makam*, and *makam* is a concept of classical Turkish music whose rules determine tonal relations and the overall indication of the melodic contour and patterns. *Beste* is a vocal composition of four verses, each of which is followed by the same melodic passage.

A Pronunciation Guide to Turkish

A, a   Open a, like the *u* in *fun, sun* or the *o* in *son*

B, b   Same sound as the *b* in *boy, bat*

C, c   Pronounced like the English *j* in *joy, jump*

Ç, ç   Pronounced like the *ch* in *chip*

D, d   Same sound as the *d* in *day*

E, e   Open *e*, as in *net, bet*

F, f   Same sound as the *f* in *fame*

G, g   Hard g, as in *go, get*

Ğ, ğ   Called a soft g, this almost mute consonant functions as a diphthong or glide. Between two identical vowels, it becomes a long vowel: *ağa* sounds almost like *aa* or *aah*. Between different vowels, it functions as a diphthong and lengthens the second vowel, so that *ağır* ("heavy") sounds like a-ıır. After a vowel and before a consonant or at the end of a word after a vowel, it also functions as a diphthong and lengthens the preceding vowel: *dağ* ("mountain") sounds like *daa* or *dah*, and *sağlık* ("health") like *saa-lık*. The letter is often transliterated as *gh*, but it is much softer than that, almost inaudible. It never occurs at the beginning of a word.

H, h   Same sound as the *h* in *home, happy*

I, ı   This is a schwa (ə) in linguistic terminology. Also called an indeterminate vowel, it is pronounced like the *er* in *mother*.

İ, i   A front vowel, pronounced like the *i* in *kid* or *mid* or like the *ee* in *peek*

J, j   Pronounced like the soft *zh* in the middle of the words *leisure, measure* or like the *j* in the French word *je*

K, k   Same sound as the *k* in *king* or the *c* in *cold*

L, l   Same sound as the *l* in *leaf, lamp*

M, m   Same sound as the *m* in *most*

N, n   Same sound as the *n* in *nest*

O, o	An open o, as the *o* in *sorry* or the *au* in *fault*
Ö, ö	*O* with an umlaut, as in the German *ö*; as in the *u* in *purr, fur*
P, p	Same sound as the *p* in *pal*
R, r	Same sound as the *r* in *room*. It is always sounded when it occurs at the end of the word.
S, s	Same sound as the *s* in *soap, sun*
Ş, ş	Pronounced like the *sh* in *ship, shop, sure*
T, t	Same sound as the *t* in *tea*
U, u	As in the *u* in *put* (with the same stress as in the English word); or the *oo* in *pool* and the *ou* in *tour*
Ü, ü	*U* with an umlaut, as in the German *ü* or as the letter *u* in the French word *sur*
V, v	Same sound as the *v* in *very*
Y, y	Same sound as the consonant *y* in *yes* or the diphthong *y* in *toy*
Z, z	Same sound as the *z* in *zip*

Modern Turkish Novels in English Translation

Adıvar, Halide Edib. *The Daughter of Smyrna*. Lahore, India: Dar-ul-Kutub Islamia, 1941.

A retranslation of *The Shirt of Flame,* with modifications by Muhammed Yakub Khan.

———. *The Shirt of Flame* [*Ateşten Gömlek*]. Trans. Adıvar. New York: Duffield, 1924.

Ağaoğlu, Adalet. *Curfew* [*Üç Beş Kişi*]. Trans. John Goulden. Austin: U of Texas P, 1997.

The author's foreword is a fine introduction to Ağaoğlu's work and philosophy of writing.

Atasu, Erendiz. *The Other Side of the Mountain* [*Dağın Öteki Yüzü*]. Trans. Atasu and Elizabeth Malsen. London: Milet, 2000.

Bilbaşar, Kemal. *Jemmo* [*Cemo*]. Trans. Esin B. Rey and Mariana Fitzpatrick. London: Owen, 1976.

Eray, Nazlı. *Orpheus* [*Orphée*]. Trans. Robert Finn. Austin: Center for Middle Eastern Studies; U of Texas, Austin, 2006.

This translation is introduced by Sibel Erol's informative and critically astute essay.

Erdoğan, Aslı. *The City in Crimson Cloak* [*Kırmızı Pelerinli Kent*]. Trans. Amy Spangler. New York: Soft Skull, 2007.

I translated this title as "The City with the Red Cape," since the city of Rio de Janeiro is metaphorically depicted as a city of killing streets, as a matador in a red cape who confronts the marginals, exiles, and outsiders with the intent to kill.

Güntekin, Reşat Nuri. *Afternoon Sun* [*Akşam Güneşi*]. Trans. Wyndham Deedes. Melbourne: Heinemann, 1951.

Deedes's short foreword provides much insight into Güntekin's appeal as a novelist and a craftsman of the Turkish language.

———. *The Autobiography of a Turkish Girl* [*Çalıkuşu*]. Trans. Wyndham Deedes. London: Allen, 1949.

An excellent translation, which captures the tone of the original.

Karasu, Bilge. *Death in Troy* [*Troya'da Ölüm Vardı*]. Trans. Aron Aji. San Francisco: City Lights, 2002.

————. *The Garden of Departed Cats* [*Göçmüş Kediler Bahçesi*]. Trans. Aron Aji. New York: New Directions, 2003.

Aji received the American Literary Translators Association 2004 National Translation Award for this translation.

————. *Night* [*Gece*]. Trans. Güneli Gün and Karasu. Baton Rouge: Lousiana State UP, 1994.

Karasu, a gifted translator himself, collaborated with another novelist-translator, and the result is a work that preserves the complexity and the phantasmagoric tone of the original.

Kemal, Yaşar. *The Birds Have Also Gone* [*Kuşlar da Gitti*]. Trans. Thilda Kemal. London: Collins, 1987.

————. *Iron Earth, Copper Sky* [*Yer Demir Gök Bakır*]. Trans. Thilda Kemal. London: Harvill, 1996.

————. *The Legend of Ararat* [*Ağrı Dağı Efsanesi*]. Trans. Thilda Kemal. London: Collins, 1975.

————. *The Legend of the Thousand Bulls* [*Binboğalar Efsanesi*]. Trans. Thilda Kemal. London: Collins, 1976.

————. *The Lords of Akchasaz, I: Murder in the Ironsmiths Market* [*Akçasazın Ağaları: Demirciler Çarşısı Cinayeti*]. Trans. Thilda Kemal. New York: Morrow, 1980.

————. *Memed, My Hawk* [*İnce Memed*]. Trans. Edouard Roditi. New York: New York Rev. Books, 2005.

Roditi's excellent translation secured the enduring appeal of this novel for English-speaking readers of modern Turkish literature.

————. *Salman the Solitary* [*Kimsecik I*]. Trans. Thilda Kemal. London: Harvill, 1997.

————. *The Sea-Crossed Fisherman* [*Deniz Küstü*]. Trans. Thilda Kemal. New York: Braziller, 1985.

————. *Seagull* [*Al Gözüm Seyreyle Salih*]. Trans. Thilda Kemal. New York: Pantheon, 1981.

————. *They Burn the Thistles* [*İnce Memed II*]. Trans. Margaret E. Platon. New York: New York Rev. Books, 2006.

————. *To Crush the Serpent* [*Yılanı Öldürseler*]. Trans. Thilda Kemal. London: Harvill, 1991.

————. *The Undying Grass* [*Ölmezotu*]. Trans. Thilda Kemal. London: Harvill, 1996.

————. *The Wind from the Plain* [*Ortadireki*]. Trans. Thilda Kemal. London: Harvill, 1999.

Virtually all the novels of Yaşar Kemal have been ably translated by his late wife, Thilda Kemal.

Mağden, Perihan. *The Messenger Boy Murders* [*Haberci Çocuk Cinayetleri*]. Trans. Richard Hamer. London: Milet, 2003.

A darkly comic tale from one of Turkey's most sharp-witted and quirky columnists.

————. *Two Girls* [*İki Genç Kızın Romanı*]. Trans. Brendan Freely. London: Serpent's Tail, 2005.

Makal, Mahmut. *A Village in Anatolia*. Trans. Wyndham Deedes. London: Vallentine, 1954.

A collection of the main chapters of Makal's *Bizim Köy* ["Our Village"] and *Köyümden* ["From My Village"]. Güntekin's translator, Deedes, does an excellent job with this book also, but the editorial decision to leave out some of the chapters from the original *Our Village* takes away from the work's ethnographic value.

Nesin, Aziz. *Hayri the Barber Surnâmé* [*Surnâme*]. Trans. Joseph S. Jacobson. Holladay: Southmoor Studios, 2001.

Humor is always difficult to translate, but Jacobson is one of Nesin's greatest fans and does justice to this extraordinary vintage Nesin tale.

Ören, Aras. *Please, No Police* [*Bitte, nix Polizei*]. Trans. Teoman Sipahigil. Austin: Center for Midddle Eastern Studies; U of Texas, Austin, 1992.

This English translation is from an original unpublished Turkish manuscript. Like Aysel Özakın, Ören is currently better known as a Turkish German author. He lives in Germany, writes in Turkish, and all his works are made available in German translation.

Özakın, Aysel. *The Prizegiving* [*Genç Kız ve Ölüm*]. Trans. Celia Kerslake. London: Women's, 1980.

A fine translation of a novel by one of the most accomplished women writers to come out of Turkey. Özakın was already a well-known name in Turkey when she sought political asylum in West Germany in 1981. She gained fame as a Turkish German writer during her years in Germany, although all her novels were in Turkish. Whatever she wrote was translated into German and issued by leading publishers. She has also written two novels in English, which were published not in English but in German translation.

Pamuk, Orhan. *The Black Book* [*Kara Kitap*]. Trans. Güneli Gün. New York: Farrar, 1994.

Although the second translation by Maureen Freely is supposed to redress the "somewhat opaque"—in Freely's words—quality of this translation, I find Gün's version more faithful to the spirit of Pamuk's idiom than Freely's domesticating translation. The opaqueness of the translation is an outcome more of Pamuk's abstruse mode of expression than of Gün's translational skills. The terms *domesticating* and *foreignizing* translation have been used in translation theory to refer, respectively, to translations that bend the work to the will of the target language and erase the work's cultural and linguistic specificity and those that keep intact the otherness of the original language. Obviously, a successful translation is one that negotiates these two approaches.

———. *The Black Book*. Trans. Maureen Freely. New York: Vintage, 2006.

———. *My Name Is Red* [*Benim Adım Kırmızı*]. Trans. Erdağ M. Köknar. New York: Knopf, 2001.

A fine translation, which was instrumental in putting the novel on many course syllabi at American colleges.

———. *The New Life* [*Yeni Hayat*]. Trans. Güneli Gün. New York: Vintage, 1998.

As in *The Black Book*, Gün's translation stays close to the tone of the original.

———. *Snow* [*Kar*]. Trans. Maureen Freely. New York: Knopf, 2005.

———. *The White Castle* [*Beyaz Kale*]. Trans. Victoria Holbrook. New York: Braziller, 1991.

This first novel by Pamuk to appear in English is by far the best translation of any of his books into English. It captures in idiomatic English all the metaphoric nuances of Turkish. I found reading the translation more enjoyable and rewarding than reading the original.

Şafak Elif. *The Flea Palace* [*Bit Palas*]. Trans. Müge Göçek. London: Boyars, 2006.

The translation buckles under the weight of Şafak's vintage overwrought style.

———. *The Gaze* [*Mahrem*]. Trans. Brendan Freely. London: Boyars, 2006.

Tanpınar, Ahmet Hamdi. *A Mind at Peace* [*Huzur*]. Trans. Erdağ Köknar. New York: Archipelago, 2008.

———. *The Time Regulation Institute* [*Saatleri Ayarlama Enstitüsü*]. Trans. Ender Gürol. Madison: Turco-Tatar, 2001.

This translation is introduced by an excellent essay by Berna Moran on *The Time Regulation Institute*. The essay was translated by Zekeriya Başkal, from Moran's study *Türk Romanına Eleştirel bir Bakış* ["A Critical Look at the Turkish Novel"].

Tekin, Latife. *Berji Kristin: Tales from the Garbage Hills* [*Berci Kristin: Çöp Masalları*]. Trans. Ruth Christie and Saliha Paker. London: Boyars, 1993.

———. *Dear Shameless Death* [*Sevgili Arsız Ölüm*]. Trans. Saliha Paker and Mel Kenne. London: Boyars, 2001.

———. *Swords of Fire* [*Buzdan Kılıçlar*]. Trans. Saliha Paker and Mel Kenne. London: Boyars, 2007.

Uzuner Buket. *Mediterranean Waltz* [*Kumral Ada, Mavi Tuna*]. Trans. Pelin Arıner. London: Milet, 2000.

———. *The Sound of Fishsteps* [*Balık İzlerinin Sesi*]. Trans. Pelin Arıner. Istanbul: Remzi Kitabevi, 2002.

Chronology

1729: İbrahim Müteferrika, founder of the first Ottoman publishing house, publishes the first book in Turkish, a dictionary from Arabic to Ottoman Turkish.

1831: The first periodical in Turkish, *Takvim-i Vekayi* ("Calendar of Events"), is published.

1833: The Tercüme Odası ("Translation Office") is established.

1839: The Gülhane-i Hatt-ı Şerif ("The Noble Script of Gülhane"), a liberal charter of political, social, and legal rights, is promulgated, launching the Tanzimat ("Reorganization") era. All races and creeds are declared equal. However, the implementation of the charter in its totality proves untenable.

1840: *Ceride-i Havadis* ("News Journal"), the first nongovernment journal in Turkish, appears.

1856: The Young Ottoman movement pushes for reform.

1859: İbrahim Şinasi publishes the first literary book in Turkish, an anthology of French verse in Turkish translation.

1862: The first Turkish newspaper, *Tasvir-i-Efkâr* ("Description of Ideas"), is founded.

1872: The first Turkish novel, *Taaşşuk-ı Talât ve Fıtnat* ("The Love of Talat and Fitnat"), by Şemseddin Sami, is published.

1876: Sultan Abdülhamid II accepts the new constitution and allows for a parliament to form (1877), but he dissolves it within a year.

1889: The secret organization İttihâd-ı-Osmânî ("Ottoman Union") is founded by opponents of the Abdülhamid regime. It eventually becomes İttihat ve Terâkkî Cemiyeti or Fırkası ("Committee of Union and Progress"), the first political party in the Ottoman Empire.

1891: The journal *Servet-i Fünun* ("Treasury of Science") is founded. What begins as a journal of general science becomes a full-fledged literary journal, when the famous poet Tevfik Fikret assumes its editorship in 1896. The

literary movement named after this journal and also known as the Edebiyat-
ı-Cedide (1896–1901; "Modern Literature"), brings a strong Western literary influence into Turkish letters.

1898: Halit Ziya Uşaklıgil's popular novel *Aşk-ı Memnu* ("Forbidden Love") is
published.

1908: The Committee of Union and Progress (CUP) revolts. It is composed
largely of members of the Young Turks movement, who want a parliamentary system to replace the monarchy.

1909: Abdülhamit II is forced to declare the constitution. He is deposed by the
parliament. Constitutional sovereignty is established.

1910–12: *Genç Kalemler* ("Young Pens") is founded, a journal that initiates the
Yeni Lisan ("New Language") movement, which strives for a clearer, sim-
pler, more colloquial language. Ömer Seyfettin, the prominent short story
writer, and Ziya Gökalp are contributors.

1912: The First Balkan War. Serbia, Greece, and Bulgaria attack Macedonia.

1913: The Second Balkan War. The Balkan League dissolves over dispute regard-
ing the division of spoils. CUP seizes power through a military coup and
rules until the end of the First World War.

1914–18: The First World War. The Ottoman Empire enters the war on the side
of Germany. CUP leaders are widely regarded as responsible for getting
the empire into the war, for the decimation of its remaining lands, and for
the forced deportation and massacre of the Armenians in northeastern
Anatolia. Treaty of Mondros is signed on 30 October 1918.

1919: The Turkish War of Independence begins.

1920: The Treaty of Sèvres is signed, virtually dissolving the Ottoman Empire.
The sultan accepts the terms of the treaty. The treaty is not recognized by
the rival nationalist government of Mustafa Kemal (Atatürk), whose armies
fight the occupying forces of Italy, France, and Greece.

1922: The Turkish nationalist forces under Mustafa Kemal are victorious, leading
to the armistice of Mudanya.

1923–50: The First Turkish Republic.

1923: The sultanate is abolished, the Treaty of Lausanne is signed, and the
Cumhuriyet Halk Partisi ("Republican People's Party") is founded under
the leadership of Kemal. The Republic of Turkey is proclaimed. Kemal is
elected the first president of the republic.

1924: The caliphate is abolished by the Turkish Grand National Assembly. The Ministry of Religious Affairs is abolished and all religious schools are closed.

1925–28: Various modernization reforms are instituted, including a Turkish civil code based on the Swiss civil code, a dress code that outlaws religious garb, and abolition of the lunar calendar in favor of the Western calendar.

1926: Civil rights are granted for women. Polygamy is banned.

1928: *Harf devrimi* ("alphabet reform"). A new alphabet based on the Roman alphabet replaces the Arabic letters that Turkish was using.

1931: The Measurements Law is instituted; it abolishes the Arabic system of measurements, replacing it with the metric system.

1932–34: Noted Republican intellectuals and writers publish the journal *Kadro* ("Cadre"). It is closed on suspicion of leftist propaganda.

1932: Turkey becomes a member of the League of Nations.

1933: The old university Dar-ül-Fünûn ("House of Science") becomes the University of Istanbul.

1934: The *soyadı kanunu* ("surname law") is established. Last names replace former honorific and other titles, such as Bey, Efendi, Pasha, and Hanım, and the use of the name of the father as the family name or surname.

1934: Women are granted the right to vote and be elected to the parliament. In the following elections, eighteen women are elected to the Turkish Grand National Assembly.

1938: Mustafa Kemal Atatürk dies. He is succeeded by İsmet İnönü, his comrade in arms, a former general, and a hero of the War of Independence.

1939–45: The Second World War. Turkey strives to stay neutral, and İnönü manages to keep the country out of the war, using diplomacy and political calculation. As the German defeat becomes clear, Turkey declares war on Germany.

1940: The *köy enstitüleri* ("village institutes") are founded. A generation of socially engaged writers, including Mahmut Makal, Talip Apaydın, Mehmet Başaran, and Fakir Baykurt, graduate from the village institutes.

1946: The Demokrat Partisi ("Democrat Party") is founded.

1950: The Democrat Party wins the national elections. The multiparty period begins.

1952: Turkey becomes a member of NATO.

1954: The village institutes are closed.

1960–80: The Second Turkish Republic.

1960: A coup d'état on 27 May results from the growing threat to the secularist principles of the state, accusations of the depletion of the treasury by leaders of the ruling party, and the killing of students demonstrating against governmental corruption and repression.

1961: Trials of Democrat Party leaders take place, including the former president and the prime minister. The prime minister is sentenced to death along with his two ministers. The Adalet Partisi ("Justice Party"), a reincarnation of the Democrat Party, is founded. The new constitution is approved.

1961–65: Four coalition governments in four years create political and economic instability. Under the protection of the 1961 constitution, however, a wave of intellectual freedom ushers in a marked growth in translations of Western leftist literature and the production of politically engaged works.

1966: The Justice Party wins parliamentary majority in national elections.

1967: Founding of DİSK: Devrimci İşçi Sendikaları Konfederasyonu ("Revolutionary Confederation of Workers' Unions").

1970: There are labor riots in Istanbul, 16–17 June.

1971: The Muhtıra ("Memorandum") of 12 March is issued. An army intervention forces the formation of an advisory committee to control the increasing anarchy caused by clashes between fascist and leftist groups. Although the army does not take over, it has considerable power and creates a culture of oppression and persecution. This dark period gives rise to the publication of a series of novels, including a trilogy by Adalet Ağaoğlu.

1973: General elections take place. Uneasy coalitions among ideologically opposed political parties, a declining economy, and ongoing street battles between the ultranationalists and the leftists create a dangerous instability.

1974: The overthrow of the Cypriot president, Archbishop Makarios, by the Greek junta leads to the Turkish invasion of the northern part of the island on Prime Minister Bülent Ecevit's watch. Under the terms of the Treaty of Guarantee (1960), either or all of the three guarantor countries (Greece, Turkey, United Kingdom) have the right to intervene militarily to restore peace on the island. The invasion leads to a practical partition of the island, and the situation remains unresolved.

1980: A second coup d'état takes place, 12 September.

1980 TO THE PRESENT: The Third Turkish Republic. The history of the third republic is marked by both the further liberalization of the political system and an increase in political repression and the growth of an export-oriented free market economy and rampant inflation. Political instability and unrest reach new heights because of the unstoppable rise of radical Islam and the Kurdish insurgence in the southeast border area. The insurgency, aggravated by the Gulf War and the massacres of the Kurdish terrorist group PKK, is countered by the often brutal attacks of the Turkish army.

1983: The military steps down, and the constitution of 1982 goes into effect. Leaders of pre-1980 political parties who were banned from entering politics reemerge behind numerous proxy parties. Turgut Özal, head of the Anavatan Partisi ("Motherland Party"), wins the elections and becomes prime minister. His regime is marked by the growth of a globally oriented economic program combined with conservative social values, the emergence of a nouveau riche, and impoverishment of the middle class.

1989: Özal becomes the second civilian president after Celâl Bayar. He dies unexpectedly in office, of a heart attack.

1990s: Political instability returns, with assassinations of journalists, professors, and writers by militant fundamentalists and right-wing extremists.

1993: Tansu Çiller of the Doğru Yol ("True Path") Party becomes the first and the only Turkish woman prime minister and heads a coalition government. The withdrawal of the Republican People's Party from the coalition in 1996 brings down her government. She is later investigated by the parliament on serious corruption charges. Although she is cleared on a technicality, her name becomes a symbol of the self-serving, Westernized intellectual politicians, who are now widely held responsible for the turn of the masses to Islamic leaders.

1997: A postmodern coup takes place. Necmettin Erbakan, the first Islamist prime minister of Turkey, who took office in 1996, is asked by the military to step down, on the grounds that his government's support of religious policies is undermining the secular character of the state. He obliges.

1999: Former Prime Minister Bülent Ecevit's Demokratik Sol Partisi ("Democratic Left Party") wins big in the elections, and a coalition government is formed by the Democratic Left Party, the Motherland Party, and the Milli Hareket Partisi ("National Action Party"). Though this coalition, like many preceding it, is not a harmonious assemblage, it succeeds in implementing much-needed economic reforms and passing human rights laws.

2002: The Islamist Adalet ve Kalkınma Partisi ("Justice and Development Party") wins an overall majority in the Grand National Assembly in parliamentary elections.

2003: Prime Minister Tayyib Erdoğan, of the Justice and Development Party, assumes office on 14 March.

2005: The European Union starts accession talks with Turkey on 3 October. Negotiations are expected to take at least a decade to complete.

2007: The cultural divide between the Islamists and the secularists reaches a critical point, as major demonstrations take place in April in Istanbul and Ankara against the candidacy of Justice and Development Party leaders for the presidency.

Adak, Hülya. "An Epic for Peace." Introduction. *Memoirs of Halidé Edib*. Piscataway: Gorgias, 2004. v–xxvii.

Adıvar, Halide Edib. *Ateşten Gömlek* [Shirt of Fire]. 4th ed. Istanbul: Özgür, 1998.

———. *The Daughter of Smyrna*. Trans. of *Ateşten Gömlek*. Rev. Muhammed Yakub Khan. Lahore, India: Dar-ul-Kutub Islamia, 1941.

———. *House with Wisteria: Memoirs of Halidé Edib*. Introd. Sibel Erol. Charlottesville: Leopolis, 2003.

———. *Inside India*. Ed. Mushirul Hasan. New Delhi: Oxford UP, 2002.

———. *Memoirs of Halidé Edib*. Introd. Hülya Adak. Piscataway: Gorgias, 2004.

———. *Mor Salkımlı Ev* [The House with Wisteria]. Istanbul: Özgür, 1996.

———. *The Shirt of Flame*. Trans. Adıvar. New York: Duffield, 1924.

———. *The Turkish Ordeal: Being the Further Memoirs of Halide Edib*. New York: Century, 1928.

———. "Yakup Kadri Bey'e Açık Mektup" [An Open Letter to Yakup Kadri Bey]. Adıvar, *Ateşten Gömlek* xiii–xvi.

Ağaoğlu, Adalet. "Author's Foreword." Ağaoğlu, *Curfew* vii–ix.

———. *Curfew*. Trans. John Goulden. Austin: U of Texas P, 1997.

Ahmad, Feroz. *The Making of Modern Turkey*. London: Routledge, 1993.

Alcott, Louisa May. *Little Women*. Signet Classics. New York: Penguin, 2004.

Anderson, Benedict. *Imagined Communities*. Rev. ed. London: Verso, 1991.

Andrews, Walter G. *Poetry's Voice, Society's Song: Ottoman Lyric Poetry*. Seattle: U of Washington P, 1985.

Andrews, Walter G., and Mehmet Kalpaklı. *The Age of Beloveds: Love and the Beloved in Early Modern Ottoman and European Culture and Society*. Durham: Duke UP, 2004.

Andrić, Ivo. *The Bridge on the Drina*. Trans. Lovett F. Edwards. Chicago: U of Chicago P, 1977.

Atiş, Sarah Moment. *Semantic Structuring in the Modern Turkish Story: An Analysis of "The Dreams of Abdullah Efendi" and Other Short Stories by Ahmet Hamdi Tanpınar*. Leiden: Brill, 1983.

Aytaç, Demir. "Reşat Nuri Güntekin ve 'Mektuplar'" [Reşat Nuri Güntekin and "Letters"]. *Bütün Dünya* Jan. 2004: 47–53.

Bakhtin, M. M. *The Dialogic Imagination*. Trans. Caryl Emerson and Michael Holquist. Ed. Holquist. Austin: U of Texas P, 1981.

Benjamin, Walter. "Die Aufgabe des Übersetzers." *Illuminationen*. Frankfurt am Main: Suhrkamp, 1977. 50–63.

———. *Der Begriff der Kunstkritik in der deutschen Romantik*. Benjamin, *Gesammelte Schriften* 1.1: 9–122.

———. *Gesammelte Schriften*. Ed. Rolf Tiedemann and Hermann Schweppenhäuser. Frankfurt am Main: Suhrkamp, 1974.

———. "Theses on the Philosophy of History." *Illuminations*. Trans. Harry Zohn. Ed. Hannah Arendt. New York: Schocken, 1969. 253–64.

———. *Ursprung des deutschen Trauerspiels*. Benjamin, *Gesammelte Schriften* 1.1: 205–430.

———. "Zentralpark." Benjamin, *Gesammelte Schriften* 1.2: 657–90.

Berger, John. "Rumour." Preface. Tekin 5–8.

Berkes, Niyazi. *The Development of Secularism in Turkey*. New York: Routledge, 1999.

Berman, Antoine. *The Experience of the Foreign: Culture and Translation in Romantic Germany*. Trans. S. Heyvaert. Albany: State U of New York P, 1992.

Berman, Marshall. *All That Is Solid Melts into Air: The Experience of Modernity*. New York: Penguin, 1988.

Bermann, Sandra. Introduction. *Nation, Language, and the Ethics of Translation*. Ed. Bermann and Michael Wood. Princeton: Princeton UP, 2005. 1–10.

The Book of Dede Korkut. Trans. and ed. Faruk Sümer, Ahmet E. Uysal, and Warren S. Walker. Austin: U of Texas P, 1972.

Borges, Jorge Luis. *Labyrinths: Selected Stories and Other Writings*. Ed. Donald A. Yates and James E. Irby. New York: New Directions, 1964.

———. "Pierre Menard, Author of the *Quixote*." Trans. James E. Irby. Borges, *Labyrinths* 36–44.

———. "Tlön, Uqbar, Orbis Tertius." Trans. James E. Irby. Borges, *Labyrinths* 3–18.

Bourdieu, Pierre. *The Rules of Art: Genesis and Structure in the Literary Field*. Trans. Susan Emanuel. Cambridge: Polity, 1996.

Bradbury, Malcolm. *Possibilities: Essays on the State of the Novel*. London: Oxford UP, 1973.

Calvino, Italo. *If on a Winter's Night a Traveler*. Trans. William Weaver. San Diego: Harcourt, 1981.

———. *Invisible Cities*. Trans. William Weaver. San Diego: Harcourt, 1972.

———. *Six Memos for the Next Millennium*. Trans. Patrick Creagh. New York: Vintage Intl., 1993.

Certeau, Michel de. *The Practice of Everyday Life*. Trans. Steven Rendall. Berkeley: U of California P, 1984.

Cixous, Hélène. "The Laugh of the Medusa." Trans. Keith Cohen and Paula Cohen. *Signs* 1 (1976): 875–93.

Compagnon, Antoine. *Literature, Theory, and Common Sense.* Trans. Carol Cosman. Princeton: Princeton UP, 2004.

Connor, Steven. Introduction. *The Cambridge Companion to Postmodernism.* Ed. Connor. Cambridge: Cambridge UP, 2004. 1–19.

Crimp, Douglas. "On the Museum's Ruins." *The Anti-Aesthetic: Essays on Postmodern Culture.* Ed. and introd. Hal Foster. Port Townsend: Bay, 1983. 43–56.

Critchley, Simon. *On Humour.* London: Routledge, 2002.

Deedes, Wyndham. Foreword. *The Afternoon Sun.* By Reşat Nuri Güntekin. Trans. Deedes. Melbourne: Heinemann, 1951. v–vii.

Derrida, Jacques. "White Mythology: Metaphor in the Text of Philosophy." *Margins of Philosophy.* Trans. Alan Bass. Chicago: U of Chicago P, 1982. 207–71.

Djaout, Tahar. *The Last Summer of Reason.* Trans. Marjolijn de Jager. Saint Paul: Ruminator, 2003.

Djebar, Assia. *Algerian White.* Trans. David Kelley and Marjolijn de Jager. New York: Seven Stories, 2000.

Donald, James. "This, Here, Now: Imagining the Modern City." *Imagining Cities: Script, Signs, Memory.* Ed. Sally Westwood and John Williams. London: Routledge, 1997. 181–201.

Dostoevsky, Fyodor. *The Brothers Karamazov.* Trans. Richard Pevear and Larissa Volokhonsky. New York: Vintage, 1991.

Ecevit, Yıldız. *Türk Romanında Postmodernist Açılımlar* [Postmodernist Trends in the Turkish Novel]. Istanbul: İletişim, 2002.

Eco, Umberto. *The Name of the Rose.* Trans. William Weaver. New York: Warner, 1984.

Edib, Halide. *See* Adıvar.

Eliot, T. S. *Four Quartets.* New York: Harcourt, 1971.

Erdoğan, Aslı. *The City in Crimson Cloak.* Trans. Amy Spangler. Brooklyn: Soft Skull, 2007.

———. *Kırmızı Pelerinli Kent* [The City with the Red Cape]. Istanbul: Türkiye İş Bankası Yayınları, 2001.

Evin, Ahmet Ö. *Origins and Development of the Turkish Novel.* Minneapolis: Bibliotheca Islamica, 1983.

Fiedler, Leslie A. "The Death and Rebirth of the Novel." *The Theory of the Novel: New Essays.* Ed. John Halperin. New York: Oxford UP, 1974. 189–209.

Findley, Carter Vaughn. *The Turks in World History.* Oxford: Oxford UP, 2004.

Foucault, Michel. *Discipline and Punish: The Birth of the Prison.* Trans. Alan Sheridan. New York: Vintage, 1979.

———. *The Order of Things: An Archeology of the Human Sciences.* New York: Vintage, 1973. Trans. of *Le mots et les choses.* Paris: Gallimard, 1966.

Freud, Sigmund. "Der Humor." *Gesammelte Werke*. Vol. 14. Ed. Anna Freud et al. London: Imago, 1948. 383–89.

———. "Humour." Trans. Joan Riviere. Freud, *Standard Edition* 21: 159–66.

———. *The Standard Edition of the Complete Psychological Works of Sigmund Freud*. Ed. James Strachey. London: Hogarth, 1961.

———. "The Uncanny." Trans. Alix Strachey. Freud, *Standard Edition* 17: 217–56.

Gellner, Ernest. "The Turkish Option in Comparative Perspective." *Rethinking Modernity and National Identity in Turkey*. Ed. Sibel Bozdoğan and Reşat Kasaba. Seattle: U of Washington P, 1997. 233–51.

Goethe, Johann Wolfgang von. *The Sorrows of Young Werther*. Signet Classics. Trans. Catherine Hutter. New York: Penguin, 2005.

Gökalp, Ziya. *Turkish Nationalism and Western Civilization: Selected Essays of Ziya Gökalp*. Trans. and ed. Niyazi Berkes. New York: Columbia UP, 1959.

———. *Yeni Hayat*. Ed. Yalsın Toker. Istanbul: Toker Yayınları, 2005.

Göktürk, Akşit. "Sunuş" [Introduction]. *Gece* [Night], by Bilge Karasu. 5th ed. Istanbul: Metis, 2004. 5–8.

Goytisolo, Juan. *Estambul otomano*. Barcelona: Planeta, 1989.

———. "Orhan Pamuk'un Kara Kitap'ı" [Orhan Pamuk's *Black Book*]. Trans. Gül Işık. *Kara Kitap Üzerine Yazılar* [Writings on *The Black Book*]. Ed. Nükhet Esen. Istanbul: İletişim, 1996. 295–313.

Güntekin, Reşat Nuri. *The Autobiography of a Turkish Girl*. Trans. Wyndham Deedes. London: Allen, 1949.

———. Rev. of *Yaban* [The Alien], by Karaosmanoğlu. Karaosmanoğlu 261–64.

———. *Yeşil Gece* [The Green Night]. 26th ed. Istanbul: İnkilâp, n.d.

Gürbilek, Nurdan. "Dandies and Originals: Authenticity, Belatedness, and the Turkish Novel." Güzeldere and Irzık 599–628.

Güvenç, Bozkurt. *Türk Kimliği: Kültür Tarihinin Kaynakları* [Turkish Identity: Sources of Cultural History]. Istanbul: Remzi Kitabevi, 1996.

Güzeldere, Güven, and Sibel Irzık, eds. *Relocating the Fault Lines: Turkey beyond the East-West Divide*. Spec. issue of *South Atlantic Quarterly* 102 (2003): 283–666.

Halman, Talat Sait. Foreword. Nesin 1–3.

Haq, Asrarul [Majaz]. "To Khâlide Edib Khanam." Adıvar, *Inside India* lxxvii–lxxix.

Hegel, Georg Wilhelm Friedrich. *Phänomenologie des Geistes*. Frankfurt am Main: Suhrkamp, 1973.

Heidegger, Martin. *Gesamtausgabe*. Ed. Friedrich Wilhelm von Herrmann. Vol. 5. Frankfurt am Main: Klostermann, 1976.

Heine, Heinrich. *Zur Geschichte der Religion und Philosophie in Deutschland*. 1834. *Werke*. Vol. 4. Ed. Helmut Schanze. Frankfurt am Main: Insel, 1968. 44–165.

Hobsbawm, E. J. *Bandits*. London: Weidenfeld, 1969.

Holbrook, Victoria Rowe. *The Unbearable Shores of Love: Turkish Modernity and Mystic Romance*. Austin: U of Texas P, 1994.

Horkheimer, Max, and Theodor W. Adorno. *Dialektik der Aufklärung*. Frankfurt am Main: Fischer, 1986.

Hutcheon, Linda. *A Theory of Parody: The Teachings of Twentieth-Century Art Forms*. New York: Methuen, 1985.

İleri, Selim. "Bugüne Bir 'Ateşten Gömlek' " [A "Shirt of Fire" for Our Time]. Afterword. Adıvar, *Ateşten Gömlek* 225–29.

———. " 'Mor Salkımlı Ev'in Hikâyesi" [The Story of *The House with Wisteria*]. Afterword. Adıvar, *Mor Salkımlı Ev* 299–301.

İnci, Handan. "İlk Dönem Türk Romanlarında Etkiler Sorunu" [The Question of Influence in Early Turkish Novels]. *Varlık* 73 (2005-08): 60–62.

Jameson, Fredric. *The Political Unconscious: Narrative as a Socially Symbolic Act*. Ithaca: Cornell UP, 1981.

———. *Postmodernism; or, The Cultural Logic of Late Capitalism*. Durham: Duke UP, 1991.

Jauss, Hans Robert. *Toward an Aesthetic of Reception*. Trans. Timothy Bahti. Minneapolis: U of Minnesota P, 1982.

Kant, Immanuel. *Kritik der Urteilskraft*. Ed. Gerhard Lehmann. Stuttgart: Reclam, 1963.

Karaosmanoğlu, Yakup Kadri. *Yaban* [The Alien]. Istanbul: Birikim, 1977.

Karasu, Bilge. *Night*. Trans. Güneli Gün and Karasu. Baton Rouge: Louisiana State UP, 1994.

Kazan, Frances. *Halide's Gift*. New York: Random, 2001.

Kemal, Yaşar. Introduction. Trans. Sungur Savran. Kemal, *Memed* vii–xiii.

———. *Memed, My Hawk*. Trans. Edouard Roditi. New York: New York Rev. of Books, 2005.

———. *The Sea-Crossed Fisherman*. Trans. Thilda Kemal. New York: Braziller, 1985.

Khadra, Yasmina. *The Swallows of Kabul*. Trans. John Cullen. New York: Anchor, 2005.

Köksal, Sırma. "Cumhuriyet Kızı Feride" [Republican Daughter Feride]. *Kitap-lık* May 2005: 100–02.

Kongar, Emre. "Turkey's Cultural Transformation." *The Transformation of Turkish Culture: The Atatürk Legacy*. Ed. Günsel Renda and C. Max Kortepeter. Princeton: Kingston, 1986. 19–68.

Kundera, Milan. *The Art of the Novel*. Rev. ed. Trans. Linda Asher. New York: Harper, 2000.

———. *The Curtain: An Essay in Seven Parts*. Trans. Linda Asher. New York: Harper, 2006.

————. *Testaments Betrayed: An Essay in Nine Parts*. Trans. Linda Asher. New York: Harper, 1996.

Lewis, Bernard. *The Emergence of Modern Turkey*. 3rd ed. New York: Oxford UP, 2002.

Loti, Pierre. *Constantinople in 1890*. Trans. David Ball. Istanbul: Ünlem, 2002.

Lukács, Georg. *Realism in Our Time: Literature and the Class Struggle*. Trans. John Mander and Necke Mander. New York: Harper, 1971.

————. *The Theory of the Novel: A Historico-Philosophical Essay on the Forms of Great Epic Literature*. Trans. Anna Bostock. Cambridge: MIT P, 1977.

Lynch, Deidre, and William B. Warner. "The Transport of the Novel." Introduction. *Cultural Institutions of the Novel*. Ed. Lynch and Warner. Durham: Duke UP, 1996. 1–10.

Lyotard, Jean-François. *The Postmodern Condition: A Report on Knowledge*. Trans. Geoff Bennington and Brian Massumi. Minneapolis: U of Minnesota P, 1984.

Makal, Mahmut. *Bizim Köy* [Our Village]. 10th ed. Istanbul: Sander, 1973.

————. *A Village in Anatolia*. Trans. Wyndham Deedes. Ed. Paul Stirling. London: Vallentine, 1954.

Mango, Andrew. *Turkey*. London: Thames, 1968.

Marx, Karl. *The Communist Manifesto*. Trans. Samuel Moore. Ed. Frederic L. Bender. New York: Norton, 1988.

————. "Speech at the Anniversary of the People's Paper." *The Marx-Engels Reader*. Ed. Robert C. Tucker. New York: Norton, 1978. 577–78.

Mitchell, W. J. T. *Image, Text, Ideology*. Chicago: U of Chicago P, 1986.

Moran, Berna. *Türk Romanına Eleştirel Bir Bakış* [A Critical Look at the Turkish Novel]. 3 vols. Istanbul: İletişim, 2003.

Naci, Fethi. *Reşat Nuri'nin Romancılığı* [Reşat Nuri as Novelist]. Istanbul: YKY, 2002.

Nafisi, Azar. *Reading* Lolita *in Teheran: A Memoir in Books*. New York: Random, 2003.

Nesin, Aziz, ed. *Cumhuriyet Döneminde Türk Mizahı* [Turkish Humor in the Republican Era]. Istanbul: Akbaba, 1973.

————. *Hayri the Barber Surnâmé*. Trans. Joseph S. Jacobson. Holladay: Southmore Studios, 2001.

Nietzsche, Friedrich. *Werke*. 6 vols. Ed. Karl Schlechta. München: Hanser, 1980.

Novalis (Friedrich von Hardenberg). *Werke*. Ed. Gerhard Schulz. München: Beck, n.d.

Ortega y Gasset, José. *La deshumanización del arte e ideas sobre la novela*. 2nd ed. Madrid: Revista de Occidente, 1928.

Paker, Saliha. Introduction. Tekin 9–14.

Pamuk, Orhan. *The Black Book*. Trans. Güneli Gün. New York: Farrar, 1994.

———. "International Books of the Year." *Times Literary Supplement* 7 Dec. 2001: 11.

———. *Istanbul: Memories and the City*. Trans. Maureen Freely. New York: Knopf, 2005.

———. *My Name Is Red*. Trans. Erdağ M. Köknar. New York: Knopf, 2001.

———. *Öteki Renkler: Seçme Yazılar ve Bir Hikâye* [Other Colors: Selected Writings and a Story]. Istanbul: İletişim, 1999.

———. *Snow*. Trans. Maureen Freely. New York: Knopf, 2005.

Paz, Octavio. *Corriente alterna*. Mexico City: Siglo veintiuno, 1969.

———. *The Labyrinth of Solitude and Other Writings*. Trans. Lysander Kemp. New York: Grove, 1985.

Redfield, Marc. *The Politics of Aesthetics: Nationalism, Gender, Romanticism*. Stanford: Stanford UP, 2003.

Ricoeur, Paul. *Oneself as Another*. Trans. Kathleen Blamey. Chicago: U of Chicago P, 1992.

Schiller, Friedrich. *Sämtliche Werke*. 5 vols. Ed. Gerhard Fricke and Herbert G. Göpfert. München: Hanser, 1962.

Schlegel, Friedrich. *Kritische Ausgabe*. Ed. Ernst Behler. Vol 2. Paderborn, Ger.: Schöningh, 1957.

Tahir, Kemal. *Bozkırdaki Çekirdek* [The Seed in the Steppe]. Istanbul: İthaki, 2006.

———. *Rahmet Yolları Kesti* [Mercy Blocked the Road]. Istanbul: Adam, 1994.

Tanpınar, Ahmet Hamdi. *Ahmet Hamdi Tanpınar: Bir Kültür, Bir İnsan* [Ahmet Hamdi Tanpınar: A Culture, A Person]. Ed. Turan Alptekin. Istanbul: İletişim, 2001.

———. *Beş Şehir* [Five Cities]. 13th ed. Istanbul: Dergâh, 1999.

———. "Edebiyatımızda Tesirler (Influence'lar) Meselesi" [The Problem of Influence in Our Literature]. Tanpınar, *Ahmet Hamdi Tanpınar* 137–46.

———. *Huzur* [Peace]. 13th ed. Istanbul: Dergâh Yayınları, 2003.

———. *Mahur Beste*. Istanbul: Dergâh Yayınları, n.d.

———. *A Mind at Peace*. Trans. Erdağ Göknar. New York: Archipelago, forthcoming.

———. *Mücevherlerin Sırrı* [The Secret of Jewels]. Ed. İlyas Dirin, Turgay Anar, and Şaban Özdemir. Istanbul: YKY, 2004.

———. "Roman ve Meseleleri" [The Novel and Its Problems]. Tanpınar, *Ahmet Hamdi Tanpınar* 152–70.

Tekin, Latife. *Berji Kristin: Tales from the Garbage Hills*. Trans. Ruth Christie and Saliha Paker. London: Boyars, 1993.

Updike, John. "Murder in Miniature." Rev. of *My Name Is Red*, by Orhan Pamuk. *New Yorker* 3 Sept. 2001: 92–95.

Woolf, Virginia. *Collected Essays*. Vol. 2. London: Hogarth, 1966.

Yıldırım, İbrahim. *Vatan Dersleri*. Istanbul: Ekim, 2006.

Zengotita, Thomas de. "Common Ground: Finding Our Way Back to the Enlightenment." *Harper's* Jan. 2003: 35–44.

Zürcher, Eric J. *Turkey: A Modern History*. Rev. ed. London: Tauris, 1998.

If citations in the text are from the Turkish original, page numbers are given under the Turkish titles. Of the works listed in appendix B, "Modern Turkish Novels in English Translation," this index includes only those cited in the text. Some Turkish names before the surname law was passed (1934) are like a first name and middle name (usually the second is the father's first name; in rare cases it is a pseudonym). So a name like Namık Kemal appears in the index as "Namık Kemal" and not as "Kemal, Namık."